Please remember that this is a library book,
and that it belongs only temporarily to each
person who uses it. Be considerate. Do
not write in this, or any, library book.

THE PIAGET PRIMER
Thinking · Learning
Teaching

ED LABINOWICZ

THE PIAGET PRIMER
Thinking · Learning Teaching

ED LABINOWICZ

Illustrations by
Susie Pollard Frazee

Addison-Wesley Publishing Company
Menlo Park, California • Reading, Massachusetts • London • Amsterdam • Don Mills, Ontario • Sydney

To teachers willing to learn from children;
To children, who have so much to teach us about thinking and learning.

This book is published by the Addison-Wesley Innovative Division.

ISBN-0-201-04090-5
ABCDEFGHIJK-WC-854321079

About the Author

Ed Labinowicz (LabiNOwich) began his teaching career in Canada where he taught in public schools for several years. He studied both science and education at the University of Manitoba, did graduate work in chemistry at the University of Hawaii, and completed the PhD program in Science Education at Florida State University in 1969. His dissertation research incorporated aspects of Piaget's work. He is currently Professor of Education at California State University, Northridge, where he has taught since that time, applying his interest in Piaget's findings to his work with elementary school teachers in the areas of science and mathematics education. His methods courses actively involve teachers in thought-provoking activities with materials. These activities, in turn, serve as models for the elementary school classroom. In 1975~76 he served as director of the Elementary Science Study Teacher Institute, a funded project for the implementation of an innovative science program which provided children with materials to explore rather than textbooks to read. He has also published articles in a variety of teacher journals. As this book goes to press he is undertaking a research project in early childhood mathematics education in preparation for a second book.

Contents

Before Beginning

As teachers, we teach children.
Since we teach children,
Then we understand
How children think and
How they learn . . .
Or, do we just think we do?

Do children have anything to *teach* teachers? Jean Piaget believes that they do. As a beginning teacher, I focused on elaborate preparation of explanations and demonstrations of content. To Piaget and his co-workers I owe a special debt for their ingeneous methods of exploring children's *thinking* and their theory of intellectual development. A study of Piaget's work, together with direct observations of children, has been instrumental in my transition to another stage of development as a teacher. This has enabled me to begin to subordinate my *teaching* to a more meaningful focus—*learning*.

A study of Piaget's explorations with children can drastically change our understanding of how children *think* and *learn*. Despite the fact that interpretations of his work have been available in this country for more than ten years, there is little evidence that how we *teach* is in tune with how children *learn*.

Piaget has a compelling message for people who are *thinking, learning,* and *teaching* in a world in rapid transition. Unfortunately, some of his writings are difficult to read. However, this book attempts to remove this difficulty, so that there may no longer be an excuse for avoiding his message. The book presents the essence of Piaget's ideas with a minimum of technical vocabulary. Although its approach is graphic and informal, its intent is serious—to make Piaget's ideas accessible to you and to provoke you to interact with these ideas. Not only does the book clarify Piaget's theory, its design puts this theory into practice. The book is organized so that you have many opportunities to *think* and *learn* as you read it. Illustrated sequences depict children's *thinking* and *learning* in action, with some subtle detail that may surprise you. These sequences take some of the mystery out of the process of equilibration which is central to Piaget's theory. If you choose to interact with the ideas illustrated in the book, you may begin to reorganize some of your existing ideas about *thinking, learning,* and *teaching*. You may then begin to observe aspects of children's *thinking* which you hadn't noticed before.

Another intent of this book is to bridge the gap between Piaget's theory, his research methods, and classroom practice. Although the applications of Piaget's work to the classroom are not made explicit until Chapters 9 and 10, the earlier chapters raise serious questions about current methods of teaching and suggest alternatives. In Chapter 9 and 10, Piaget's general guidelines for the "active" classroom are interpreted and illustrated with selected, classroom-tested practices, and the teacher's role is clearly defined. Piaget's statements on education and the classroom examples are placed side by side so that you can decide whether a gap between theory, research methods, and classroom practice really does exist or should exist. In the final chapter, the book deals with the complexities of changing schools to provide environments that encourage the development of logical thinking.

The writing of this book began out of the frustration of preparing teachers in active methods of teaching mathematics and science, without the time to develop a conceptual framework of learning and teaching from which the teachers could defend these methods in an alien school system. The book was a problem of my own choosing from which to grow. In the process of researching the book I have reorganized and refined my understanding of Piaget's work considerably.

This book has been many years in the making and reflects the cumulative efforts of many individuals and groups. In addition to the monumental works of Jean Piaget and his colleagues, Barbel Inhelder, Hermine Sinclair and Magali Bovet, at the University of Geneva, I acknowledge the interpretations of Piaget's work which provided initial access to his ideas for me and motivated me to read the original works. These interpreters of Piaget theory include: John Flavell, Milton Schwebel, and Jane Raph, Constance Kamii, Eleanor Duckworth, George Hein, Barry Wadsworth, Mary Ann Pulaski, and others. In the area of science education I acknowledge the contagious enthusiasm of Darrell Phillips for Piaget's work, the creative classroom research and theory of Mary Budd Rowe, and the innovative curriculum products of the Elementary Science Study (ESS) and the Science Curriculum Improvement Study (SCIS) groups. In math education I acknowledge my enthusiastic introduction to the area through team teaching with Van Dyk Buchanan, as well as the pioneering efforts in curriculum development made by Mary Baratta-Lorton and Robert Wirtz. In the areas of reading, language arts, and social studies I received a child-oriented introduction through team teaching with Brenda Wash. In addition, I am indebted to my wife, Shirley, for countless hours of insightful discussion of children, thinking, learning, and teaching. She provided anecdotes and personal observation's of her classroom and was the teacher in the Explorations in the book which were originally videotaped, as well as a reviewer of the manuscript. Groups of children at Osceola Elementary School* and at Calahan Elementary School* and classrooms at Sherman Oaks Elementary School in Los Angeles provided support for the feasibility of applying Piaget's

---

*These children participated in videotaped exploration of their thinking which appear in Chapters 1 and 7. The names of the children have been changed to protect their privacy.

theory in the classroom. Furthermore, I am indebted to the National Science Foundation which supported my study of curriculum innovations at various times, beginning in 1962 with Chemical Bond Approach (CBA) chemistry and later culminating in 1975 with the funding of an ESS implementation project, which served to integrate my earlier experiences. All of these experiences and ideas have interacted with Piaget's ideas and have allowed me to construct personal meanings of his theory. In turn, I was able to view curriculum innovations from this framework.

In the direct preparation of this book I wish to thank Susie Pollard Frazee for bringing the Explorations to life through her sensitive and insightful illustrations of children.

I am greatly indebted to the following people who reviewed various parts of the manuscript: to Elizabeth Lamey for her review and encouragement of some crude beginnings; to Eleanor Duckworth of the University of Geneva for communicating some Genevan concerns on the early chapters; to Larry Lowery of the University of California at Berkeley for his suggestions and contributions; to the late Mary Baratta-Lorton, of the Center for Innovation in Education, for her support and contribution of ideas; to Brenda Wash of California State University at Northridge, who not only reviewed the early chapters but also encouraged an early completion of the remaining chapters by undertaking an overload in our teaching/supervising team; to Jane Raph of Arizona State University for her enthusiastic review of the early chapters which made the publishers take notice, and for her continuing support, critical feedback, and editorial assistance. Interacting with the critical feedback received from the reviewers was invaluable in clarifying my understanding of Piaget's theory and my communication of it.

It is my sincere hope that at the completion of this book you will have gained an appreciation and understanding of a spiral of activity that is central to our challenging profession. You can continue this spiral by *learning* more about children through direct observation and interviews, and by a deeper study of Piaget's work. This should stimulate your *thinking* about other ways to adapt your *teaching* to your children's natural ways of learning.

Ed Labinowicz

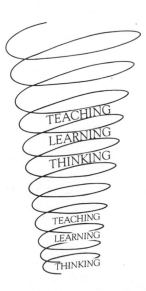

Exploring Children's Thinking and Learning: Displacement Volume

1

This chapter illustrates an example of how Piaget and his colleagues find out about children's thinking and learning. It describes a teacher on sabbatical leave who found time outside her classroom to explore in depth the way children think and learn about displacement volume. The children are three 11–12 year olds who are about to complete the sixth grade. The ingenious set of tasks used in the exploration is one of many devised by Piaget and his colleagues.[1] The exploration is illustrated so that you can readily share in the surprising observations the teacher encounters as the thought-provoking materials help her to open a small window to the children's minds.

First Comes Thinking

Before we look at the children studying similar materials, try thinking about them yourself.[2]

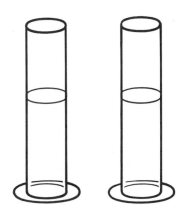

These two cylinders are the same size and contain equal volumes of water.

Here are two rods of equal size. One is made of glass and the other of steel. Although the steel rod is heavier than the glass rod, they both sink in water.

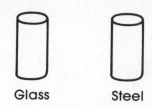

Glass   Steel

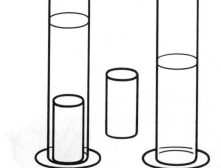

When the glass rod is lowered into the cylinder, notice the new water level.

Predict what will happen to the water level in the second cylinder when the steel rod is put in.

Can you explain your prediction?

. . . And now, the children

INTRODUCTION*

Jimmy, Rosa, Victor and their teacher are seated around a table. On the table are pairs of film cans, cylinders containing equal volumes of water and an equal-arm balance. The teacher has eight cans which are paired according to specific combinations of variables.

	Volume	Weight
Pair A (1,2)	Same	Same
Pair B (3,4)	Different	Same
Pair C (5,6)	Same	Different
Pair D (7,8)	Different	Different

One film can in each pair is lowered into one of the containers . . .

Then . . . the children predict the position of the water level before the second can is lowered into the other cylinder. They use colored rubber bands to mark their predictions. The teacher also asks them to justify their predictions.

After the second can has been lowered into the water, the children are encouraged to compare the results with their predictions and to explain what they have observed.
The general sequence is repeated for each pair of cans.

*This sequence is illustrated from a videotaped exploration of children's thinking.

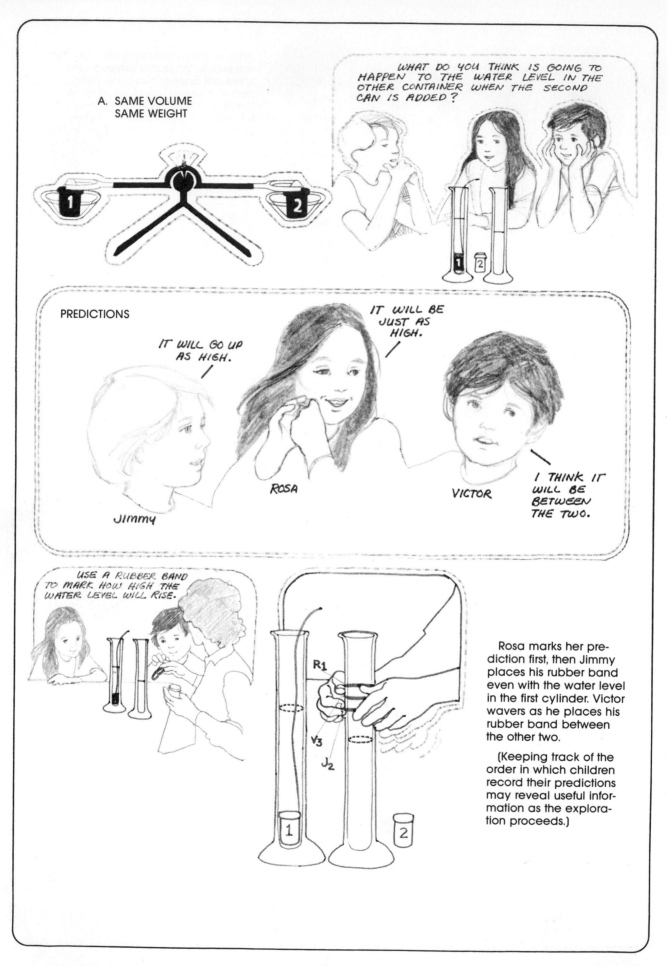

Rosa marks her prediction first, then Jimmy places his rubber band even with the water level in the first cylinder. Victor wavers as he places his rubber band between the other two.

(Keeping track of the order in which children record their predictions may reveal useful information as the exploration proceeds.)

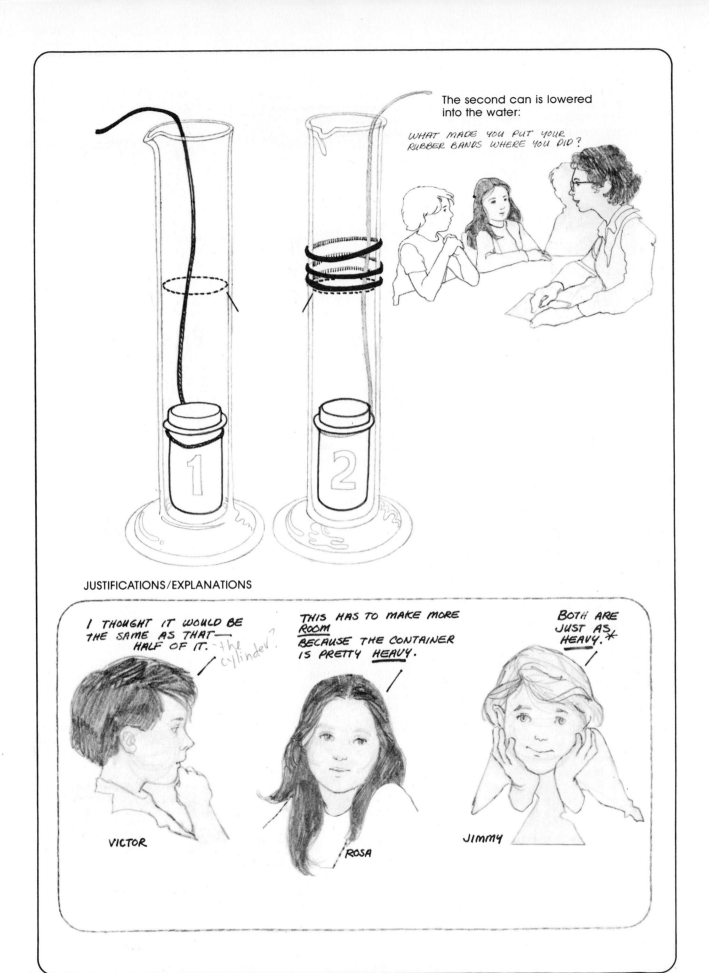

The second can is lowered into the water:

JUSTIFICATIONS/EXPLANATIONS

B. SAME WEIGHT
DIFFERENT VOLUME

After examining the new pair of cans with the aid of a balance, they lower the smaller can into the water.

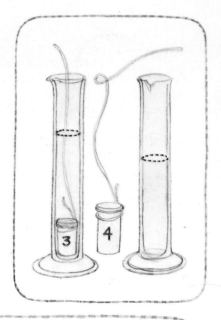

PREDICTIONS:

IT'S THE SAME (SECOND LEVEL). THIS IS JUST AS HEAVY.

IT'S GOING TO BE HIGH. THE CAN IS JUST ABOUT THE SAME SIZE (WIDTH) AS THE CYLINDER. THE WATER WILL GO UP THE SAME SIZE AS THE CAN TO MAKE ROOM FOR IT.

THAT ONE IS BIGGER.

JIMMY

ROSA

VICTOR

RECORDED PREDICTIONS:

IT HAD TO MAKE MORE ROOM. THIS ONE (CAN 4) IS BIGGER THAN THIS ONE (CAN 3). IT (SECOND LEVEL) HAD TO GO HIGHER.

THOSE GUYS WERE RIGHT—THEY CAME CLOSER. IT'S BIGGER AND NEEDS MORE ROOM. IT WEIGHS THE SAME. IT DOESN'T MATTER VERY MUCH HOW MUCH IT WEIGHS. IT'S JUST THE TALLER ONE.

IT HAD TO MAKE MORE ROOM. THIS ONE (CAN 4) IS BIGGER THAN THIS ONE (CAN 3) IT (SECOND LEVEL) HAD TO GO HIGHER!

THAT'S BIG (CAN 4) AND HAS TO PUSH UP MORE WATER.

After observing the results for the last pair of cans, the children agree that it's the volume of the immersed cans that is responsible for the displacement of water.

Predict what the children will say and do when given:

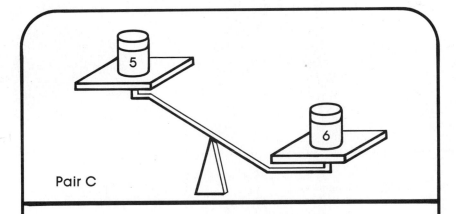

Pair C

cylinders having the same volume but different weights.

C. SAME VOLUME
DIFFERENT WEIGHT

The heavier of the pair is lowered into the water after the cans are examined by all children with the aid of the balance.

Then the children mark their predictions.

$*$
R_1
J_2
V_3

JUSTIFICATIONS:

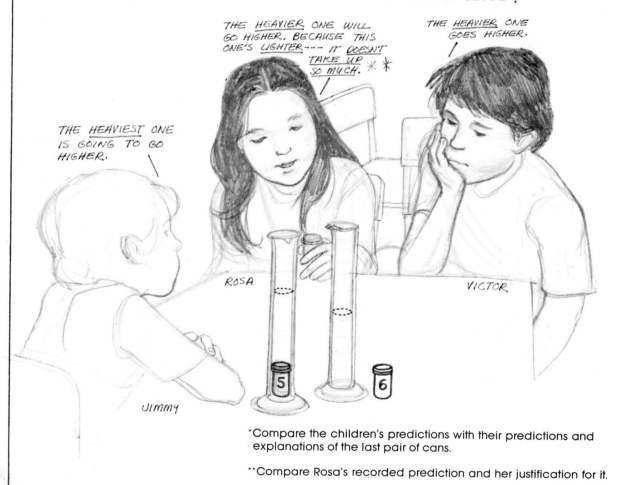

TEACHER: WHAT MADE YOU DECIDE ON THE WATER LEVEL?

THE HEAVIER ONE WILL GO HIGHER. BECAUSE THIS ONE'S LIGHTER --- IT DOESN'T TAKE UP $*$ $*$ SO MUCH.

THE HEAVIER ONE GOES HIGHER.

THE HEAVIEST ONE IS GOING TO GO HIGHER.

ROSA

VICTOR

JIMMY

*Compare the children's predictions with their predictions and explanations of the last pair of cans.

**Compare Rosa's recorded prediction and her justification for it.

The children observe the water level as the lighter can is lowered into the water. Jimmy looks dumbfounded. Rosa also shows some surprise. Victor's expression is relatively unchanged. They all agree that the resultant water levels are the same.
    Their teacher then asks them: What do you think happened?

EXPLANATIONS:

Predict what the children will say
and do when given:

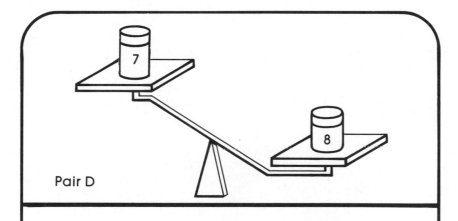

Pair D

cylinders of different weight* and
different volume.
(*Notice which one is heavier)

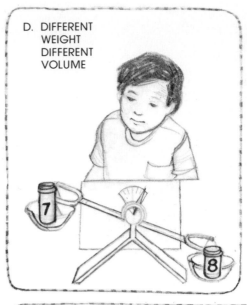

D. DIFFERENT WEIGHT DIFFERENT VOLUME

The larger can is also the lighter can of the pair.

This can is lowered first and then the children record their predictions.

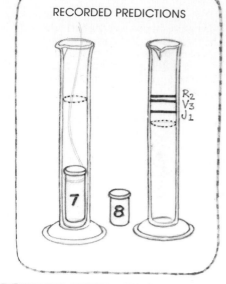

RECORDED PREDICTIONS

R_2
V_3
J_1

JUSTIFICATION

CAN YOU TELL ME WHY YOU DECIDED THAT WAY?

THIS TALL ONE (CAN 7) WILL GO HIGHER IF THE OTHER (CAN 8) WAS THE SAME SIZE IT WOULD BE THE SAME (LEVEL).

?

THIS ONE IS SMALLER * SO IT WON'T TAKE UP AS MUCH ROOM. IT WILL GO ABOUT UP TO___ THERE.

The children observe the water level as the smaller, heavier can is lowered into the water and find that it does not raise the water level as high as the larger, lighter can.

EXPLANATION

WOW!

IF THEY (CANS) WERE THE SAME SIZE IT (LEVEL) WOULD GO UP JUST AS HIGH.

IT DOESN'T MATTER HOW HEAVY IT (SECOND CAN) IS. IT COULD WEIGH THREE OR FOUR POUNDS AND STILL NOT GO ANY HIGHER!

What can we infer from Jimmy's facial expressions after he observes the results of pair C and pair D?

* Notice the inconsistencies between Rosa's marked prediction and her justification.

The teacher wasn't satisfied with her knowledge of the children's level of understanding; she referred to a pair of cans used previously, cans five and six in pair C.

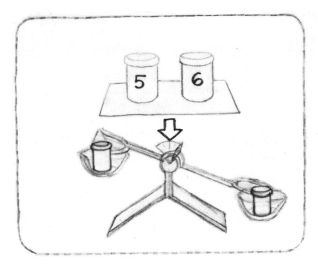

The cans are lowered into the water, one at a time, and the levels are checked.

- What else could the teacher have done here to learn more about the children's understanding?

- What can we infer from the expressions of Rosa and Victor after seeing the results for pair D and the results here?

EXTENSION

All pairs of cans are now examined.

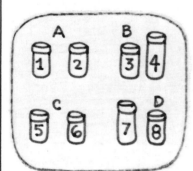

The children agree that the tallest ones will push the water up higher. The teacher removes the taller cans.

NO, THEY'RE JUST THE SAME SIZE.

THESE TWO MIGHT BE LOWER

WOULD SOME OF THESE MAKE THE WATER LEVEL GO UP LOWER THAN OTHERS?

A spontaneous comparison of weights of the remaining cans begins.

WHAT DO YOU THINK WOULD HAPPEN IF I PUT ONE OF THE LIGHT-WEIGHT ONES AND ONE OF THE HEAVY ONES IN THE WATER?

THIS ONE (THE HEAVIER CAN) MIGHT GO UP HIGHER.

IT WILL PROBABLY BE THE SAME.

I THINK IT WILL STAY THE SAME.

VICTOR   ROSA   JIMMY

YOU HAVE A DISAGREEMENT HERE—WHAT COULD YOU DO CHECK IT OUT?

The children and teacher take turns in lowering a can. The lighter of the two cans is lowered last.

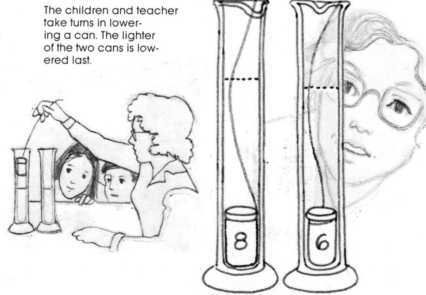

Jimmy and Rosa look surprised, as well as the teacher. The level of the water is higher in the cylinder with the heavy can.

- How can you explain the surprising result? (There is a clue on the preceding page.)

- Predict what Rosa and Jimmy will do and say?

- Is there something else the teacher could have done before checking the predictions?

Although the cans were carefully paired for the sequence, they became mismatched when all were mixed together.

Both cans were the same height but the heavier one also had a larger diameter.

TEACHER:

YOU SEEM TO HAVE A DISAGREEMENT HERE. WHAT CAN YOU DO TO CHECK IT OUT?

TAKE THE CANS OUT OF THE WATER TO SEE IF THE WATER LEVEL IS THE SAME.

JIMMY   ROSA

. . . After much discussion, they agree the water levels are equal.

TEACHER:

DO YOU SUPPOSE THE DIFFERENCE COULD BE SOMEWHERE ELSE?

THE HEAVIER ONE COULD BE BIGGER.

JIMMY   ROSA

THIS ONE IS ROUNDER AND---- THIS ONE IS THINNER.

THEY'RE A DIFFERENT SIZE.

Are these children thinking?

The following statements are typical responses of people who are unfamiliar with Piaget's theory:

"Surely the vacillations in the children's predictions and explanations would disappear if they were serious about their thinking. All they need to do is to pay attention to see that it's the volume that makes the difference."

"Isn't this kind of thinking unusual for children going into junior high school?"

- Do you consider that the children were thinking?
- If so, how would you describe the thinking of Jimmy, Rosa, and Victor?
- If not, why not?

Are these children learning?

"How can children understand something one moment and not the next?"

"This episode took more than thirty minutes; surely learning can be more efficient than that!"

- Do you believe that the children are learning through this approach of alternate predicting and testing?
- If so, what evidence is there that the children are learning?
- If not, why not?

Couldn't the teacher be teaching?

"How can a child learn if the teacher doesn't correct his wrong answers? The teacher just accepted the children's responses even though they were obviously wrong. Why didn't she praise (reinforce) a child's answer when it was given correctly?"

"Why didn't the teacher just tell the children the rule and demonstrate an example? Surely she could do this in much less time and the children would know the correct answer!"

"Would you let Victor leave this exploration without setting his thinking straight?"

"Couldn't the teacher facilitate the children's thinking and learning by alerting them to the inconsistencies in their thinking and action from one moment to the next?"

• Do you believe that direct teaching (demonstrating, telling, and reinforcing) could improve the children's thinking and learning?

• Could any indirect teaching help the children's thinking and learning about displacement volume? Justify your responses.

Piaget: The Man, His Methods, and His Ideas

2

Piaget's ideas on intellectual development provide some surprising answers to the deep concerns raised at the end of Chapter 1. Before we can begin an in-depth discussion of this Exploration of children's thinking and learning, we need to take a brief look at Piaget, at his methods, and at the most pertinent aspects of his theory.

Piaget, the Man will outline the broad background from which Piaget approaches children's thinking.

Piaget's Method and Observations will discuss his clinical method which revealed surprising observations of children's thinking. It will include selected examples of these observations.

Piaget's Ideas on the Development of Thinking will argue the position that intellectual development is a process in which ideas are restructured and improved as a result of an individual's interaction with the environment. It will also provide you with some direct experience in restructuring your own ideas.

Piaget, The Man

Nature seems to have been playing a trick on adults since the beginning of time. We quickly forget what it was like to be a child. Instead, we create arbitrary expectations of what children should be like and assume we were that way as children. Our trap is that we can't really see what children are like because our expectations get in the way. We are too busy telling children how they should be to really observe what they say and do. Underlying our behavior is the assumption that children are helpless without our teaching (telling), and that there is nothing they can teach us. [1,2]

Jean Piaget is a Swiss psychologist who is internationally renowned for his studies of the development of children's thinking processes. Piaget's insight and empathy penetrated this illusion. At a time when childhood was given little acknowledgment as being different from adulthood, Piaget recognized and accepted children as different from adults. [2]

In 1920, Piaget, as a brilliant young graduate in both biology and psychology, was invited to use the children of a laboratory school in Paris, to standardize a reasoning test. He was to tabulate statistical data based on children's correct responses. Rather than approach the task with typical adult expectations and thus focus only on correct responses, *Piaget actually listened to what the children were saying.* He soon became so fascinated by the patterns emerging from the children's incorrect responses that he undertook his own studies to reveal the thinking processes behind these responses. This fascination led to a lifetime study of how children view the world—how they organize and reorganize their thinking about the world around them. Since that time Piaget has published over 35 books and numerous articles on his findings. The unexpected nature of his findings has served as a catalyst for considerable research activity around the world.

Piaget's Method and Observations

Piaget's ability to listen to children as well as his fascination with children's error patterns reflects an openness to accepting children as they are, independent of arbitrary adult expectations. From this acceptance evolved a method that became his trademark. Piaget's natural rapport with children led one writer to describe him as a "papa-experimenter."[3]

In a method typical of Piaget, the child is presented with physical objects from his environment, e.g., balls of clay, glasses of water, etc. The interviewer observes what the child does and listens intently to what the child says in response to the materials.[2]

The interviewer not only raises questions about the materials, but also asks questions aimed at uncovering the thinking processes underlying a child's responses. As he asks the questions, he accepts the child's responses. He imposes neither adult expectations of correctness nor adult explanations. This acceptance allows the interviewer to follow a child's intricate thought patterns without deforming them.

Questions are phrased in the child's language and may be restated in different ways to clarify his thinking processes. The child's actions and responses suggest new questions to the interviewer, who is free to follow his intuitions. In a word, flexibility is the key to Piaget's interview method, with each interview adapted to the individual child.[3,4]

Although he is interested in what children know, Piaget's chief concern is in how children come to know.

The combination of his ingenious tasks with physical materials and his penetrating questions has altered our knowledge of how children think and learn.

Piaget noticed patterns in children's responses to intellectual tasks which he interpreted as reflections of children's level of reasoning.

Children of like age groups responded in ways that were remarkably similar to each other and remarkably different from adult responses and expectations.

Piaget observed that children have their own ways of figuring out, organizing ideas, or recalling a visual presentation.

Most five-year-old children focus on the height of the water level as the indicator of the amount of liquid in a glass. To them equal height indicates equal amount regardless of the diameter of the container.

Representative drawings made from memory by six-year-olds one hour following exposure to example.[5]

This drawing was made from memory immediately following exposure. It is representative of most five- to six-year old children.[5]

When the perceptual attraction of the most striking dimension is pitted against the developing system of logical thought of young children, the perceptual attraction typically wins out. This way of interpreting the world is typical of most children below six to seven years of age. They believe the basic amount of something changes when its appearance changes.

Adults, too, are aware of their environment from a different perspective or framework than children. They also view many matters differently from friends of the same age.

Yet they often express surprise or disappointment when observing their children's thinking in progress, and they try to counteract this "fuzzy" thinking with a logical explanation.

Piaget's Ideas on the Development of Thinking

As systematic differences between children's and adult's view of the world reappeared in more and more situations, Piaget set out to explain these patterns.

Since so little was known about the complex functioning of the brain Piaget could only infer internal, mental differences from his observations of children's thinking in action. He explained these external differences with ideas that made sense to him. These ideas developed into a comprehensive theory of the development of thinking.

In this section we will look at thinking in action, somewhat as Piaget might, and examine processes of restructuring ideas that result in more effective ways of dealing with the environment.

How Our Minds Interpret Reality

Rather than passively record a mental copy of reality, as a camera makes a physical copy, our minds actively interpret and construct a representation of it in the manner of a creative artist. Our mental image resembles a painting rather than a photograph of reality.[1]

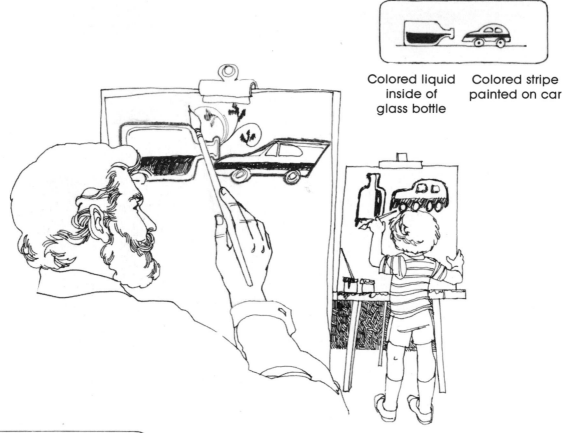

Colored liquid inside of glass bottle

Colored stripe painted on car

A camera copies reality.

People interpret and construct their reality.

The interpretation or reconstruction of reality is initiated by the present organization of our existing knowledge or framework that we bring to a situation. In this example a person's current understanding of spatial relations interacts with his input from the senses. We bend reality to the way we have organized our understandings to receive it. The drawings made from memory several minutes after a visual presentation reflect the mental images of the child and adult in contrast to their common sensory input. The contrasting interpretations of the same environment by a young child and an adult suggest that the organization of their mental frameworks differ considerably. Major differences in mental organization account for the differences in perspective, with smaller variations in organization accounting for differences in personal style.

A Child's Construction of a New Concept[6,7]

Consider three-year-old Betty, who meets cats in her neighborhood daily. From her observations, she is able to organize a mental category or concept built on cats' similarities, despite their differences. She can recall the category for use when needed. Organizing her observations in this way gives her an effective means of handling new observations. We can infer this from Betty's observed behavior.

One day she notices a squirrel for the first time . . .

Having focused on the squirrel's similarities with cats only, she mentally placed this new information from the environment into her category for cats. However, curiosity aroused, she approaches the squirrel and it runs off.

Later in the day, she is surprised to see a squirrel standing on its hind legs. After a momentary puzzlement her expression changes as she calls after the squirrel.

Having focused on a difference between squirrels and cats, the child found the "cat" category was no longer useful here. She formed a new category based on the differences she observed. The squirrel can fit into this new category. Her facial expression suggests that she has reached a solution that is satisfying to her mental framework and is compatible with her experience.

On another occasion, when she used the "funny kitty" label in her mother's presence, she was given the correct label. The name "*squirrel*" fitted into her framework. Earlier, Betty, through her framework of personal experiences, interacted with the new experience and constructed a new mental category in response to the demands of reality. This new category is put into relation with previous knowledge and becomes part of a more discriminating framework that could handle information from the environment more efficiently. As Betty makes further observations of squirrels she will further refine her category.

You might say that Betty's mother taught her daughter the difference between two, somewhat similar, furry animals. You could also say that the mother's teaching was incidental to the child's learning. Although perhaps incidental, its timing was effective because her child had already constructed the preliminary understanding on her own.

A Child's Construction of a Solution to the Succession Puzzle Problem[8]*

To shed further light on Piaget's ideas of how we learn let's observe this child solve a tangram puzzle.

I'll be giving you some pieces and asking you to put them together with the ones you already have to make a regular geometric shape that's easy to describe to someone over the phone, e.g., square, triangle, parallelogram, etc.

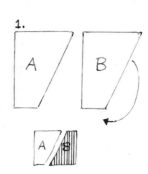

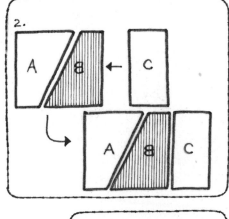

Here's how Johnny put the puzzle together . . .

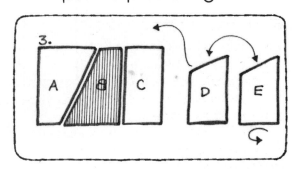

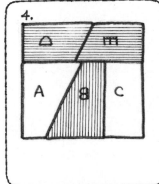

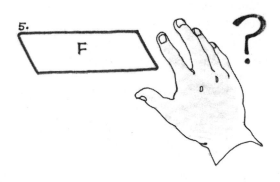

*(This puzzle is adapted from Edward de Bono's *Lateral Thinking*, New York: Harper & Row, Publishers, 1970.)

If you were Johnny, how would you solve the problem?

(This puzzle is adapted from Edward de Bono's *Lateral Thinking*, New York: Harper & Row, Publishers, 1970.)

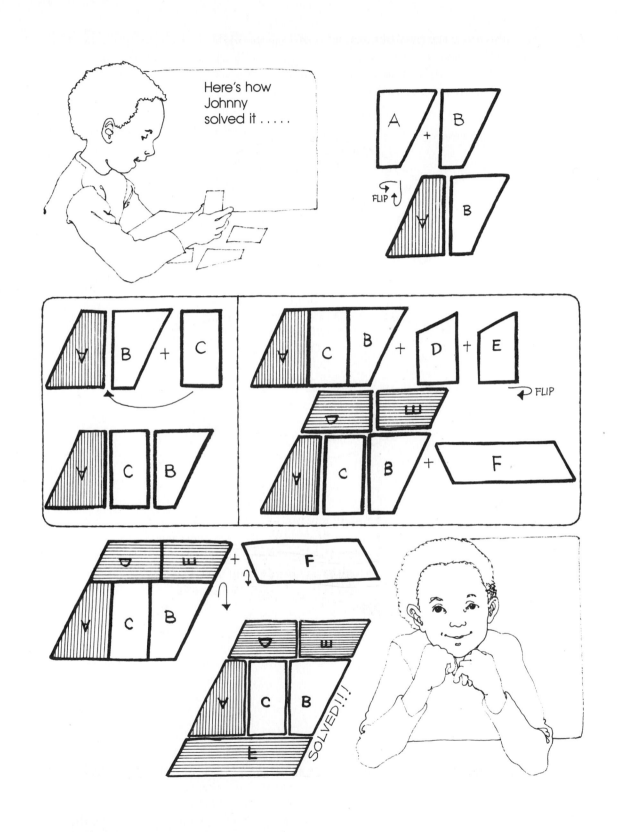

Here's how Johnny solved it . . . . .

(This puzzle is adapted from Edward de Bono's *Lateral Thinking*, New York: Harper & Row, Publishers, 1970.)

Before discussing the previous examples of constructing and reconstructing our ideas about the environment in terms of Piaget's ideas, the following clarification of terms may be helpful. Although Piaget refers to the mental framework in more precise terms, we will use a variety of descriptive terms to get across the general idea.

The following metaphors will be used interchangeably to communicate the way in which individuals organize the seemingly random input from the environment so as to be able to infer regularities or reorganize their ideas. The *product* of this organization, the current mental framework of ideas, in turn, becomes involved in the *process* of its own reorganization. The metaphors reflect this "duality" to different degrees.

Framework

Structures

Organizers

Categories

Concepts

Thought patterns

Strategies

Starting with a few basic structures available at birth, the child begins interacting with his environment to reorganize these structures and to develop new ones. The new mental structures result in more effective ways of dealing with the environment. Beyond birth, Piaget believes that the personal framework of organized knowledge that a person brings to a situation is actively constructed from previous interactions with the environment.

In Piaget's view, knowledge:

is NOT being absorbed passively from the environment,

is NOT being preformed in the child's mind and ready to emerge as the child matures, but

IS being constructed by the child through his interactions between his mental structures and his environment.

For Piaget, intellectual development is the process of restructuring knowledge:

The process starts with a structure or a way of thinking proper to one level;

Some external disturbance or intrusion on this ordinary way of thinking creates a conflict and disequilibrium;

The person compensates for the disturbance and solves the conflict by means of his own intellectual activity;

The final state is a new way of thinking and structuring things, a way that gives new understanding and satisfaction,

In a word, a state of new equilibrium.[9,p.95]

Towards a Balance Between
Stability and Change: Equilibration

In the last two examples of children's thinking and learning you've seen two processes in action, the resistance to change and the need for change. One leads to stability and the other to growth. Both processes operate simultaneously.

In the process of *assimilation* — incorporating our perceptions of new experiences into our existing framework — we resist change even to the extent that our perceptions may be "bent" to fit the existing framework. If this process were totally dominant, our mind would have only a few large and very stable categories for incoming information. We would be handicapped by being unable to differentiate between inputs. For example, the squirrel would never have its own category as distinct from the cat because all four-legged furry animals would be in the same category.

On the other hand, we modify and enrich structures in our framework as a result of new input demanding changes. If this process of *accommodation* were totally dominant it would greatly increase the number of categories for handling input. Each cat would be thought of as a different species and would have its own category. As a result we would have difficulty in generalizing to a class of cats.[7]

Obviously some balance between these processes is essential if the child's interactions with the environment are to lead to progressively higher levels of understanding. Piaget calls this active intellectual balance with the environment *equilibrium*. The overall process of reaching the state of balance has been illustrated in the Displacement Volume Problem and the Succession Puzzle problem. This process is known as *equilibration*. The state of imbalance, or *disequilibrium*, which includes the discomforting inner conflict between opposing interpretations, provides the motivation to find a solution. This solution restores the intellectual balance and inner contentment.

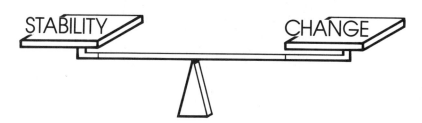

Assimilation of new information into our existing structures causes us to resist change, therefore ensuring that intellectual development is deliberate and continuous. As a child faces a basically familiar world, this process allows him time to connect structures that he has already constructed *internally*.

Contrarily, accommodation of new input (modifying existing structures) ensures change and extension of our understanding. This modification may involve reorganization of existing structures or construction of new ones, thus allowing more information to fit. Such accommodation to environmental events forces the child to move beyond his present understandings by testing them in novel situations.[10]

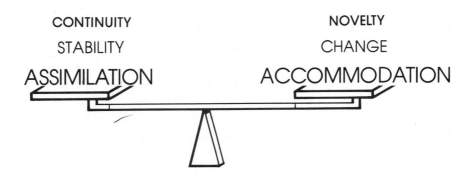

CONTINUITY   NOVELTY

STABILITY   CHANGE

ASSIMILATION   ACCOMMODATION

The Succession Puzzle sequence can serve as a physical model for what may take place in the child's mind. Each input from the environment interacts with the existing organization and is assimililated into this structure. The shape of the structure is not greatly changed.* The structure is, however, enlarged.

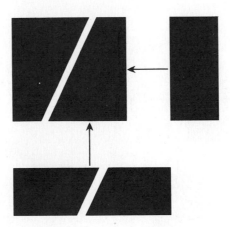

---

*It begins as a square—a special case of a rectangle—and continues to be a rectangle.

Sometimes new inputs from the environment no longer fit into the existing structure, thus creating a discrepancy. The solution comes from the intellectual interaction between the environment and the existing structure. The end result is that the existing structure is modified or accommodated.

Following the restructuring, more information from the environment can be assimilated, thus enlarging the new structure.

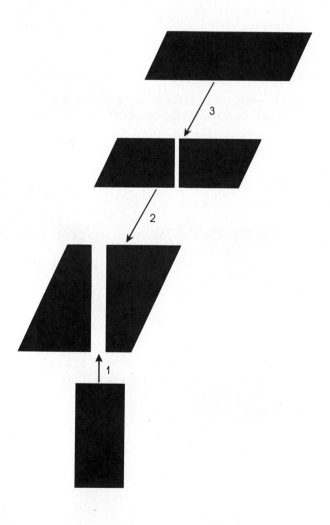

To distinguish between the processes of assimilation and accommodation, we have considered the two separately and sequentially. In reality, Piaget views them as interacting simultaneously Although some learning requires much accommodation and some requires much assimilation, neither exists in a pure form.[11]

Assimilation is the predominant process in the formation of the rectangle shown. However, some accommodation also takes place, that is, the sides are no longer equal as in the square when the structure is enlarged.

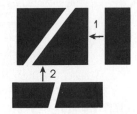

Accommodation is the main process when the original square is restructured to form a parallelogram. However, previous assimilation of spatial relations of geometric shapes permitted the restructuring.

New structure

Assimilation predominates once again as the parallelogram is enlarged. Although the superstructure still retains the shape of a parallelogram, the relationship between the lengths of its sides has been accommodated.

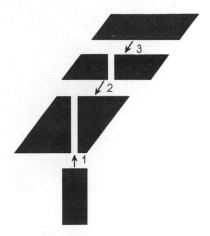

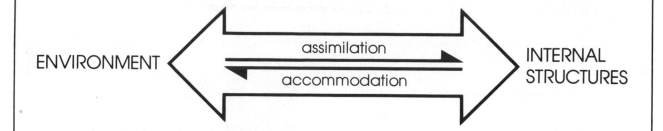

ENVIRONMENT

assimilation

accommodation

INTERNAL
STRUCTURES

Equilibrium is the balance between interacting factors, inside and outside the child.

Equilibration consists of complementary processes operating simultaneously.

These twin processes of assimilation and accommodation operate simultaneously to allow the child to reach progressively higher states of equilibrium. At each level of higher understanding, he is equipped with a more comprehensive structure or complex thinking patterns. Though each level is more stable than the last, each is nonetheless a temporary state. The more powerful thinking patterns, in turn, generate more intellectual activity as they point out gaps and inconsistencies in other existing patterns.[12] With possibilities for interaction with the environment expanded, the child can more readily assimilate external input into a framework that is not only expanding but also becoming more integrated. As he encounters more of the environment, he receives further stimulation for development of internal structures. Thus intellectual development may be visualized as a continuous spiraling process, with equilibration being the driving force behind this adaptation of the individual to his environment.[13]

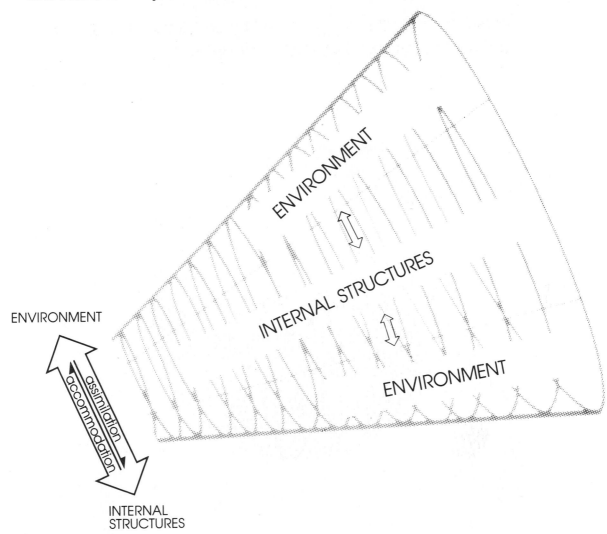

Before trying to clarify this process of restructuring knowledge any further, let's briefly examine three other factors of intellectual development.

Other Factors Affecting Intellectual Development

1. Maturation

The older a child is, the more likely that he will have more mental structures that act in more coordinated ways. The nervous system controls the potentialities available at a given time. It is not fully matured until about age 15 or 16. A maturation of supporting motor and perceptual abilities also takes place during this time.

2. Physical Experience

The more experience that a child has with physical objects in his environment, the more likely that related understanding will have developed.

Mexican children who help their parents make pottery develop related concepts earlier than Mexican children lacking this experience. The experience in a pottery shop helps the children to understand that altering the appearance of a piece of clay doesn't affect the amount of clay.[14]

A child can obtain *physical knowledge* — identify physical properties — directly from perceiving the objects themselves.

The child derives *logical knowledge* not from the objects themselves, but from manipulating them and the internal structuring of her action.[14] (Which objects that are used is unimportant.)

The buttons were in a random pile, without order. Through her actions the child introduced order.

In discovering that the sum is independent of the arrangement, the child discovered a property of her actions and not just a property of buttons.[15]

In a pile, the buttons had no sum. Through her actions of putting together and counting she made a sum.

3. Social Interaction

The more opportunities children have to interact with peers, parents and teachers, the more viewpoints they will hear. This experience stimulates children to think through their viewpoint and to approach objectivity. This type of interaction is also an important source of information on customs, labels, etc., which make up *social knowledge*.

The Sum of Intellectual Development

Taken individually, neither maturation nor physical or social experience can explain intellectual development.

Maturation is not enough. Age is only a crude indicator of intellectual development. Although more potentialities for furthering intellectual development of a child emerge with age, other factors are also important in actualizing this potential.

Physical experience is not enough. Children are unable to view water levels in a bottle relative to the horizon and independent of the bottle's position until about age nine. This happens despite rich experiences with drinking, pouring, bathing, and swimming during the preceding years. Factors other than physical experience are also involved in influencing intellectual development.

Social interaction is not enough. Some children are brought up in relative isolation. Yet, they do not appear to be seriously handicapped in developing basic understandings of the physical world around them. Other factors, however, are essential for refining these understandings.

No single factor can account for intellectual development by itself. It is a combination of all of these factors:

Maturation
Physical experience
Social interaction
EQUILIBRATION

and the interactions between and among them that influence this development. Equilibration is seen by Piaget as playing a principal, coordinating role in these interactions.

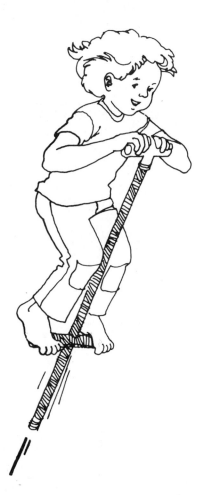

Equilibration is the most fundamental of the four factors influencing intellectual development—it coordinates the other three. It involves a continuous interaction between a child's mind and reality. Not only does the child assimilate experience into his existing mental framework, he also accommodates the structures of his framework in response to his experience.

This cycle of repeated interactions between the child and his environment depends on the child as the mainspring to his own development. The child's activity not only uncovers new problems, and thus initiates disequilibrium, it also constructs a solution and attains a higher level of equilibrium. Since the child has such an active role in the process, equilibration is also known as *self-regulation*.

The child is the mainspring to his own development.

Piaget's view of the child's internal construction of knowledge through a cycle of repeated and self-expanding interactions between his mental framework and his environment is called *an interactionist position*. Similarly, Piaget's view of the child's active role in constructing this knowledge is known as a *constructivist position* in developmental psychology.

Experiencing Equilibration

Since equilibration plays such an important role in Piaget's view of intellectual development, you are asked to consciously experience this process to make it more meaningful to you. For the exercise you will need a rectangular hand mirror, a pencil and a large book.

Mirror Reading:[16]

←—— Place mirror along this line. ——→

> Put your mirror along this line and look into it.

CAN YOU READ THIS IN THE MIRROR?

Now read these words in the mirror. →

CARBON DIOXIDE

How can you explain what you see? Take a couple of minutes to think about it.
If you still can't explain it, place your mirror along the line of letters below.

    Look at the first six letters.
    Now predict the mirror image of the others.
    Check your prediction if you're not sure.

(Place mirror here.)

A B C D E F G H I J K L M N O P Q R S T U V W X Y Z

Mirror Writing:[16,17]

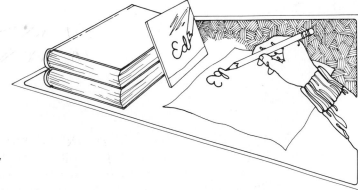

Write your name while looking into the mirror. In other words, change your style of writing so that its mirror image appears "normal."

Mirror Drawing:[16,17]

Trace the drawings below while looking into the mirror and not lifting your pencil.

A book placed between you and the mirror can be used to block out your view of the drawing.

Copy these shapes while looking into the mirror:

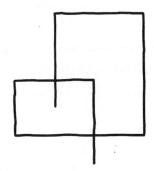

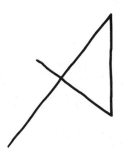

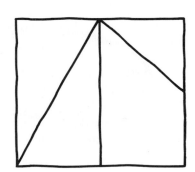

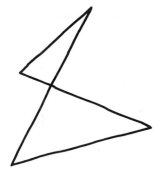

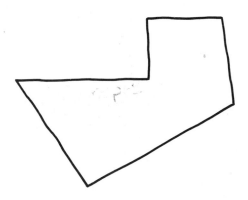

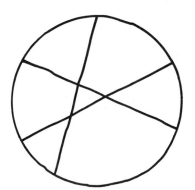

Unless you make a living at mirror drawings you've just experienced disequilibrium. Your old thinking patterns weren't very helpful in this situation. What you saw yourself drawing was contrary to your expectations based on previous experience. In the mirror

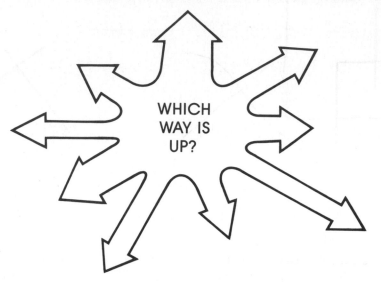

drawing you experienced a discomforting awareness of a conflict between your "up" and "down" commands and the direction of your hand movements. Your input from the mirror demanded that you do some accommodating. Like most people, you probably experienced frustration with your initial attempts. If you stayed with the task and reflected on the changes needed to coordinate your movements with your mirror image feedback, you eventually experienced success. In moving from a state of disequilibrium to one of equilibrium, you must have been quite aware of your initial resistance to change as you slipped back into old patterns several times before reaching a stable behavior pattern. Only then could you assimilate a variety of new drawings with relative ease.

Putting It Together

Reflect on your understanding of Piaget's view of intellectual development, and then record these ideas. In accordance with Piaget's view of learning you are encouraged to construct a summary of the chapter in your own words.

Revisiting the Thinking and Learning Exploration with Piaget as a Guide

3

Now that you've experienced equilibration directly as well as having read about it and reflected on the process, you are ready to take a second look at the Exploration of Children's Thinking and Learning in Chapter I. You are asked to do this prior to reading any further. By this time you may have some different ideas about the exploration. Approaching the exploration from a modified personal framework may alter your ideas about it. If you've done some accommodating of your views on thinking and learning, you can now assimilate more information from the sequence. Also, you should have more empathy for the children as they pit their developing logic against the perceptual pull of the heavy objects in their hands.

This chapter will re-examine the concerns raised in Chapter I. It will discuss the children's *thinking* and *learning* as well as the teacher's method of *exploring,* from Piaget's viewpoint.

Introduction

The Exploration of Children's Thinking and Learning about displacement volume in Chapter 1 is a group adaptation of a sequence designed by Magali Bovet, one of Piaget's associates.[1] It was devised following a preliminary study of children's spontaneous approaches to the understanding of displacement volume. This preliminary study revealed that children often  have two misconceptions that interfere with their understanding of displacement volume: (1) Larger objects are usually heavier, and (2) An object's weight is what displaces the water when submerged. The objects and situations from the Exploration would normally be encountered in random order over a much longer period of time. Here, in the Exploration, the encounters with relevant objects are sequenced and compressed into a shorter, more intense period. The children are actively engaged in making predictions, checking the outcomes, and constructing explanations in each encounter. By exposing children to a range of related tasks, a conflict between opposing interpretations is initiated which may lead to a successful reorganization of ideas.

The purpose of this sequence of tasks in the context of Piaget's research is to reveal the moments of children's internal reorganization through their responses, actions, and facial expressions. An analysis of the Exploration, therefore, will shed light on the children's *thinking* and *learning* processes. An analysis also will offer insights into methods of *exploring* and facilitating children's thinking and learning.

Exploring Thinking and Learning [1,2,3]

These children are serious about their thinking. Their thinking and learning behavior is predicted by Piaget's theory.

Victor did not seem bothered by the results, which appear contradictory to an adult. His face lacked any expression to suggest that he was aware of the discrepancies between his observations, predictions, and explanations. As compelling as was the feedback provided by the immersed materials, just seeing the results didn't auto-  matically trigger his internal restructuring to greater understanding. An awareness of the contradictions in his thinking would be a clear indicator of disequilibrium and, thus, an initiation of the equilibration process. Could it be that the level of thinking required by the tasks to allow Victor to be aware of the problem is beyond the reach of his existing framework at this point?

During the same sequence of tasks, Jimmy and Rosa eventually reached a stage of expectancy for greater regularity. They began to perceive their predictions and subsequent observations as contradictory. From their responses you can infer that the thinking demands of the tasks were matched closely enough with their existing mental frameworks to trigger the equilibration process successfully. They were able to let go of an old notion—"It seems that heavier objects should make the water go higher"—and construct a new concept.

Learning begins with recognition of a problem (disequilibrium).

The demands of the task must match the child's framework if there is to be a problem.

The episode illustrates the children's characteristic of alternating focus on opposing variables, i.e., weight and volume, during disequilibrium.

JIMMY'S PREDICTIONS AND EXPLANATIONS

	Volume	Weight	Prediction/Justification	Explanation
A.	Same	Same	*same* level	Both are just as *heavy* so this level is the same as that.
B.	Different	Same	*same* level because this one is just as *heavy*.	It's *bigger* and needs more *room*. It doesn't matter very much how much it weighs.
C.	Same	Different	The *heavier* one is going to go *higher*.	I think he's right, it's just the *size*.
D.	Different	Different	The *tall* one will go *higher*. If the other can was the same *size* it would be the same (level).	*It doesn't matter how heavy* the smaller can is. It could weigh three to four pounds and still not go any higher!

As shown above, Jimmy made a retroactive correction based on observation of the second pair of cans. He then blithely ignored his conclusion when the third pair was introduced, making a prediction that clearly contradicts his explanation for the second pair. However, upon seeing the results of the third pair, he looks astonished. This awareness of the contradiction between his thinking and the feedback from the materials initiated his equilibration. For the fourth pair of cans, his prediction is consistent with all previous outcomes.

THE HEAVIER ONE WILL GO HIGHER. BECAUSE THIS ONE'S LIGHTER --- IT DOESN'T TAKE UP SO MUCH. ✳ ✳

ROSA

Rosa was the first to predict a difference in the water level owing to a difference in the volumes of the cans. Following this correct prediction, she vacillated twice before her responses became consistent. After first stating and marking her prediction based on volume in situation B, she also marked her prediction for situation C on the same basis. However, she fluctuated in her focus on the variables while making a verbal prediction for the same pair of cans. In making her statement, Rosa did an about face and favored the heaviest can. Furthermore, as she completed her justification she constructed an original solution taking both weight and volume into account. Another vacillation in Rosa's focus can be observed in her predictions within situation D. In a state of disequilibrium what we say and do does not always agree.

In a state of disequilibrium what we say and do does not always agree.

Is there an alternative explanation to Rosa's vacillations in a group situation?

During disequilibrium, when the child begins to sense contradictions in his reasoning, there seems to be a breakdown in the existing, stable intellectual structures followed by reorganizations of thought patterns into new structures. Until these structures are fully integrated, they produce largely unpredictable behaviors, for example, vacillating judgments, sometimes logical, sometimes illogical. These rapid alternations in judgments seem to increase the probability of internal reorganization. What is predictable about these behaviors is the increasing probability of logical judgments until equilibrium is reached. Often, children who experience the most confusion during the sequence arrive at the highest level of understanding.

In the preceding examples it is apparent that children's notions about water displacement don't proceed from being totally wrong to being totally correct. There are many vacillations in which these notions appear to almost exist side by side before the advanced notion appears consistently. Furthermore, even the wrong notions contain some degree of correctness. In these activities it is not entirely wrong to consider weight as a determining factor in water displacement. Weight actually does play a role here. Sufficient weight is necessary to make an object sink in order for it to displace an amount of water equal to its volume. Beyond that minimum weight, the range of possible weights does not affect the displacement. The weight response, therefore, has some logical basis and may be regarded as incomplete. The tasks require the child to dissociate water and volume from a complex relationship which he is in the process of constructing.

Teachers usually consider such switching from one kind of reasoning to another as being errors for eradication. In contrast, Piaget views such responses as uncoordinated and incomplete, but necessary, intermediate steps towards a higher level of understanding.

A child's errors are actually natural steps to understanding.

The attainment of a stable equilibrium is reflected in the children's increased confidence. This can be inferred from their facial expressions and their emphatic justifications. Jimmy's explanation, which generalizes beyond his immediate experience with these materials, clearly indicates his confidence.

IT DOESN'T MATTER HOW HEAVY IT (SECOND CAN) IS.
IT COULD WEIGH THREE OR FOUR POUNDS AND STILL NOT GO ANY HIGHER!

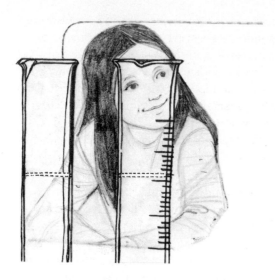

The level of the children's confidence can be tested in their response to a discrepant event or by a verbal challenge from the teacher. The stability of Jimmy's and Rosa's new understanding was reflected in their insistence on a logical explanation of a discrepant event which resulted when slightly mismatched pair of cans displaced unequal amounts of water.

Other children might demonstrate their confidence by treating further questions as amusing or exasperating, since the answer is at this point obvious to them.

Exploring Thinking and Learning[2,3]

Throughout the exploration in Chapter 1 the teacher maintained a very accepting manner but gave no verbal sanctions to any responses. She accepted answers that were wrong according to adult logic and did not use praise to reinforce correct responses. She recognized the wrong answers as being normal to the children's developmental level and part of the equilibration process. This attitude provided an atmosphere of freedom in which the children were able to express exactly what they experienced and believed. In other words, acceptance leads to unADULTerated thinking by children.

The use of praise to reinforce correct responses creates pressure to learn through social conformity rather than by active equilibration. Such pressure interferes drastically with children's confidence in how they experience their environment, as well as with the development of their reasoning processes.

Acceptance leads to unADULTerated thinking by children.

Following 30 minutes of related experiences together with compelling feedback from the materials, Victor had not arrived at an adult understanding of displacement volume. By this time, even though it was an exploration of thinking, it would be very tempting for a teacher to tell him the "correct" answer. That Victor apparently ignored the conflicting evidence of the immersed materials suggests that his internal structures define his experience. His observations of the reality of volume displacement are interpreted by his internal structures. Consequently, his interpretation may not agree with that of Jimmy or Rosa. Piaget believes the child actively constructs knowledge internally through continuous interaction with the environment, rather than passively absorbing it from the environment. Since Victor failed to perceive the compelling physical evidence as conflicting, it is unlikely that telling him the "correct" answer could lead to a true understanding, even though Victor could repeat the response successfully for the teacher.

The teacher, in her exploration of children's thinking and learning, might have facilitated the equilibration process by alerting them to the inconsistencies in their thinking. In Rosa's situation she might have asked her to repeat her earlier prediction and compare it to her recorded prediction. The teacher might ask if the predictions "mean the same thing." Similarly, questions which encouraged comparisons of predictions on different pairs of cans might have helped Victor to initiate a disequilibrium. Such questions might also have sharpened the contradictions which were recognized later by Jimmy and Rosa. Note that although the teacher might attempt to alert the children to the discrepancies, it is the children's mental framework and activity that are responsible for recognizing them.

Teaching involves more than merely telling.

According to Piaget's theory,
the equilibration processes
of
experiencing discrepancies
between
ideas, predictions, and outcomes,
whether
compressed and sequenced as in the exploration
or
randomly experienced in real life,
are
important factors in the acquisition of knowledge
they are the basis of life-long learning.

THE EXPLORATION CONTINUED

The teacher followed her intuitions about Victor's readiness to tackle the problem and spontaneously moved into ten minutes of unplanned activities. They successively stacked pairs of cans in the cylinders of water. Predictions and discussion took place at each step.

Suddenly, Victor became very active at predicting outcomes. He had arrived at a definite expectancy and was anxious to have it verified. His facial expression, though neutral throughout most of the episode, now reflected a mental engagement, and finally an inner satisfaction at his new-found expectancy.* Meanwhile, Jimmy, who had solved the problem earlier, showed much less involvement.

*Since the task was quite similar to the original sequence, Victor may have arrived at his correct responses through social conformity in the group, rather than through equilibration. A truer measure of his understanding would be another displacement volume task requiring totally different materials, and no input from the others.

Putting It Together

- Construct your own summary of personal meanings gained from the analysis of the Thinking and Learning Exploration.

- The teacher who conducted the Exploration reflected back on it and identified an important implication for her teaching of children.

The Exploration was certainly a thinking and learning experience for me and affected my subsequent work with children in my third-grade classroom. It revealed to me that as a teacher I can't assume what appears to be apparent about children's learning. I better appreciate how slowly concepts are developed. Just because a child demonstrates some understanding of a math concept one day, I can't assume that his understanding is stable and therefore check it off as being taught.

Identify and record an implication of this Exploration for your work with children.

Piaget's Stages-Levels of Children's Thinking

4

Piaget noticed patterns in children's responses to intellectual tasks. Children of like ages responded in ways that were at the same time remarkably similar and yet remarkably different from adult responses and expectations. Likewise, children at different situations, Piaget categorized levels of children's thinking into four major stages.

On the basis of the patterns that he observed repeatedly in different situations, Piaget categorized levels of children's thinking into four major stages:

	STAGE	AGE RANGE*	CHARACTERISTICS
Preparatory, prelogical stages	Sensori-motor	Birth– 2 years	Coordination of physical actions; prerepresentational + preverbal.
	Preoperational	2–7 years	Ability to represent action through thought + language; prelogical.
Advanced, logical thinking stages	Concrete operational	7–11 years	Logical thinking, but limited to physical reality
	Formal operational	11–15 years	Logical thinking, abstract and unlimited

This chapter will describe and contrast children's thinking at each of the four stages. To aid in this comparison, the characteristic reactions of different-aged children to the same task will be placed side by side whenever possible. Part A of the chapter will describe children's thinking in the first two preparatory stages, while Part B will describe and

---

*Age ranges quoted in this chapter represent averages reported for Swiss children. Departures from these ages can be expected for individuals and for different cultures.

contrast children's thinking in the advanced, logical thinking stages. In Part C, Piaget's concept of stage will be clarified with references to earlier examples of children's thinking. You will be invited, in Part D, to explore levels of children's thinking yourself and will be provided with some necessary background which allows you to do so.

A. The Preparatory, Prelogical Stages

First Comes Thinking

Which statement in the following pairs do you think is true?
Think of past observations of children which support your choice.

a. Babies are helpless creatures who are totally dependent on their mothers' care and must wait until they develop language before they can receive instructions and begin to learn from their mothers.

b. Babies actively pursue the development of intelligence in the first months after birth through expanding encounters with their environment. Considerable intelligence is developed before language is even spoken.

a. Play is a necessary activity in the child's intellectual development, e.g., through "make believe" play the child not only develops his capacity for mentally letting something stand for something else, but also develops a foundation for logical thinking.

b. Play is something that children do to amuse themselves and to while away the time until they are old enough to attend school.

Some adults have commented that babies don't interest them until they walk, talk, and think. Even mothers express gratification as their infants become less dependent and are judged to understand better what the mother says or wants. Part of the genius of Piaget's contribution to theory is his careful observation of the child's beginning intelligence being manifested even in the first months of life. From observations of his own three children he documented six levels in the child's sequential origins of intelligence during its first two years.[1] Subsequently the general sequence of the child's development in this sensori-motor stage has been verified by others.[2,3] Beyond this initial stage, Piaget expanded his observation of children to include a broader sampling. A summary of children's characteristic behaviors during the two preparatory, prelogical stages—the sensori-motor stage and the preoperational stage, follows.

Sequence of Development in Sensori-Motor Stage[1,4,5]

	DIFFERENTIATION OF REFLEXES (0–1 mo.)	FORMATION OF FIRST ACTION PATTERNS (1–4 mo.)
GENERAL DEVELOPMENT	The infant comes into the world equipped with all his senses and a few reflexes for survival such as sucking and crying. Initially, the infant's sucking reflex is triggered automatically by anything placed in his mouth. In a widening search for objects to suck he exercises this reflex. He also learns to recognize objects by sucking on them and begins to discriminate between objects to suck. Since sucking his thumb is performed differently from sucking his mother's breast, the infant learns to accommodate his activity to differences in size, shape and position.	Some of the infant's random movements produce interesting results; for example, his thumb may fall into his mouth, trigger sucking, and drop out. He immediately attempts to rediscover the behavior so that the pleasurable sucking can be repeated. After considerable trial and error the infant is able to coordinate his erratic movements and produce a repeatable action pattern. The infant does not intentionally invent new behaviors but merely reproduces familiar ones through a cycle of self-stimulation. Initially, these action patterns—or habits—are restricted to the infant's body.
	NO EXPECTATIONS (0–2 mo.)	PASSIVE EXPECTATION (2–4 mo.)
OBJECT PERMANENCE	The infant will not look for an object or person that leaves his visual field. Out of sight is out of mind. He has no knowledge that objects or people exist independent of his perceptions. The infant's world is limited to himself and his actions.	The infant develops the ability to follow a moving object with his eyes. When the object disappears, he will continue to look in that direction as if expecting it to reappear. This expectation, however, is passive as the infant does not actively search for it.

THE NEWBORN CHILD ENTERS THE WORLD EQUIPPED WITH ALL HIS SENSES AND ONLY A LIMITED NUMBER OF REFLEXES.

	FORMATION OF ACTION PATTERNS WITH THE EXTERNAL WORLD (4–8 mos.)	COORDINATION OF FAMILIAR ACTION PATTERNS (8–12 mos.)
GENERAL DEVELOPMENT	The infant exercises his grasping reflex and manipulates objects he encounters in his immediate vicinity, developing eye-hand coordination. His ability to crawl expands his horizons to include more of the external world. Acts which were initiated by chance, if they interest the infant, can now be repeated purposefully. An infant lying in a crib may make chance contact with a mobile while kicking his feet. He will then reproduce this action pattern to recreate the interesting movement of the mobile. Such goal-directed activity is initiated only after chance discovery of the connection between kicking and the mobile's movement. When presented with a pair of objects, the infant will reach for the moderately novel one as opposed to a familiar one.	The child will move to strike down a barrier such as an adult hand which is placed between it and an interesting object. (The object is placed above the barrier so that it remains visible to the child.) The child is able to coordinate two familiar action patterns—one of striking and one of grasping an object. One of his actions serves as the means to the goal while the other serves as the goal itself. At this level of development the child is able to coordinate familiar actions into larger patterns. He is still unable to invent new action patterns. Since the child had a goal in mind (intention) prior to the action, Piaget views his behavior as an indicator of intelligence.
OBJECT PERMANENCE	SEARCH FOR PARTLY COVERED OBJECTS (4–8 mos.) The infant learns to anticipate the landing place of dropped objects. He will actively search for the object in the expected location, particularly when he has thrown or dropped it. Through manipulation of objects the infant develops an ability to recognize partially visible objects, and will search for partly hidden ones.	SEARCH FOR COMPLETELY HIDDEN OBJECTS (8–12 mos.) The child will now search for a completely hidden object, even though another person has moved it. But, after the child has successfully retrieved a hidden object from a pillow on the adult's right, he will be unable to find it when next hidden under a sweater on the adult's left. The child will ignore the object's displacement to a second location and will look for it in the first location.
THE CHILD ACTIVELY SEARCHES OUT STIMULATION AND INITIATES ACTION.		

EXPERIMENTS TO DISCOVER PROPERTIES OF OBJECTS AND EVENTS (12–18 mo.)

GENERAL DEVELOPMENT

A kind of experimentation is now initiated by the child. Rather than merely repeating the same action pattern to produce the same result, he varies the behavior to produce different results. These experiments are not always random—they may build on the results of preceding ones. The child may explore the dropping of objects by varying the height of release and the kind of objects in order to produce variation in landing position, noise produced, height of bounce, etc. The child appears to be actively seeking novelty as it varies its behaviors, as if checking the objects' properties. The child's ability to walk further expands his world of objects.

SEARCH FOR HIDDEN OBJECTS AFTER VISIBLE DISPLACEMENT (12–18 mo.)

OBJECT PERMANENCE

Now when an object is hidden in a second location the child will search where he last saw the object. In repeated trials he will resist returning to the location where he last found the object. To the child, object permanence is real only when all the displacements are visible. When some displacements are not visible they must be imagined. At this point the child is not equipped to hold a mental image of the object to infer its position. It reverts to an earlier type of behavior.

The adult hand encloses the pencil. The pencil is then moved under the sweater, the beret, and then the handkerchief. The hand is kept closed throughout the sequence when not covered with an object. If the child were to retrieve the pencil from under the handkerchief he would need to form a mental image of the pencil and maintain it throughout the sequence. This level of behavior is demonstrated after 18 months.

MODIFYING FAMILIAR ACTION PATTERNS TO FIT NEW SITUATIONS (12–18 mos.)

The child's experimentation at this level of development facilitates his discovery of new means of reaching a goal.

Although the child's initial move was groping, he then adapted his behavior to continue the movement of the box. Although pushing was a familiar action pattern he used for moving objects, he hadn't used it previously to rotate objects. The child adapted a familiar pattern to fit a new situation.

SEARCH FOR HIDDEN OBJECTS AFTER INVISIBLE DISPLACEMENT (18–24 mos.)

A child may see a shiny ring placed under a sweater. When she searches for it she finds a beret. Rather than give up, the child immediately lifts up the beret with the expectancy of finding the ring.

This behavior is demonstrated by a child between 12 and 24 months (usually after 18 months). He needs a mental image of the object to search for it when he doesn't see it hidden. Furthermore, he displays a coordination of activity that reflects what Piaget calls a kind of *logic of actions*.

THROUGH HIS INTERACTION, THE CHILD MODIFIES AND SUPPLEMENTS HIS INITIAL CAPABILITIES, THUS INCREASING HIS POTENTIAL FOR INTERACTING WITH AN EVER-EXPANDING WORLD.

THE BEGINNING OF THINKING BEFORE ACTING (18–24 mos.)

A matchbox containing a shiny watch chain is closed to a slit, through which the child can see the chain. The slit is not big enough to allow the child to stick his hand in and grasp the chain; he tries but fails.

He thus focuses on the slit and opens and closes his mouth, progressively wider, several times.

With no further hesitation he puts his finger into the slit. Rather than trying to reach the chain he pulls out the inner box to make the opening larger.

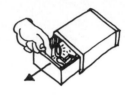

He succeeds and grasps the chain.

The child's mouth movements suggest that he is thinking through the problem and inventing a solution. Until now the child's actions have been based on immediate sensory experience. At this new level he is able to retain mental images beyond his experiences.

OBJECT PERMANENCE AND A SENSE OF SPACE (18–24 mos.)

A child throws a ball under a sofa. Rather than searching for the ball directly under the sofa, he anticipates that it crossed under the sofa to the other side. To retrieve the ball from behind the sofa he must turn his back on the location of its disappearance and take a different route from that of the ball. Successful retrieval of the ball not only demonstrates a knowledge of object permanence but also a sense of space.

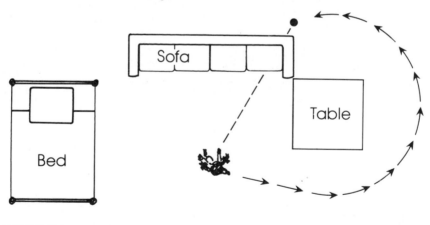

Piaget proposes that the "logic of actions" described here are responsible for the simultaneous development of early notions of space, time, causality, and object permanence. Since the development of the concept of object permanence is easily observed, progress with this notion is used as an indicator of parallel progress in the other notions.

The Preoperational (Representational) Stage[4-8]

The preoperational stage is a period (two—seven years) marked by a breakthrough in thinking in terms of images, symbols, and concepts. The child no longer needs to act out all situations externally. Actions become more internal as the child is increasingly able to represent an object or event with a mental image and a word. This internalized acting or representational thinking also frees the child from the present, as reconstruction of the past and anticipation of the future become increasingly possible. The child can now mentally re-present prior experiences to himself and attempt to represent them to others. Some of this activity begins to emerge during the transition period (18—24 months) to this stage and has already been illustrated.

Deferred Imitation

In the sensori-motor stage the child uses various forms of simple imitation. Initially he gives a representation of a model's actions in its presence; later, simple actions are imitated in the model's absence. Eventually, at about 18 months, the child is able to imitate a complex act in the absence of a model. This *deferred imitation* suggests to Piaget that the child has progressed from representation in action to representation in thought and marks the transition of the child to the preoperational stage. Piaget stresses that these actions must first be carried out physically before they can be later constructed in thought. This explains the need for such a long period of pure physical activity in the first stage.

In order to imitate the second child's behavior several hours later, the first child must recall an image or mental representation of that event. Since the child does not copy reality, but interprets it through internal structures, the imitation is not an exact copy. This internal representation is an example of what we call thinking.

Symbolic Play

Emerging almost simultaneously with deferred imitation is a form of play based on imitation, called *symbolic play*. In imitating behaviors the child uses something to stand for something else. In imitating his own sleeping behavior, the child can use another object to represent his pillow. He is also capable of generalizing his mental representation of "pretending to sleep." It seems that his mental image becomes detached from its immediate context, he extends "sleep" play to putting his teddy bear and dog to sleep.

 As the child imitates behaviors he must accommodate or reorganize his structures for physical activity. In turn, he forms a mental representation of the act that now serves as a structure through which he can assimilate objects in symbolic play. The object becomes a symbol for something else already existing in the mind of the child. The baseball glove can suggest the pillow in the sleep representation. In symbolic play, the child bends reality to his mental representation, ignoring all the similarities between the object and what he chooses to represent. Since play is such an important characteristic of this stage, a more detailed discussion of variation of play follows.

Practice Games   One of the earliest kinds of play to appear, it helps the child to improve his motor performance in activities such as throwing, stacking blocks, jumping rope. These activities are marked by their repetition with variations usually introduced by chance, and by pleasing results.

Symbolic (Pretend/Fantasy) Play   These games have no rules or limitations.

1. One form of symbolic play is *the generalization of earliest patterns for mental representation to new objects:* after the child pretends to telephone he involves the doll in telephoning. Other objects, such as a shoe, can be used to represent the telephone.

2. Children's *use of their bodies to represent other people or things* is a second example of symbolic play. A child's fingers walking can represent the father, the dog, etcetera.

3. In a more advanced form of symbolic play, the children *incorporate previous play bits into extended play sequences* involving imaginary companions.

These conversations are later internalized and become daydreams.

4. *Compensatory play* allows the child to act out actions that are ordinarily forbidden. Also, the child can recreate an unpleasant situation in fantasy. For example, a scene at lunch is replayed later that day with dolls and brought to a happier ending. Similarly, a frightening experience with a big dog will trigger a reenactment in which the child is braver or the dog friendlier.

Symbolic play has no rules or limitations. Anything can stand for anything else in the child's experience. Play therefore becomes a creative experience in which the child bends reality to his own wishes, incorporating his social experiences, reliving his pleasures, and resolving his conflicts, thus ensuring survival. Freedom from fixed social roles such as authority provides for an extension of self.

Social Games and Games with Rules In the latter part of the preoperational stage, children increasingly become involved in social play with real companions. Social play evolves from parallel play, in which children play beside each other and interact occasionally. Eventually children undertake roles and act them out with some awareness of each other. This type of play provides a way of adapting to social rules with minimum risks.

Games such as marbles and hopscotch have rules that are passed from child to child. Although the pre-operational child may know some of the rules, he does not heed them. Each child plays alongside another, aiming and throwing independently. Since each child plays for himself he always wins. During the preoperational stage children's participation in social games is limited by their inability to take another's perspective.

Games of Construction After the age of four, the child's play with materials increasingly reflects more organization and approximate reality. The houses, castles, garages, etcetera that the children construct as part of this play reflect greater attention to detail. The underlying themes may remain symbolic but the details are realistic. This kind of construction often involves a reconstruction or accommodation to meet the needs of reality and may be an opportunity for intelligent creations and problem-solving. This shift towards reality is accompanied by greater awareness of the physical properties of materials involved in construction.

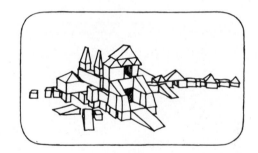

Play in Advanced Stages of Development For children in the pre-operational stage, play is reality. A child who reports seeing a lion in the shrubs reports from his reality. Once children enter the concrete operational stage they can distinguish play from reality. In the advanced stages of development, play continues to be more adaptive to reality. Children begin to play games with rules cooperatively. Socio-dramatic play, role-playing, and simulations are all important activities in the child's continued adaptation to his environment.

Language

Language also emerges from the sensori-motor structures and is closely related to the other processes of representation that emerge at about the same time. The preoperational period is marked by both the emergence and rapid development of language ability. Language is not restricted to the speed of physical actions. It is more mobile and can represent instantly a long chain of actions. While the physical action is restricted to immediate space and time, language liberates thought from the immediate and allows it to range over stretches of space and time.[3] (Language in thinking, learning, and teaching is the topic of Chapter 6.)

B. The Advanced, Logical Stages

In this section the focus will be on the logical thinking of the advanced stages, the concrete operational stage (7–11 years) and the formal operational stage (11–15 years). In order to appreciate the new capacities for logical thinking at each of these stages, they will be contrasted with children's thinking in the preoperational stage (2–7 years). This contrast will be repeated for a variety of tasks which sample different aspects of logical thought. Piaget attributes these new capacities for logical thinking at each stage to a combination of increased maturation and physical and social experiences which provide opportunities for equilibration. Each stage is considered as a higher level of equilibrium. Once again, the reported ages represent averages which are open to individual and cultural variability. Some children may enter the concrete operational stage at age five, two years earlier than the average. Similarly, some children may not enter this stage until age nine, two years later than average.

WARNING: TO BE TAKEN IN SMALL DOSES ONLY

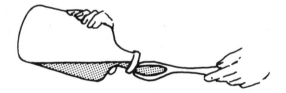

You cannot read the remainder of this chapter in a single sitting and be able to assimilate very much unless you bring a wealth of prior experience with children to your reading. For this reason it is important to intersperse your reading with:

- administering similar tasks to children (see Part D).
- viewing filmed interviews given by experienced interviewers. (See Appendix B for sources.)
- experiencing some tasks yourself and reflecting on the level of your own thinking. (See First Comes Thinking on pp. 71-72).
- discussing these experiences with others.

This is not a chapter to be mastered in detail before moving on to the remainder of the book. Rather, it is organized to serve as a valuable reference when reading the other chapters and when working with children. As you continue your work with children it will take on new meaning.

First Comes Thinking

Here's an opportunity to experience some tasks yourself and to reflect on your own thinking.

1 YOUR FRAME OF REFERENCE[9]*

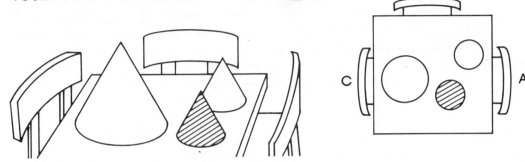

Draw the perspective of the scene as viewed from the three different positions, A, B, and C.

At which age can children recognize pictures or draw the changing perspective of objects? (Children's approaches to this task are described on page 78.)

2 COMBINING COINS

Select four different coins.

Arrange them in all the possible combinations. Noting these combinations on paper may help you to generate more ideas.

At which age can children generate an exhaustive list of arrangements or combinations? (A problem involving similar thinking is found on page 84.)

*Adapted from *The Origins of Intellect: Piaget's Theory,* Second Edition, by John S. Phillips, Jr. W. H. Freeman and Company. Copyright © 1975.

3 BALANCING WEIGHTS/BALANCING IDEAS[10]

CONSTRUCTING A STRAW BALANCE

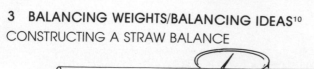

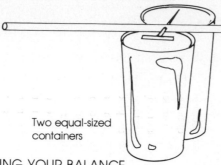

Two equal-sized
containers

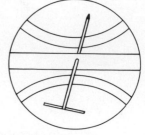

Stick the pin in the middle of the soda straw—
in the upper portion, for stability. Arrange the
materials so that the straw can swing freely.

EXPLORING YOUR BALANCE

Use paper clips as weights. (The common-sized paper clip will not slip if squeezed
sightly.) Hang the clips on the left side of the straw as shown. Predict where you will
need to place the paper clips on the right-hand side. Test your ideas.

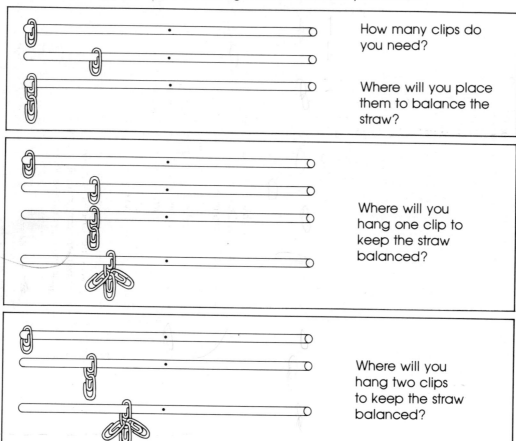

How many clips do
you need?

Where will you place
them to balance the
straw?

Where will you
hang one clip to
keep the straw
balanced?

Where will you
hang two clips
to keep the straw
balanced?

BALANCING YOUR IDEAS

Look back over the different situations and examine the role played by the number
of clips (weight) and their positions (distance from the balance point) in balancing
the straw beam. Write a rule that explains and predicts balance.

When do you think that children can balance the soda straw as suggested in
drawings and can write a rule that explains/predicts balance? See page 82 for
children's approach to the problem.

*Adapted from *Kitchen Physics.* By permission of the Elementary Science Study of Education Development Center,
Inc. © 1967.

Conservation 8.9

PICK OUT THE TWO CLAY BALLS THAT HAVE THE SAME AMOUNT OF CLAY.	NOW WATCH WHAT I DO. I'M GOING TO MAKE THIS ONE INTO A SAUSAGE.	DO YOU STILL HAVE THE SAME AMOUNT OF CLAY, OR DO YOU HAVE MORE IN ONE OF THE PIECES?	WHAT MAKES YOU THINK SO?
EQUIVALENCE ESTABLISHED	ONE OBJECT TRANSFORMED	CHILD JUDGES CONSERVATION	CHILD JUSTIFIES RESPONSE

PREOPERATIONAL (2–7)

THE SAUSAGE IS MORE. IT'S LONGER.

Preoperational children are strongly influenced by appearances. When two dimensions are altered at the same time the preoperational child will center his attention on only one dimension and ignore the other. Most children younger than 7–8 years experience *centration* as they are unable to mentally hold two dimensions at the same time. They may have already constructed rules such as "longer is more" and "skinnier is less" but are unable to coordinate the rules.

When questioned, the children may agree that it's still the same clay. This knowledge of the *identity* of the clay is not enough to overcome the perceptual pull of the dominant dimension.

Children of this age tend to focus on the end result rather than on the act of transformation that neither adds nor subtracts any clay. Their responses reflect an *irreversibility* of such transformations to return to the original state. The children are unable to take a mental round trip back to the original shape of the clay.

CONCRETE OPERATIONAL (7–11)

YOU MADE IT LONGER, BUT IT'S SKINNIER. IT'S STILL THE SAME AMOUNT.

IT'S THE SAME CLAY. YOU DIDN'T ADD ANY OR TAKE ANY AWAY.

IF YOU ROLLED IT BACK IT WOULD BE JUST AS BIG.

Seven to eight-year-olds

Each child here justifies his conservation response with at least one of three logical arguments, as above. Children seldom offer more than two logical arguments in their justification. Children in the concrete operational stage have the following logical capacities:

Compensation: To mentally hold two dimensions at the same time (decenter) in order to see that one compensates for the other.

Identity: To incorporate identity in their justification. Identity now implies conservation.

Reversibility: To mentally reverse a physical action to return the object to its original state.

These related and reversible mental actions that operate in the presence of physical objects are called *concrete operations*.

Understanding of the conservation concept applied to most other properties requires more time and experience to develop.

Does the clay ball weigh the same as the sausage, or does one weigh more?

CONSERVATION OF WEIGHT (10 YEARS)

Will the water levels still be the same or will one be higher when the sausage is put in?

CONSERVATION OF DISPLACEMENT VOLUME (11 YEARS)

FORMAL OPERATIONS (11–15)

YOU'VE GOT TO BE KIDDING!

(Look of disdain)

Since the results are so obvious to the adolescent he may refuse to take the question seriously.

The adolescent might choose to focus on minutiae such as the amount of clay left on the surface of the table during the process of rolling.

If he takes the question seriously he could consider it in the absence of objects, generating all the logical arguments.

The adolescent is no longer restricted to the immediate, testable environment. He can now consider the conservation of invisible particles and energy.

Classification [5, 11-14]

PREOPERATIONAL STAGE (2–7)	CONCRETE OPERATIONAL STAGE (7–11)	FORMAL OPERATIONAL STAGE (11–15)

PREOPERATIONAL STAGE (2–7)

Classification is the act of grouping objects according to their similarities. It is an activity in which young children naturally get involved.

"Put things together that are alike and go together."

Rather than arrange objects according to some chosen property, young children (four years) will arrange them according to the requirements of a picture.

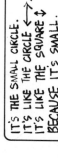

Graphic representation

Children make piles of objects that look alike in one way.

Resemblance sorting

When two colors are present the child's grouping shows a lack of consistency. The child begins by grouping according to shape but soon loses track and allows color to become the basis for grouping. The number of objects grouped consistently can be used as an indicator of progress.

Although the child's groupings become consistent between ages five and seven, he still has difficulty in grasping the relations between groups at different levels in the classification system.

CONCRETE OPERATIONAL STAGE (7–11)

Seven-eight-year-old children can place objects in two overlapping classes and justify their choice.

IT'S THE SMALL CIRCLE.
IT'S LIKE THE CIRCLE ←→.
IT'S LIKE THE SQUARE ↕.
BECAUSE IT'S SMALL.

Seven-eight-year-old children can respond to the *class inclusion* tasks in the presence of objects, e.g., green + yellow chips.

Eight- to nine-year-old children demonstrate a refinement in approaching classification. When presented with groups of flowers they are able to respond correctly to the following questions:

(invisible relationship of groups)

"Which will make a bigger bunch, all the daisies or all the yellow daisies? . . . all of the flowers or all the daisies?

"If you picked all the flowers in the garden would you have any daisies left?"

"Can you put a daisy in the box marked flowers without changing the label?

"If you take all the daisies out of the box would you have any flowers left?"

In the presence of objects, these children can *construct hierarchies* and *understand class inclusion at the different levels of a hierarchy*. They are able to hold both the part (subclass) and the whole (larger class) together mentally to make comparisons.

FORMAL OPERATIONAL STAGE (11–15)

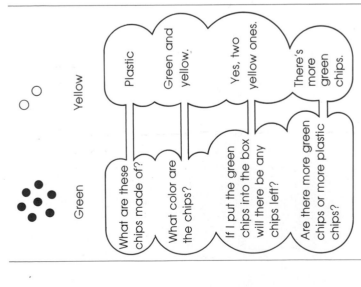

Class inclusion:

The preoperational child is unable to hold two aspects of the problem together mentally. He is unable to compare the subclass of green chips to the larger class. The child then focuses on the subgroups of green and yellow chips.

The same children have difficulty in responding to similar questions when representations of objects are used.

When children are presented with a random assortment of pictures to classify they revert to earlier behaviors. They have difficulty in constructing the hierarchy and in understanding the relations between groups at different levels of the hierarchy. This difficulty is experienced despite an introduction parallel to the "flower task."

"If all the animals were killed would there be any birds left?"

"If all the birds were killed would there be any animals left?"

"Can I put these two piles together under this label?"

Children are unable to respond to this problem when presented with representations of real objects until 10–12 years. (Common usage of the word *animal*, which is restricted to mammals and does not include birds, may also account for the systematic lag in capacity for solving this problem.)

Similarly, in the absence of concrete referents, Piaget found that 75 percent of nine-year-old Genevan children interviewed denied that they were both Genevan and Swiss. This inability was demonstrated despite the use of a representation (Venn diagram) for reference.

Formal operational thinkers readily classify and reclassify large groups of objects in different ways, realizing that each is possible at the same time. They have a realization that all arrangements are hypothetical and tentative. They are able to form classification schemes in the absence of objects and may even consider hypothetical objects, e.g., atoms. Their classification schemes may involve multiple criteria. They are also capable of constructing identification keys for biology and cataloging systems for libraries and industry.

In this stage it is possible to compare classification systems mentally and to group them according to suitability for different tasks. At this point the formal thinker would be constructing a *classification of classification systems.*

Seriation: Ordered Relationships[8,15,16]

PREOPERATIONAL STAGE (2–7)	CONCRETE OPERATIONAL STAGE (7–11)	FORMAL OPERATIONAL STAGE (11–15)
The child is shown a set of 10 sticks of graduated length in random order. He is asked: "Put down the shortest stick. Now put down one a little longer, then another a little longer. . . See if you can make it look like a staircase." The child's earliest attempts (age four) produce another random arrangement. The attempts of older children in this stage indicate a progressive approximation of order.	Most seven- to eight-year-olds are capable of coordinating the comparison of pairs of sticks and can construct the ordered series. They are able to focus on two aspects of the problem at the same time (decenter). This not only allows them to discover a system for construction but also to intersperse additional sticks of intermediate lengths after constructing the initial series.	
Ordering sticks may be based on their position in the series. This type of arrangement avoids comparing the lengths of neighboring sticks.		
The child may compare sticks in isolated pairs. However, two pairs of sticks are not compared at the same time.	A child's ordering ability is readily extended in two dimensions as he orders a set of objects according to both size and intensity of color.	
Through trial and error the child eventually constructs incomplete orderings of a small number of lengths. Starting by comparing neighboring pairs, the child soon loses track of his system.		

Pre-operational children tend to focus only on one aspect of the problem at a given time and ignore other relevant information of the total picture.

When compared to two neighboring pairs of sticks, the one in the center must be shorter than one of its neighbors at the same time that it is taller than the other. This ordering according to increasing size is known as *seriation*.

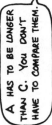

$$A < B < C$$

The following example illustrates an operation essential to seriation. The child is first shown sticks A and B. A is then hidden and stick C is placed alongside B. The child is asked to compare the lengths of sticks A (hidden) and C (visible).

To solve the task, the child is required to mentally retain the hidden relationship between A and B then coordinate it with the visible relationship between B and C.

$$\text{If } A > B$$
$$\text{and } B > C$$
$$\text{then } A > C$$

The pre-operational child is unable to coordinate two aspects of the problem to arrive at a solution. Piaget would say that pre-operational children lack the logical operation of *transitivity*.

The seven- to eight-year old is capable of mentally coordinating two relationships even though the reminder of one is no longer visible through transitivity.

The child's ability to coordinate relationships of weight develops more gradually.

LIMITATION:

Nine- to ten-year-olds experience difficulty in solving ordering problems presented verbally, even though they may be written down. "If Edith has darker hair than Lily and Edith's hair is lighter than Susan's, which of the three girls has the darkest hair?"

When verbal ordering problems are presented to nine- to ten-year-old children who are capable of solving similar problems with physical materials, they revert to the intuitive thinking of a pre-operational child. Their comparisons produce only a set of uncoordinated pairs.

These children are able to solve ordering problems only when presented with physical materials.

The 11- to 12-year-old children are capable of drawing conclusions not only through direct observation but also from hypothetical statements. At this stage they are capable of considering an infinite series.

In the verbal problem comparing hair shades, the information is presented abstractly through hypotheses having the form, "If . . . , then . . ." The formal operational thinker can reach valid conclusions even if these girls do not exist. He can ignore the content and focus on the form of the relations.

Such abstract verbal statements are called *propositions* or *hypotheses*. The ability to think in such abstract terms demonstrates *propositional logic* and *hypothetico-deductive thought*.

Egocentrism: The Child's Frame of Reference[5,9]

SENSORI-MOTOR (0–2)	PREOPERATIONAL (2–7)	CONCRETE OPERATIONAL (7–11)	FORMAL OPERATIONAL (11–15)
The infant's world begins as one without objects. His body and actions are the center of his world, so objects only exist as a result of his action. By the end of the first year the child is aware of his independent existence and permanence of objects.	Young children demonstrate an inability to take another's viewpoint. *Social interaction:*  In telling a story, a child omits large segments, assuming that the listener already has the same view. The child never clarifies "it."   Rather than talk to each other, young children tend to talk at each other. Being unable to take another's viewpoint, they are insensitive to what others need to hear. Piaget refers to this as a collective monologue. The amount of egocentric speech gradually decreases in the latter part of this stage. *Space:* The child views a mountain scene and is asked to select a drawing which would show the doll's view of the scene at A, B, and C. The preoperational child selects the drawing of his own view. He is unable to imagine an object from another's viewpoint.	Seven- to eight-year-old children show a marked decrease in egocentrism. *Social interaction:* As they show increasing ability to take another's view they are also increasingly aware of the needs of the listener—what information he has, his interests, etcetera. Discussions now involve an exchange of ideas. Explanations are more in tune with the listener. *Space:* Children in the early part of this stage demonstrate some ability to take another's view in space, but they lack consistency. It is not until age nine that children can pick correct drawings from three different positions of the doll. The child will select the following drawings for each different position of the doll. 	*Social interaction:*  The onset of hypothetical thinking results in more fruitful discussion and debate. By using hypotheses, the adolescent can adopt his adversary's viewpoint and consider the consequences of that argument. He need not believe the adversary's argument to consider it. He now sees his view as one of many possible views. The full capacity of formal operational thinking is postponed by two adolescent preoccupations: a. self-consciousness of personal physical changes; b. being enamored of idealistic possibilities, thus resisting consideration of reality. Piaget acknowledges the importance of the adolescents work experience to bring the latter into balance.

A Child's Representation of Space by Mapping[8,16]

SENSORI-MOTOR STAGE	PREOPERATIONAL STAGE	CONCRETE OPERATIONAL STAGE	FORMAL OPERATIONAL STAGE
Once a child learns to walk he soon is able to orient himself to his surroundings, i.e., home and yard. He is able to coordinate his movements of coming and going. Through a reversibility of action he returns to his original point of departure. Further, the child returns to the point of departure through a variety of detours. Although the child is able to coordinate physical displacements, he is still unable to represent these displacements mentally.	Nursery school children (four–five) are able to travel alone to a neighborhood school and back. When asked to represent their path on a physical model of the neighborhood, they are unable to do so until the next stage. They are capable of only a global representation of their path using words and gestures, without reference to the model. The children are shown two identical physical models of a village. They are asked to place a doll in one of the models according to the positions of similar dolls in the other model. Four-year-olds position their dolls in the proximity of a reference object but with little concern for left-right, before-behind, distances. Four–six-year-olds give more attention to the above relations. When his model is rotated 180° the child will ignore the rotation and place the doll in terms of himself. Older children in this stage show a gradual coordination of relationships in space. When children are presented with a physical model of a village they are given a larger number of similar materials and asked to construct an identical model. Four-year-old children neither choose a matching set of objects nor place them accurately. Objects tend to be bunched together in small groups without an overall pattern. Four–seven-year-olds demonstrate closer approximations to the model without achieving a close representation.	Seven–eight-year-olds are able to position the doll in 15 separate situations. The rotation of the model no longer disturbs them. Children gradually develop a coordinated system of spatial relations and can reconstruct a model village with physical objects between ages seven–ten. The same children experience more difficulty in making a 2-D drawing of a 3-D model when given a piece of paper that is smaller than the model. Although they may be capable of a true 2-D representation, there are three areas of weakness which are strengthened just prior to the next stage. The distances involved are only approximated. The distances and sizes still lack coordination. Although attempting to reduce his map to scale, the child may leave the sizes of the objects unchanged while only placing them closer together. All the relationships can't be considered simultaneously. When the child is required to change his map in response to a change in the model, he does so only through a series of approximations.	The formal thinker can draw conventional maps to a reduced scale. These maps are more abstract representations of reality. The symbols which are used for representation now bear little resemblance to the original objects. This level of map-making is possible through the integration of such ideas as horizontal and vertical coordinates, perspectives, similarity, and proportion. At this stage of intellectual development the child can interpret the symbols on maps of places he has never seen. Some of the symbols represent concepts rather than only visible features of a region, e.g., lines of longitude and latitude.

Causality [9,15,17-19]

SENSORI-MOTOR STAGE	PREOPERATIONAL STAGE	CONCRETE OPERATIONAL STAGE	FORMAL OPERATIONAL STAGE
The infant's intelligent behavior reflects a primitive notion of causality in its actions. At this stage, however, the child cannot mentally represent this action.	The young child's view of the world is the only one possible for him. An example of this view is symbolic play. For the child at this stage of development his play is reality.	Becoming aware of other's viewpoints, the child searches to justify his own viewpoint and to coordinate the views of others. His explanations gradually become more logical.	The explanations are considerably more comprehensive and theoretical in nature than those of the preceding stage. Formal thinkers are able to consider abstract models, to explain physical behavior, not only of distant objects in the solar system, but also invisible objects, e.g., molecular and atomic models.

Speech bubbles (Preoperational): "WHY ARE YOU DOING THAT?" "WHY IS THE PAINT WET?"

The young child's incessant questioning reflects his view of the world. For him things don't happen by chance. Everything is made by man or God for man and children.

Speech bubbles: "HOW DID THE WIND BEGIN?" "IT'S MADE BY BLOWING --- BY GOD." "SOMEBODY BLEW-- IT WAS MAN WHO DID IT. IT WAS THEIR WORK."

In the child's world things don't just happen by chance. Since every effect must have a cause, the child's standards for logical connections are, of necessity, rather loose. Usually the child's explanations consist of unrelated facts linked together as if one explains the other.

Speech bubbles: "THE MOON DOESN'T FALL DOWN BECAUSE THERE'S NO SUN, BECAUSE IT'S VERY HIGH UP." "I'VE LOST MY PENCILS BECAUSE I'M NOT DRAWING." "THE MAN FELL FROM THE MOTOR CYCLE BECAUSE HE BROKE HIS ARM."

Since the child views the world with the self as a model he considers everything active to be alive.

Speech bubbles: "IT'S ALIVE BECAUSE IT WRITES." PENCIL "IT'S ONLY ALIVE WHEN IT'S LIT." CANDLE "IT'S ALIVE BECAUSE IT RUNS." TRICYCLE

Speech bubble (Concrete Operational): "THE MAN FELL FROM THE MOTORCYLE AND BROKE HIS ARM BECAUSE THE ROAD WAS SLIPPERY."

However, circular explanations are still common for complex events.

The child's inclination of assigning living characteristics to inanimate objects decreases considerably in the first half of this stage. Since inanimate objects are no longer "living," children learn to deal with death in realistic terms.

Events beyond the child's reach, i.e., not manipulable in a concrete sense, still resist logical explanation.

Speech bubble: "THE SUN RISES BECAUSE WE NEED LIGHT."

Although seven-eight-year-old children can explain the dissolving of a solid in terms of tiny particles they are unable to explain changes of state, e.g., melting or boiling during this stage.

Eliminating Contradictions: Floating and Sinking[20,21]

Which of these objects will sink? Which will float?
How do you know?
After testing: What happened? How can you explain it?

A number of disparate objects   Some structured objects: sets of objects of same volume but different weight

PREOPERATIONAL (2–7)

Given pairs of identical objects, the child will predict behaviors on the basis of momentary whims. The child seems to ignore the fixed properties of these objects.

THIS ONE WILL FLOAT. THIS ONE WILL SINK. — 4 YEAR OLD

Although older children at this stage begin to link sinking to the weight of an object, they have difficulty in classifying objects as either sinkers or floaters. They associate big with heavy and predict that a large object will sink.

WHY DOES THE STICK SINK? — BECAUSE IT'S ROUND.
WHAT ABOUT THE BALL? HOW DO YOU KNOW? — IT FLOATS... BECAUSE IT'S ROUND.
HOW ABOUT THE NEEDLE? — IT STAYS ON TOP BECAUSE IT'S LIGHT.
WHAT HAPPENS WHEN YOU PUSH THE NEEDLE? — IT SINKS BECAUSE IT GETS HEAVY.

CONCRETE OPERATIONAL (7–11)

Ball floats.   Key sinks.
Wood floats.   Nail sinks.

WHICH IS HEAVIER... THE KEY OR THE BALL? — THE BALL.
WHY DOES THE KEY SINK? — BECAUSE ITS HEAVY.
WHAT ABOUT THE NAIL? — IT'S LIGHT BUT IT SINKS ANYWAY. IT'S IRON AND IRON ALWAYS SINKS. — 8 YEAR OLD

The child no longer thinks that all light objects float. She is beginning to think of weight in relative terms but only makes a vague connection between weight and volume. Now, rather than classifying objects as light or heavy, she groups them in four categories.

Small	Small	Large	Large
Light	Heavy	Heavy	Light

Older children suggest that some objects are more "full" than others. They also begin to refer to some objects being heavier than water but the amount of water is not clarified. Some children will predict that a floater will sink if there is less water in the container. A comparison to an "equal amount of water" is a difficult abstraction to construct.

The delay in ability to remove the contradiction between the effect of weight and volume is related to the late development of related conservation concepts of weight and displacement volume at ages 10–11.

FORMAL OPERATIONAL (11–15)

Eleven- to twelve-year-olds begin to classify objects as "lighter or heavier than water." The reference to water is no longer to total amount, but rather to the equal volume of water displaced by the object.

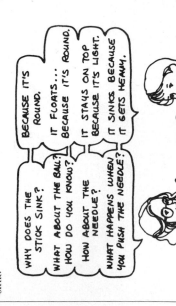

HOW COULD YOU TELL IF A COIN IS HEAVIER THAN AN EQUAL AMOUNT OF WATER? — TAKE TWO JARS OF THE SAME SIZE. FILL ONE WITH WATER, AND THE OTHER WITH COINS. YOU WOULD FIND THAT THEY WEIGH DIFFERENTLY.

The formal operational thinker can propose a hypothetical experiment and test it mentally or physically.

The concept of density relates weight and volume. The rule for floating compares the density of the object to the density of water, that is, compares the weight of the object to that of an equal volume of water. This problem requires the child to construct a *relation of relations*. The concepts of weight and volume, only recently consolidated, are now related in the concept of *density*. Density may be called a *second-order concept* because it is derived from other concepts.

A Relation of Relations: The Balance[20-22]

PREOPERATIONAL (2–7)

How can we make the beam balanced again?

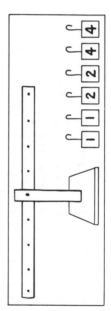

The four-year-old child adds more weight to the left side in order to balance the beam.

The child lacks the reversibility to either remove the original weight or to add weight to the other side.

The six-year-old understands that a weight is needed on both sides. The need for equal weights is not yet obvious.

The child may then push up on the left side to correct the position, since he sees himself as the primary agent of change.

CONCRETE OPERATIONAL (7–11)

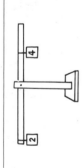

Given mismatched pairs of weights, an eight-year-old child might discover after trial and error that a large weight close to the center can balance a small weight far from the center. The child still has difficulty in verbalizing this relationship. Also, he is unable to invert the relationship from one side of the balance to the other.

THE SAME THING WEIGHS LESS WHEN I MOVE IT CLOSER TO THE CENTER.

11 YEAR OLD

An 11-year-old can verbalize the relationship of weight and length separately for each side of the balance, but he still does not state a relationship between both sides of the balance.

The child tends to limit himself to actual weights and lengths tried and does not extend himself to the possible (hypothetical).

FORMAL OPERATIONAL (11–15)

A 13-year-old may be able to quantify the relationship. She may also discover that to balance the beam a "4 weight" can be placed a quarter of the distance from the center. From this relationship she may predict that a "3 weight" would be placed at one third the distance from the center.

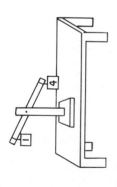

IT'S A SYSTEM OF COMPENSATIONS ... WEIGHTS AND DISTANCE ARE COMPENSATED ON BOTH SIDES.

14 YEAR OLD

SINCE THERE IS TWICE THE WEIGHT IT NEEDS TO BE HALF WAY IN TO MAKE UP FOR IT.

13 YEAR OLD

This 14-year-old is able to see the interrelation between the weights and distances on both sides of the balance. These relations form a coherent whole or system of possibilities. He is able to suggest a number of ways to balance the beam:

1. Do the same operation on the other side.
2. Cancel the original operation by removing the weight from the left side.
3. Add a different weight to the other side but compensate for it by its position. It is moved closer in if heavier than the original, or vice versa.
4. Once the weight is balanced, it can be kept balanced by doing something that produces the same result as the original operation; for example, increasing the distance produces the same effect as increasing the weight.

LEFT SIDE		RIGHT SIDE	
weight	distance	weight	distance
add	move in	subtract	move out
subtract	move out	add	move in

Study of the interrelations between weight and distance on both sides of the beam reveals the overall principle: a proportionally heavier (4) weight placed at shorter distances (1/4) will balance a lighter weight (2) at a longer distance (1/2). This *relation of relations* (proportion) permits the calculation of an unknown weight or distance when three are known: $4W \times 1/4L = 2W \times 1/2L$. Formulas make sense to formal thinkers.

Isolating and Controlling Variables—The Pendulum Problem [5,20,21]

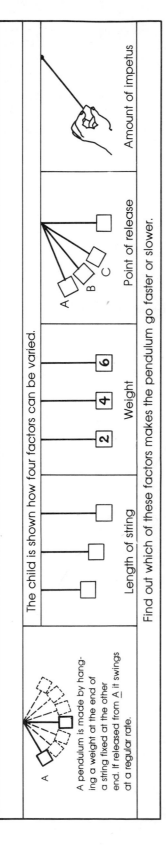

A pendulum is made by hanging a weight at the end of a string fixed at the other end. If released from A it swings at a regular rate.

The child is shown how four factors can be varied.

Length of string | Weight | Point of release | Amount of impetus

Find out which of these factors makes the pendulum go faster or slower.

PREOPERATIONAL (2–7)

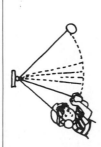

After releasing the pendulum, young children have the tendency to interfere with its movement by repeated pushes. They have difficulty separating the action of an object from their own actions. (In actuality, the time in which a pendulum makes a complete swing is not affected by a push. Once the pendulum is released it acts on its own and swings at a regular rate.) The child's actions are another example of his egocentrism.

The child's counting of swings seems to be influenced by expected outcomes and faulty observations are reported. His conclusion, therefore, may be unrelated to the evidence.

CONCRETE OPERATIONAL (7–11)

THE LENGTH MAKES IT GO SLOWER. THE WEIGHT MAKES IT GO FASTER.

LENGTH	WEIGHT	RESULTS
long	heavy	slow
short	light	fast

The child comes to this conclusion by varying two factors simultaneously:

At the same time another factor—point of release—may be varied inadvertently.

The child is an accurate observer but experiences difficulty in arriving at conclusions that fit his data.

He cannot consider all four factors simultaneously and develop a systematic plan for eliminating the unimportant factors. The child may discover that length affects the rate of swing, but this results from trial and error rather than from a clear plan of attack.

FORMAL OPERATIONAL (11–15)

This conclusion is based on data resulting from a systematic plan of attack. A design for isolating and controlling variables is held mentally or recorded on paper.

IT'S THE LENGTH OF THE STRING THAT CHANGES HOW FAST IT SWINGS. THE WEIGHT DOESN'T MATTER.

TESTS	LENGTH	WEIGHT	OBSERVED RESULT	CONCLUSION
Effect of WEIGHT ①	short	light	fast	no effect
②	short	heavy	fast	no effect
" ①	long	light	slow	no effect
②	long	heavy	slow	no effect
Effect of LENGTH ①	short	heavy	fast	+ effect
②	long	heavy	slow	+ effect
" ①	short	light	fast	+ effect
②	long	light	slow	+ effect

ALL OTHER FACTORS BEING EQUAL IT'S THE LENGTH THAT MAKES THE DIFFERENCE.

(A similar process is used to eliminate the other factors.)

The formal thinker can usually state a rule for isolating and controlling variables prior to undertaking any testing.

Systematic Combining of Possibilities: The Mixing Problem[20,21]

MATERIALS

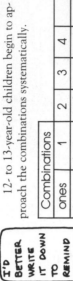

Bottles labeled 1, 2, 3, 4 and G

Colorless solutions

Watch what I do.

Colorless

1 + 3   2

G is added to two colorless solutions prepared in advance.

See if you can make the same color. You can use any or all the bottles.

Yellow	Colorless
1 + 3 + G	2 + G

A change in color is observed in one container.

The combination of 1 + 3 + G is the minimum combination to produce the color. Number 2 can be added with no effect. Conversely, 4 acts as a bleach and makes the color disappear.

PREOPERATIONAL (2–7)

"IT'S THE WATER THAT CHANGES."

"MAYBE THERE'S PAINT IN THE GLASS."

By randomly mixing two solutions at a time the young child might produce a color change by chance. However, the child's explanations lack logic.

When an expected change is not produced the child may shake the contents vigorously.

The young child has difficulty in distinguishing himself as the agent of change for change resulting from combinations of materials.

CONCRETE OPERATIONAL (7–11)

A seven-year-old may limit himself to combinations of 1+G, 4+G, 2+G, 3+G.

"I TRIED THEM ALL. I THINK I DID EVERYTHING."

When encouraged to consider other combinations he may pour all four solutions together and add G.

If the color is reproduced and then disappears on addition of 4, the child will fail to see the need for excluding the fourth solution.

Nine- to eleven-year-olds will spontaneously undertake different combinations of two or three solutions with G. The lack of a systematic approach to the combinations limits their progress at this stage.

If the child reproduces the color with 1+2+3+G he is unable to reduce the number of necessary solutions any further. His explanations tend to focus on bringing the color out from a solution rather than from a combination of solutions.

FORMAL OPERATIONAL (11–15)

12- to 13-year-old children begin to approach the combinations systematically.

"I'D BETTER WRITE IT DOWN TO REMIND MYSELF."

"THERE MIGHT BE ANOTHER WAY TO GET COLOR."

Combinations			
ones	1	2	3	4
twos	1+2	1+3	1+4	2+3	2+4	3+4
threes	1+2+3		

After successfully reproducing the color the child continues to test other combinations of twos. He also undertakes combinations of threes. His curiosity about the role played by 2 and 4 may result in further experimentation with order of combining the solutions. The tendency here is to exhaust all possibilities for combinations.

In explaining the results the formal operational thinker can focus on the combined effects of solutions.

For Piaget, the child's observable system of combinations implies a *mental combinatorial system of operations*. A system of propositions is reflected in the statements made to express the results of combination while it is being organized.

"IT IS 1 AND 3+G BUT NOT ANY OTHER COMBINATION OF TWOS. IT IS NEITHER 4 NOR 2. POUR TAKES AWAY COLOR AND 2 DOES NOTHING."

"IT'S A CHEMICAL PRODUCT OF 1+3+G"

C. Piaget's Concept of Stage

This section will summarize the thinking characteristic of children while they are in the four stages identified by Piaget. It will then look beyond the details of each stage to the common features of all stages as theorized by Piaget.

First Comes Thinking

- Reflect on children's characteristic thinking in each of the four stages:

  sensori-motor (0–2)

  preoperational (2–7)

  concrete operational (7–11)

  formal operational (11–15).

- Try to identify at least three characteristics of thought at each stage.

- Which statement in the following pair do you think is true?
  Think of past observations of children that support your choice.

  a. Stages of intellectual development are part of a continuous process in which a child's characteristic thinking is changed gradually over a period of time and integrated into better ways of thinking. A child can be in more than one stage at a time.

  b. Stages of intellectual development are distinct steps in which a child's thinking is replaced overnight by better ways of thinking. A child can only be in one stage at a time.

The Four Stages in Review

Sensori-Motor Stage — Period of Sensory Input and Coordination of Physical Actions (0–2 years)

Through his active search for stimulation the infant combines primitive reflexes into repeatable action patterns. At birth the infant's actions are his world. By the end of the first year he has altered his view of the world as he recognizes the permanency of objects outside his own perception. Other signs of intelligence include the initiation of goal-directed behavior and the invention of new solutions. The child is not capable of internal representation (what we usually consider as thinking) but the latter part of this stage reflects a kind of "logic of actions." Since the child has not developed language this emergence of intelligence is preverbal.

Preoperational Stage—Period of Representational and Prelogical Thought (2—7 years)

In the transition to this stage the child discovers that some things can stand for other things. The child's thinking is no longer tied to external actions and is now internalized. Internal representations provide a more mobile vehicle for his expanding intelligence. Forms of internal representation that emerge simultaneously at the beginning of this stage are imitation, symbolic play, mental imagery and language. This period is dominated by representational activity and a rapid development of spoken language. Despite tremendous gains in symbolic functioning the child's ability to think logically is marked by a certain inflexibility. Included in the limitations of this period are:

- inability to mentally reverse a physical action to return an object to its original state (irreversibility)
- inability to mentally hold changes in two dimensions at the same time (centration)
- inability to consider another's viewpoint (egocentrism).

Concrete Operational Stage—Period of Concrete Logical Thought (Number, Class, Order) (7—11)

The child in this stage becomes increasingly capable of demonstrating logical thinking in relation to physical objects. A newly acquired capacity of reversibility allows him to mentally reverse an action that he had previously only done physically. The child is also able to mentally hold two or more variables at a time when studying objects and to reconcile apparently contradictory data. He becomes more sociocentric, increasingly aware of the views of others. These new mental capacities are demonstrated by a rapid growth in his ability to conserve certain properties of objects (number, amount) across changes in other properties and to do relational thinking such as classifying and ordering objects. Mathematical operations are also developed in this stage. The child becomes increasingly able to think of physically absent things that are based on vivid images of past experiences. The child's thinking, however, is restricted to concrete things rather than ideas.

Formal Operational Stage—Period of Unlimited Logical Thought (Hypotheses, Propositions) (11—15 years)

This period is marked by the ability to think beyond concrete reality. Reality is now only a subset of the possibilities for thinking. In the prior stage the child developed a number of relations from interaction with concrete materials; now he can think about relations of relations and other abstract ideas, for example, proportions and second-order concepts. The formal thinker has the capacity to consider verbal statements and propositions rather than just concrete objects. He is able to think about his thinking as he becomes more conscious of his thought processes. Now he is capable of fully understanding and appreciating the symbolic abstractions of algebra and literary criticism and the use of metaphor in literature. He often gets involved in spontaneous discussions on philosophy, religion, and morality in which abstract concepts such as justice and freedom are tackled.

The Stage Concept[8,9,15,23-28]

THE ORDER IN WHICH CHILDREN PASS THROUGH THESE DEVELOP-
MENTAL STAGES DOES NOT VARY:

ALL CHILDREN *must pass through the concrete operational stage to reach the formal operational stage.*

BUT THE RATE AT WHICH CHILDREN PASS THROUGH THESE STAGES DOES VARY FROM CHILD TO CHILD. The age that Piaget associates with a behavior is one at which most of the children (75 percent) studied are capable of demonstrating that behavior, for example, most eight-year-old children were able to demonstrate conservation of solid amount.

SOME CHILDREN *reach the later stages at an earlier age than average.* A small percentage of children can demonstrate conservation of solid amount at age five.

SOME CHILDREN *hesitate in the early stages for some time.* A small percentage of children may not be able to demonstrate conservation of solid amount until 10. In different cultures the age at which most children can demonstrate similar tasks is often different.

SOME CHILDREN *never develop the mental abilities that characterize the later stages.* It is estimated that only one-half of the American adult population has reached the level of formal operational thought. Most adults reach this level of thought only in their area of expertise. This level of formal operation may be reached without advance schooling, as in auto mechanics. At the same time, a surprising percentage of college students do not function at this level.

Since Piaget has labelled his stages according to levels of thinking that are generally characteristic of them, beginning students of his work may come away with an oversimplified view of development which parallels the four stages of a butterfly's development (egg, larva, pupa, adult). In the insect, the dramatic changes in appearance occurring overnight, as its development progresses to the next stage, can be represented by a *stair-step model*. An extension of this parallel to children's intellectual development would produce an expectation that once a child enters the pre-operational stage his sensori-motor development would cease. In actuality, when a child enters the preoperational stage his sensori-motor development continues, although the novel capacity for representational thought is a dominating feature of this stage. Similarly, the stair-step model leads to an expectation that once a child is able to conserve number, he is able to do logical thinking in the presence of physical materials from all areas of his environment. However, an examination of seven-year-old children's thinking on other conservation tasks indicates gaps in their understanding of the conservation concept, e.g., children usually can't demonstrate understanding of conservation of displacement volume until age eleven. Such gaps in understanding mean that the same child who demonstrates concrete operational thinking on one conservation task would be preoperational in his thinking on more challenging conservation task. This unexpected conclusion suggests that children's intellectual development can't be represented as abrupt changes which result immediately in stable and static stages. On the contrary, it suggests that intellectual development is continuous, although simultaneously marked by the discontinuity of distinctly novel ways of thinking at each stage.

There are no discrete, static stages which appear overnight,
rather, there are overlapping stages of continuous development.

> Children are in constant transition to the next stage, respond-
> ing in ways characteristic of more than one stage.[27]

When studying children's intellectual development, sometimes its continuous nature comes into focus and at other times its discontinuous nature seems more apparent. This dual view of intellectual development can be understood if Piaget's concept of stages is viewed as a convenient framework for looking at children and the age offered as easy reference points. The age range of a stage is defined for convenience as beginning with the first stable appearance of novel thought processes, e.g., conservation of number (although this level of thinking has not been achieved in all areas) and ending with the first stable appearance of distinctly novel thought processes at the next stage. Upon entry to the formal operational stage, concrete operational thinking continues in many areas but it becomes increasingly integrated into a more comprehensive system of formal operations.

The *overlapping-stages model* of intellectual development, illustrated below, incorporates both its continuous and discontinuous nature. Here children appear to be in constant transition, responding in ways which are characteristic of more than one stage. Yet, at each stage there is a steady increase in a characteristic way of thinking following the novelty of its first appearance.

NOT DISCRETE, STATIC STAGES, BUT OVERLAPPING STAGES OF CONTINUOUS DEVELOPMENT

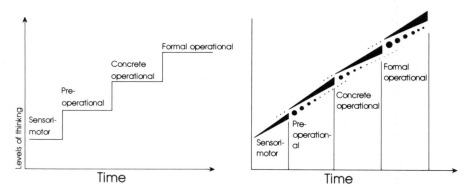

Development is a gradual process—it takes about five years after demonstrating conservation of amount before the child can demonstrate conservation of displacement volume. Upon the child's entry to the formal operational stage, his concrete operational behaviors continue and become increasingly integrated into a more comprehensive system. Formal operational thinkers do not always function at their full potential and may resort to lower-level thinking under stress. Adults often revert to concrete operational thinking, or even preoperational thinking, when exposed to new areas of learning. They benefit from concrete experiences in these areas prior to advancing to abstract levels of thinking. The overlapping stage model of intellectual development above is consistent with such gaps as well as being consistent with the adult not always functioning at full potential. The same observations are discrepant when viewed within the stair-step model of intellectual development.

Structures constructed by the child at a given stage become integrated into the new structures of the following stage. For example, the notions of object permanence and identity constructed in earlier stages become integrated into the concepts of conservation in the concrete operational stage.[8]

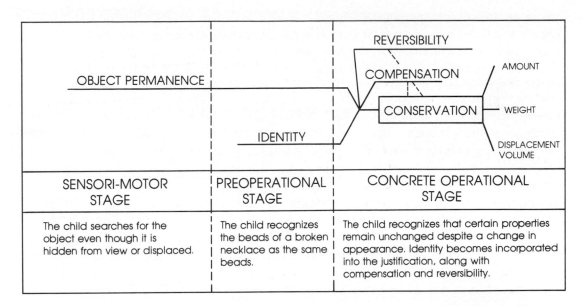

SENSORI-MOTOR STAGE	PREOPERATIONAL STAGE	CONCRETE OPERATIONAL STAGE
The child searches for the object even though it is hidden from view or displaced.	The child recognizes the beads of a broken necklace as the same beads.	The child recognizes that certain properties remain unchanged despite a change in appearance. Identity becomes incorporated into the justification, along with compensation and reversibility.

Similarly, the "logic of actions" which allow the child to search for objects despite invisible displacements, during the sensori-motor stage are later integrated in a new organization of transitivity at a later stage.[8,15]

SENSORI-MOTOR——PRE-OPERATIONAL TRANSITION	CONCRETE OPERATIONAL	FORMAL OPERATIONAL
Ring hidden under sweater / Pulling sweater reveals only beret / Child raises beret with expectancy	$A > B$ and $B > C$ so $A > C$ $A > B > C$	Edith > Lilly and Susan > Edith so Susan > Lilly Susan > Edith > Lilly
The "logic of action" at 18–24 months can be explained as a primitive form of transitivity. The ring was under the sweater The beret is under the sweater So the ring must be under the beret. It can be explained in this way, but it is based on pure physical action by the child.	At age 7–8 there's an expanded understanding. In the presence of concrete materials the operation can be explained verbally.	A 12-year-old formal thinker could handle comparable problems when presented as verbal propositions.

The actions which are effective are reorganized in a gradual developmental process and must be relearned and elaborated at another level of functioning. The period of five years separating each level emphasizes the gradual nature of the developmental process.

The proposed model of continuous intellectual development (page 88) is consistent with the relationship between stages which Piaget theorizes from the preceding observations. Perhaps a familiar puzzle can serve as a physical model for the process theorized by Piaget. At each new stage Piaget proposes a major reorganization of mental structures at the same time that he proposes an integration of previous structures. The models below suggest a way of envisioning how at each stage the mental structures from the preceding stages might be incorporated in the new mental structure. The models also suggest how the reorganization allows for further expansion of the structure as a result of this new view of the environment.

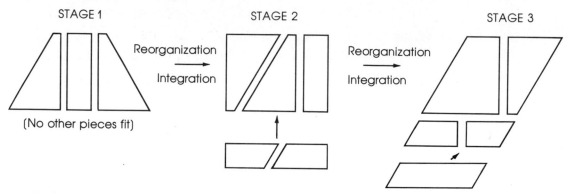

On his concept of developmental stages, Piaget says,

> **There are no static stages as such. Each is a fulfillment of something begun in the preceding one and the beginning of something that will lead to the next.**[23,pp.23-27]

Similarly, the concrete operations become integrated into formal operations. In the concrete operational stage, the child's physical and mental action on objects construct operations and relations. In the formal operational stage, mental action on these operations and relations result in operations on operations and relations of relations.

CONCRETE OPERATIONAL STAGE Thinking about actions on things and constructing ideas about reality.		FORMAL OPERATIONAL STAGE Thinking about ideas and thinking processes and constructing a universe of possibility.	
		Mental Action on ↓	
	→ Representation (of an action)	Representations ↓	→ Representation of Representation (of a possible action)
Physical and Mental Action on Objects (or on vivid images of objects)	→ Operations	Operations ↓	→ Second-Order Operations
	→ Classes	Classes ↓	→ Classes of Classes
	→ Relations	Relations ↓	→ Relations of Relations
	→ Concepts	Concepts	→ Second-Order Concepts

At each stage the structures become progressively more integrated, and in the final stage they form a total interlocking system.

The transitions from stage to stage involve the restructuring and integration of structures from the previous stage. These transitions are governed by the process of equilibration, which orchestrates the contributions from maturation and social and physical experience. Although children are in constant transition to the next stage, each stage is marked by the initial appearance of novel ways of thinking which expands with age until it dominates the period. Each mature stage can be thought of as a period of relative equilibrium in which there is relative stability and restructuring is minor.

Although the process of intellectual development is gradual and continuous, its products are discontinuous. These products of development are the stages in which thinking is characteristically different.

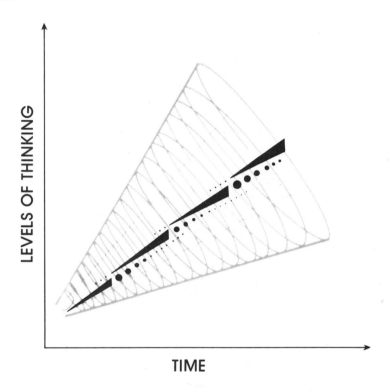

LEVELS OF THINKING

TIME

D. Exploring Children's Levels of Thinking

One of the benchmarks of a child's functioning at a concrete operational level as well as the child's progress within that stage is his ability to give conservation responses to a variety of physical tasks. In each task the child must mentally hold some property of a substance constant while it undergoes changes in other properties. When a child sees one clay ball from a matched pair being rolled into a sausage shape, he must be able to mentally hold the amount of clay constant despite its change in appearance. The justification of his response must indicate a logical necessity for conservation, regardless of perceptual suggestions. The table on the next page suggests that once a child enters the concrete operational stage and is able to give conservation responses to a variety of conservation tasks in the first year or two, more time, experience, and opportunities for equilibration are necessary before conservation responses are given for weight and volume tasks.

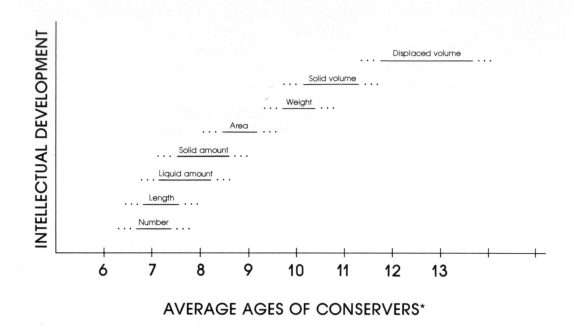

INTELLECTUAL DEVELOPMENT

... Displaced volume ...
... Solid volume ...
... Weight ...
... Area ...
... Solid amount ...
... Liquid amount ...
... Length ...
... Number ...

6   7   8   9   10   11   12   13

AVERAGE AGES OF CONSERVERS*

This section will describe the different conservation tasks in sufficient detail for you to undertake your own interviews with children and to examine the levels of thinking reflected in their responses. In undertaking a study of children, it is important to remember that these conservation tasks sample only one area of logical thought, and just represent a convenient starting point.

First Comes Thinking

Reflect on your understanding of the concept of conservation and devise:

- alternative tasks for conservation of solid amount, weight or displacement volume which have been described previously on page 73.
- tasks for conservation concepts that have not been described previously.

---

*Although the greatest difference in the average ages for success in specific tasks is indicated when comparing Western and non-Western cultures, there are also some surprising differences between ages reported for Swiss and American children. Although the developmental sequence remains the same there are many reports that American children achieve the landmarks of development at a later age, particularly in the advanced levels. This discrepancy is reflected in the surprisingly low percentage of formal operational thinkers estimated for the American adult population.

Using Conservation Tasks to Assess Children's Level of Thinking[29]

All conservation tasks are similar. They each involve four phases as illustrated below.

EQUIVALENCE IS ESTABLISHED	ONE OF MATERIALS TRANSFORMED	CHILD JUDGES EQUIVALENCE	CHILD JUSTIFIES RESPONSE
Is there the same amount of water in each glass or does one glass have more water? What can you do to make it the same? (if necessary)	Now, watch what I'm doing.	Is there the same amount of water in each glass or does one glass have more?	How do you know . . . ? THE GLASS IS TALLER BUT SKINNIER, IT'S THE SAME

1. *Establishing equivalence:* Before introducing any transformations it is essential that the child realize that the starting materials are equivalent. Note that the child can be involved in establishing as well as judging equivalence. The method on page 73 indicates another variation. If the child is unable to establish equivalence you may decide to terminate the task.

2. *One of the materials is transformed:* One of the materials is transformed or rearranged in full view of the child; the other material is left unchanged for comparison. Focus the child's attention on the change by saying, "Now watch what I do."

3. *The child judges equivalence again:* You check whether the child is able to conserve the tested property despite appearances by asking, "Is the amount of water still the same in each glass or does one glass have more water?"

4. *The child justifies his response:* Questions like "How do you know?" "What makes you think so?" will encourage the child to give a reason.

The clinical method:

a. Avoid any verbal or nonverbal responses that would cue the child to the correctness of the response or lead him during the justification.

b. Encourage the child to expand on his justification by asking, "Can you say anything else about the _____ being the same?" This additional information may suggest a second variation of the task, which will allow you to follow the direction of the child's thinking.

c. Be prepared with a planned variation of the task to check the consistency of the child's thinking. The task illustrated above might be varied by changing the shape of the second container or by changing the number of containers.

d. Reword the questions when the child seems unclear about their meaning. Use his vocabulary whenever possible to convey your intent. Presenting the task in the form of a story also facilitates communication.

e. Use countersuggestion to check the strength of the child's conviction; "The other day a girl told me that . . . What do you think about that?"

Judging the Levels of the Child's Responses

PRECONSERVER	TRANSITIONAL	CONSERVER
The child centers on only one of the dimensions and states that the tall glass has more or less water than the short glass.	The transitional child is inconsistent in his replies to two related tasks. He may conserve liquid amount in one situation but not in the other. This inconsistency may be noted even after the child logically justifies his first conservation response.	The child judges that the amount of water is conserved regardless of the container(s) involved. One logical justification is sufficient for each variation of the task (see page 73). Piaget considers a logical justification to be critical to judging a conservation response.

CONSERVATION TASKS:	ESTABLISH EQUIVALENCE	TRANSFORM OR REARRANGE	CONSERVATION QUESTION AND JUSTIFICATION
Conservation of Number Number is not changed despite rearrangement of objects.	○○○○○○○○ ○○○○○○○○	Rearrange one set.	Are there the same number of red & green chips or . . .?
Conservation of Length The length of a string is unaffected by its shape or its displacement.	——————— ———————	Change shape of one string.	Will an ant have just as far to walk, or . . .?
Conservation of Liquid Amount The amount of liquid isn't changed by the shape of the container.		Transfer liquid.	Do the glasses have the same amount of water, or . . . ?
Conservation of Substance (Solid Amount) The amount of substance does not change by changing its shape or by subdividing it.	○ ○	Roll out one clay ball.	Do you still have the same amount of clay?
Conservation of Area The area covered by a given number of two-dimensional objects is unaffected by their arrangement.	Grass / Garden	Rearrange one set of triangles.	Is there still the same amount of "room" for planting, or . . .? Is there still the same amount of grass to eat, or . . . ?
Conservation of Weight A clay ball weighs the same even when its shape is elongated or flattened.		Change shape of one ball.	Do the balls of clay still weigh the same, or . . . ?
Conservation of Displacement Volume The volume of water that is displaced by an object is dependent on the volume of the object and independent of weight, shape or position of the immersed object.		Change shape of one ball.	Will the water go up as high, or . . . ?

Getting Started

Locate some children and work with them individually using some of Piaget's conservation tasks. Classify their responses as conserver, transitional, or preconserver. Record your interview and listen to the tape for evidence that you were getting at the children's level of understanding. The presence of an adult observer can provide you with additional feedback on your interaction with the individual children.

Putting It Together

- Reflect on your experiences with children and on Piaget's ideas of stages of logical thinking and record your most significant learnings, in your own words.

- Reflect on how these learnings might affect your future work with children.

- Construct some clarifying questions to ask your instructor.

Children's Levels of Thinking About Numbers

5

First Comes Thinking

Verbal counting is one of the first number ideas learned by children. Many young children can impress us with how far they can count verbally.

Do these children have any concept of number?

What kind of thinking is involved in:
    verbal counting?
    counting objects?

• What do these dogs and apples have in common? Try to imagine how a young child would arrive at a response.

- Select one response from each of the following pairs. Justify your choice.

a. The learning of addition must precede subtraction which, in turn, must precede multiplication and division.

b. The learning of all four operations takes place simultaneously when children have constructed a beginning concept of number.

a. An understanding of number is related to an understanding of basic ideas of logic. Mathematics should not be taught formally until children have constructed these logical ideas.

b. An understanding of number bears no relation to logical ideas. Mathematics can be taught to children at an early age.

In the preceding chapter describing children's four stages of intellectual development, a survey was made of the range of children's thinking in a variety of areas, as revealed by Piaget's unique tasks. This chapter will focus on one such area—the concept of number.

You will see how Piaget probes beyond children's superficial rote methods to the depths of their understanding of number. Piaget's findings will reveal several logical ideas that "count" in the child's understanding of number. Once these logical ideas have been developed, the child can deal with number operations as part of a system of related operations. Piaget's theory of how such understanding of logical and number ideas develops will bring us back to his view of the child as an active learner.

Probing Beyond Young Children's Verbal Counting

Verbal counting is one of the first number ideas learned by children. This generation of television children demonstrates a great capacity for verbal counting. However, Piaget cautions that this ability can easily mislead an adult to assume that the child who can count can also understand the numbers.[1] We must not overlook children's ability, with little understanding of their actions, to mimic adults. Reciting number names in the absence of real objects is a mindless activity.

> Reciting number names in order has about the same relation to mathematics that reciting the alphabet has to reading.[2]

When young children know the number names, they seldom understand their meaning. Although they can mouth them in correct order, they usually have difficulty assigning them correctly to a set of objects.[3,4]

In the second activity the child superficially associates the number name with each object. She does not yet see the *logical need to include the objects previously counted in a set*.

A closer look at both activities reveals how easily an adult can be misled by a child's "correct" response. The second activity suggests the child's possible lack of understanding behind that "correct" response in the first activity. The child's approach might be compared to naming the objects "Tom, Dick, Harry, Jane . . . Jane!" He could then reply to "How many?" by repeating the last name in the sequence.[3]

When asked to count objects, young children (four–five) will often count an object more than once or even skip it altogether.

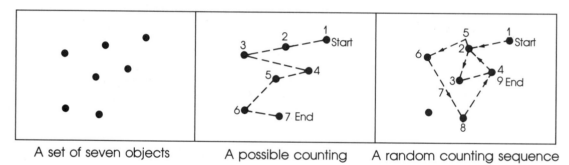

| A set of seven objects | A possible counting sequence | A random counting sequence of a four-year-old |

Although the child counts verbally in correct order, he does not recognize *the logical need to order the objects*. The end result is an incorrect count. Without ordering, the child counts randomly and can't avoid skipping or duplicate counting.[5]

Children who can complete the above task successfully may experience difficulty in counting only seven objects from a larger collection. They simply may not be able to remember when to stop the counting sequence.

When asked to pick up *red* blocks, a young child can usually do so successfully. He will observe blocks with that property and pick them up. *Physical properties exist in actual objects*.

A number cannot be picked up. When asked to pick up three blocks, a child can correctly comply; however, he has not picked up a number. Before the child picked up the blocks they were separate entities in a larger collection of blocks. As he picked them up he mentally placed them into a relationship: the set has a property of "threeness." This "threeness" is also shared by the dogs and apples on the opening page. It is an abstraction, being a step removed from actual objects. The *"threeness" does not exist in any one of the objects in the set, but is abstracted from the entire set and exists in the mind of the child*. Furthermore, it is an abstraction from all conceivable sets of three objects: three blocks, three dogs, three apples, or even a set containing a block, a dog, and an apple.[5]

A number is more than a name.
A number expresses a relationship.
Relationships do not exist in the actual objects.
Relationships are abstractions, a step removed from physical reality.
Relationships are constructions of the mind that are imposed on the objects.[5]

Piaget was interested in probing beyond the rote processes of verbal counting, addition, and multiplication facts. He studied a kind of number readiness, which is both more subtle and more basic than number studies found in most primary classrooms. The broad base of his studies helped him uncover a simultaneous development of overlapping logical ideas that count in the child's understanding of number.

For number readiness, logical ideas "count."

Logical Ideas That Count

Equivalence Through One-to-One Correspondence[6,7]

Matching is the simplest and most direct way of comparing whether collections of objects are equivalent.

Scene: The adult lays out a row of eight candies. He hands the child a box of ten peanuts and suggests an activity.

Can you put on the table as many peanuts as there are candies?

How do you know there are as many peanuts as candies?

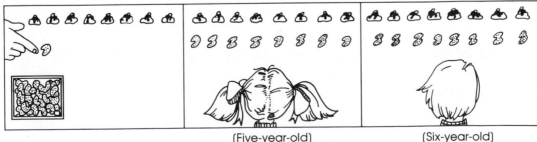

(Five-year-old)   (Six-year-old)

The younger child makes a row of nine objects beside the original row of eight. He decides that they are equivalent because the ends of both rows coincide, ignoring the fact that his row is more crowded. The older child has no difficulty in placing one peanut beside each candy.

Young children (up to age six) experience difficulty in making a one-to-one correspondence of the objects in two rows even when using objects that usually go together, such as eggs and egg cups.

This comparison without counting is a prenumber idea because the one-to-one correspondence doesn't depend on an understanding of number. Rather, it forms a foundation for such understanding.

Counting as One-to-One Correspondence

Real counting involves more than reciting names; it involves matching number names with objects. This is a more abstract example of one-to-one correspondence than matching two sets of objects.

Multiplication as a Correspondence

One-to-one correspondence also builds the foundation for understanding multiplication as the correspondence between several sets.

Three sets of eight

Can the child who matches sets in a one-to-one correspondence also recognize that their number won't change when one of the sets is rearranged?

Does the child's ability to count objects help him to conserve the number of these equivalent sets?

Logical Ideas That Count

Conservation of Number–A Lasting Equivalence[6,7]

For nonconservers, the ability to count objects is not a guarantee that the equivalence of two sets of objects will be a lasting one. This understanding of conservation develops gradually. Even though the rearrangement is carried out in full view, most children below age seven will focus on the end result rather than on the process. To them the length of the rows indicates number.

By the time the children are seven, three out of four will be capable of not only conserving number but also of providing a convincing justification for their responses*. The logic of these responses falls into the following general categories:

"They're still the same things. You just spread them out." (Identity)

"You could see they'd be the same if you pushed them back together." (Reversibility)

"They're more spread out in one line so the line is longer." (Compensation)

One of the children described by Piaget in a comparable situation said: "Once you know, you know for always."

Piaget discounts the ability to conserve up to five objects because it is possible perceptually without the use of logic. He recommends that at least eight objects be used for the task. The ability to conserve larger numbers (beyond ten objects) continues to develop gradually. Eight-year-olds are often observed having difficulty in conserving number when regrouping objects in different combinations of tens and ones and renaming the combinations.

---

*Piaget assigns an age level to a task once 75 percent of the children tested achieve success. Consequently, at that age one out of four children are unable to complete such tasks. It is also possible that some children are completing such logical thinking tasks at the age of six or earlier.

Logical Ideas That Count

Ordering in a Series (Seriation)[6,7]

Ordering builds on comparing. A comparison puts objects in relation to each other. Young children are able to compare the size of two objects at a time, however, when the number of objects is increased they have difficulty in coordinating the relationships. To place dolls in order of size, the child must view the middle doll in a series of three as being *larger than the preceding one at the same time that it is smaller than the following one.*

The dolls and umbrellas are disarranged
when presented to the child.

"These dolls are going for a walk in the rain. Each one will need an umbrella to stay dry. How can you put them so that it's easy for every doll to find its own umbrella?"

When the child completes the task successfully, as shown above, the teacher displaces the row of dolls by pushing them closer together. Now each umbrella is no longer directly below its corresponding doll. As the teacher points to one of the dolls, he asks, "Which umbrella goes with this doll?"

Five-year-olds usually have difficulty in constructing a single series. They may isolate pairs of objects on the basis of their comparisons or might complete an occasional series of three. Sometimes they manage to build a "staircase" with the umbrella tops without seeing the need for a common baseline. Using this approach, they can place any umbrella in any position.

Gradually, a sense of order develops. Most children by age six and a half are able to build a double series by trial and error. However, when the dolls are pushed together, the child will have difficulty matching the doll with its umbrella. If the teacher pointed to the fourth doll, the child would count the three dolls preceding it then locate the third umbrella. Such an approach is common for children of this age.

By the age of seven and a half most children can systematically construct a series by first locating the largest or smallest object. They find the umbrella that goes with the doll by counting from one end of the row even if one of the rows is displaced or reversed.

Each object in an ordered series is larger than the object
before it at the same time that it is smaller than the object
following it.

Ordinal Number

In the preceding activity children use number to indicate the position of objects in a series. They are applying number in its ordinal sense.

When counting objects, children must consider them in some order to ensure that they count each only once. Sometimes children will mentally order the objects without moving them.

Once the child begins to grasp the notion of ordering in his physical world he can begin to look at the order of abstract numbers. He will realize that each member of the counting series is one more than the preceding one and one less than the following one.

$$1 < 2 < 3 < 4 < 5 < 6 < 7 < 8 < 9$$

Each member of the counting series is one more than the one before it at the same time that it is one less than the one following it.

Logical Ideas That Count

Class Inclusion[6,7]

Scene: Adult presents a child (five–six) with a box containing 20 green and 7 yellow plastic counters, spread out and grouped loosely.

A: What do you think the yellow chips are made of?
C: Plastic.
A: What are the green chips made of?
C: Plastic.
A: Are there more green chips or more plastic chips?
C: More green chips.

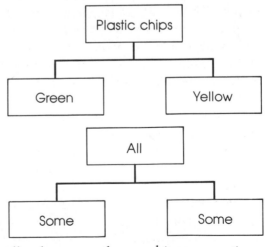

Most children below age seven will give the same response, even when the last question is restated. They have difficulty in considering the idea that *all of one group* (green chips) *can be some of another* (plastic chips) *at the same time*.

These children are unable to include, mentally, the group of green chips as a portion of the plastic chips when attempting to make a comparison. Since they have difficulty coordinating this relationship, they end up basing their responses on appearances. The biggest visible set is the green set. Only after age seven do most children gain the mobility in thinking to coordinate the relationship between "some" and "all."

Number Inclusion

When the child counts unlike objects, he overlooks their differences in size, color, and texture. He *includes* each object in a common class and assigns it a unit of one. (The only difference in these objects would be due to their position in a counting series.)

In counting to discover the number of objects in a set, the child mentally places them into a class-inclusion relationship. Now counting becomes the naming of successive sets.*

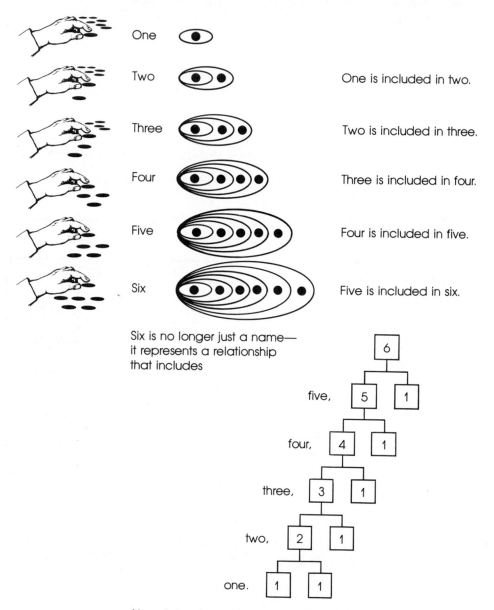

One is included in two.

Two is included in three.

Three is included in four.

Four is included in five.

Five is included in six.

Six is no longer just a name—it represents a relationship that includes five, four, three, two, one.

Also, six involves a one-more relationship. Six is one more than five, which is one more than four . . .

*The number of all the objects included in a counted set is known as the *cardinal* number.

Young children are unable to think of five in relation to adjacent numbers. The seven-year-old has grasped the relationship and arrives at the solution without unnecessary counting. He is able to *count on* from the first set of five and arrive at the solution sooner.

Once again, the ability to place numbers into a mental relationship gives the seven-year-old greater flexibility in dealing with problems. Without "seeing" the relationship between each activity, the younger child approaches each one in isolation.[8]

Logical Ideas That Count

Class Inclusion/Class Addition[6,7]

The class inclusion problem involving yellow and green plastic chips can also be considered a problem in class addition.

The child is able to consider either the whole set or its parts, but cannot consider them *at the same time.* As soon as he views one part separately, he no longer conserves the whole. Since he cannot compare the whole and its parts simultaneously, the young child ends up comparting the two parts.

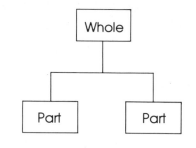

Most children below the age of seven do not see the incongruity of thinking that the part (green chips) is greater than the whole (plastic chips).

To solve the problem, children need the ability to add the parts to obtain the whole and to consider them simultaneously. They must also be able to reverse this process mentally.

Number Addition

The previous problem with addition and comparison of classes has an interesting parallel involving addition of numbers.

Even when the questions are rephrased and his understanding is probed further, the child will persist in this view. As yet, he is unable to:

- keep the sum constant regardless of how its parts are distributed;
- notice that 7+1 seems both larger and at the same time smaller than 4+4 (compensation)
- consider the parts (subsets) in relation to each other and consider both parts in relation to the sum.

Without a grasp of these logical ideas the child solves the problem perceptually.

$$
\left.\begin{array}{l}
\text{Addition} \\
\text{is an operation} \\
\text{relating the parts} \\
\text{to the whole}
\end{array}\right\}
\left.\begin{array}{l}
4 + 4 = 8 \\
5 + 3 = 8 \\
6 + 2 = 8 \\
7 + 1 = 8
\end{array}\right\}
$$

$$
\left.\begin{array}{l}
\text{while} \\
\text{renaming the whole} \\
\text{in terms of} \\
\text{its parts.}
\end{array}\right\}
\left.\begin{array}{l}
8 = 4 + 4 \\
8 = 5 + 3 \\
8 = 6 + 2 \\
8 = 7 + 1
\end{array}\right\}
$$

For Piaget, the understanding of addition presupposes the logical ideas described earlier. He cautions that children without this logical foundation are only able to memorize addition facts mindlessly.

Some research done in the United States reinforces his contention that children's ability to memorize is misleading parents and educators.[9] Of 100 first-grade children, almost all could correctly complete the following number sentences using symbols, $2+3=$ _____ and $5+4=$ _____ . When the problem was presented with materials distributing five cookies for morning and afternoon on different days, 54 children were able to solve the problem logically. When nine cookies were distributed in a similar problem, only 45 children said that the number for each day hadn't changed.

The findings show that children can memorize addition facts without a firm understanding of the meaning of number. Half the children's superficial understanding of number seemed to have little or no connection with real-world objects. Since the focus in American schools is generally on the end product rather than on the thinking processes that underly it, such discrepancies in classroom learning go largely unnoticed.

Methods of Teaching/Learning Number Ideas

Teaching by Telling[5]

Early teaching is usually done by telling. Children repeat the number names until they are committed to memory. These number names, like other labels, are usually chosen arbitrarily and vary from country to country. The only way to communicate arbitrary labels is by telling; such knowledge is called *social knowledge*.

el caballo
le cheval
koń

Other knowledge can be perceived directly from objects with little difficulty. By examining different objects, a child may notice color, size, weight, texture, whether they float or sink, etcetera. Such *physical knowledge* is knowledge of external reality. Teaching by telling can provide the child with the names for these properties as a way to facilitate discussion. However, teaching by telling can be meaningless when conducted in the absence of direct experience with the objects.[5]

Learning as Active Construction

Piaget cautions that the relationships imbedded in the concept of number cannot be taught by telling.

Number is not just a name for something. It is a relationship that

- indicates its place in an order,
- represents how many objects are included in a set, and
- is lasting despite spatial rearrangements.

Piaget refers to such relationships as *logical mathematical knowledge.*[7]

The buttons were in a random pile without order. Through her actions the child introduced order, e.g., linear, circular, etc.

In a pile, the buttons had no sum. Through her actions of putting together and counting she made a sum.

In discovering that the sum is independent of the arrangement, the child discovered a property of her actions and not just a property of buttons. The action of putting together is independent of the action of ordering.

In contrast to the arbitrary labeling in social knowledge, number relationships are coordinated into an internally consistent system. In any culture, 8 = 7+1 = 4+4. Similarly, the statement that "the whole will always be greater than any of its parts" is universally accepted. Both statements are logically consistent.

Piaget believes that these number relationships cannot be taught directly, in the verbal sense. Relationships are constructions of the mind that cannot be transmitted verbally. Words and symbols can serve as useful labels or reminders only after the child has constructed the relationship through his own experience with objects. The child derives logical knowledge not from the objects themselves, but from manipulation of them and internally structuring his actions.[5]

For Piaget, a real understanding of number implies the child's invention or active construction of relationships through her own activity.

Mathematics begins with action on things.[10]

Both physical knowledge and logical mathematical knowledge involve action on objects. Physical knowledge of the buttons is readily obtained from such individual actions as touching, rubbing, squeezing, pushing, throwing, etc. Logical mathematical knowledge, on the other hand, requires a coordination of mental and physical activity. The physical actions themselves are also coordinated in different ways, e.g., joining, ordering, placing in correspondence.[11] In the above example, the child generalized from her coordination of actions what mathematicians call the commutative property of addition[12]

Logical ideas do "count." They cannot be transmitted by word of mouth. They must be constructed by the child through his action on objects.

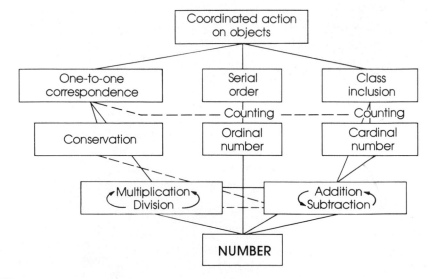

*In depicting this complex web of relationships the author wasn't able to show a clear connection between conservation and class inclusion without creating other distortions.

Piaget's concept of number includes the fusion of related ideas such as serial order and class inclusion into an integrated framework. His concept of number further implies the notions of addition and multiplication as offshoots of class inclusion and one-to-one correspondence. Children, at about age seven, gain a mobility in their thinking that allows them to mentally reverse physical operations. This reversibility gives children access to subtraction as the inverse of addition, and to division as the inverse of multiplication. Thus, no number operation exists alone. Every operation is related to a system of operations and logical ideas. It is this synthesis which Piaget identifies as a concept of number.

Putting It Together

- Reflect on the personal meanings you have constructed in this chapter. In your own words, record a summary of these understandings.

- Construct a clarifying question that you would like to ask your instructor.

- What are some implications of Piaget's findings for the grade placement of beginning mathematics concepts in elementary school?

Language in Thinking, Learning, and Teaching

6

First Comes Thinking

- Which statement in the following pairs do you think is true?

a. Language is acquired by the child through imitation of adult models.
b. Language is actively constructed by the child.

a. Language represents our only mode of thinking: we think only when we talk to ourselves.
b. Language represents only one mode of human thought: thinking can take place in ways other than inner speech.

a. Words have no meaning in and of themselves: meaning is given to the words by the framework of the receiver; we change the content to "hear" only what we understand.
b. Words have meaning in and of themselves: the logical relationships are built into the words; we hear exactly what is being said.

- Participation in the following activity will provide you with some insight into your effectiveness at communication directions to an entire class of children using language as the only vehicle.

- Obtain two sets of Tangram pieces for you and your partner. Sit across from your partner and place a full visual barrier between you. One of you will take the role of the teacher, and the other of the child. The teacher will build a geometric pattern using all seven Tangram pieces. His role is to communicate verbal directions to the child so that he can construct an identical pattern from his own set. The child is not allowed to ask questions. Once the child has completed his construction, remove the barrier and compare the patterns. Sharing your insights and feelings about this communication experience with your partner is helpful. Exchange roles and repeat the activity. Other variations are:

—The child can ask questions.
—Involve a third person as observer.
—Change to another physical activity that requires directions.

As you may have already gathered, this chapter discusses the role of language in thinking, learning, and teaching. First, you will see how Piaget's view of the active child also carries through into the area of language acquisition. We will examine the roles of language in thinking and also the role of thinking in language development and usage. Finally, the limitations of language for communication in the classroom will be considered.

The Child's Active Construction of Language

The child usually demonstrates a good grasp of spoken language by age five, independent of any formal instruction. This language development is reflected not only in the child's growing vocabulary but also in the application of many language rules. Imitation plays an important role in the young child's acquisition of language, however, his speech does not have a simple direct relationship with adult models the child hears. Without formal teaching of language the child is exposed to isolated instances of verbal application. From such an exposure he gains an intuitive understanding of the rules for an invisible language system. In the gradual acquisition of grammatical structure in his speech the child demonstrates evidence of active construction within the limits of the language. His use of "He goed" and "I taked it" are suggestive of rule-governed behavior. The child's active search for a rule is further suggested by his apparent dissatisfaction with the plural form of *foot,* his active attempt to generate other viable possibilities and, finally, his acceptance of *feet* as an exception to his rule. The cycle is reflected in the following possible patter of usage: feet, feet, foots, feets, feetses, feet, feet, feet. The child experiments freely with words in an active search for patterns in adult speech.[1]

Another example of the child's active construction is reflected in his early sentence structure; it doesn't reflect mere parrotlike imitation but, rather, a kind of selective imitation which involves construction of things he hasn't heard. In the gradual acquisition of grammatical structure, the child tends to reduce the adult sentence to a minimum of necessary information for conveying meaning. "Daddy's fixing the car" is reduced to "Daddy car." In speaking his own thoughts, the child expresses intended relationships by order in which he places the words; for example " 'Poon cup" has the intended meaning of "The spoon is in the cup." The child's abbreviated sentences suggest that he is creating rules that relate to adult sentence patterns. He is creating meaning with his order of stating selected words. In addition to active experimentation and construction of rules within his particular language system the child also enriches that language by inventing new words. [1,2]

Language: One Form of Representation

A major achievement that marks the child's development at the opening of the preoperational stage is his ability to detach thought from physical action. The child is now increasingly able to represent objects, actions, and events for himself and others through mental images and words. The child's acquisition of language is intimately linked with other forms of representation—imitation, symbolic play, and mental imagery—that emerge simultaneously in his development. [3]

As the child proceeds through the preoperational stage he becomes increasingly adept at representing objects and events in a variety of ways. He can represent both existing and absent objects for himself. He can also represent his mental representations to others through language and drawings. Although this representational process is initiated in the transition to the preoperational stage, it continues to gradually develop throughout the advanced stages. [2]

These models of representation vary both in complexity and abstractness. Language is the most complex and abstract mode of representation. Whereas other forms of representation bear some resemblance to the objects or events they symbolize, language is expressed in symbols bearing no such resemblance. Unlike other forms of representation that are personal creations, language is acquired within the limits of a socially-defined system. Although language often accompanies other forms of representation, and most rules of language have been constructed by age five, the child's grasp of the most complex rules and of the full meaning of words is more gradual.[3]

Piaget has identified three levels of representation, with two levels being preverbal.[4] The types of representation and their approximate level of complexity are illustrated in accompanying table.[5] The table begins at the bottom with the simplest level of representation, the index level.

Written Language: A Representation of a Representation

Written language is an arbitrary graphic representation of spoken language, which itself is an arbitrary, though socially determined, representation. Being twice removed from reality, written language is the most abstract form of representation. Those arbitrary configurations with characteristic shapes and arrangements called words bear no resemblance to the objects and events they represent. The letters that make up the words are arbitrary marks. Each letter has a name, a characteristic shape, and stands for one or more sounds. Decoding those markings into sounds does not automatically make the word acquire meaning. Contextual usage in a sentence provides only clues to the writer's intended meaning. Meanings are not built into written words; they are created by the reader who interprets them through his network of ideas. No two people experience a poem or story in the same way because their literary experience is personal and depends on the meanings *they* bring to the markings.[6] Similarly, mathematics is a language with its own set of markings. The relationships of mathematics are not built into these symbols. The relationships are constructed by the human mind and assigned to the symbols.

Levels and Types of Representation[5, p. 171]

LEVEL	TYPE	EXAMPLE
Sign A kind of symbol with no resemblance to a real object	**Words** A word itself evokes clear mental images and meaningful mental relations based on a variety of interactions with objects and events. Words serve to retrieve personal meanings and to express them.	
Symbol Some resemblance to real objects, yet distinct from a real object	**Pictures** Children who have rich experiences with objects and events can correctly interpret pictorial representations in terms of prior experience and understanding.	
	Physical models The child is able to represent a physical object by a three-dimensional model made from clay or a flat drawing, evoking an image of the real object from representations.	
	Make-believe play Children use objects to represent other objects (symbolic play).	
	Imitation The child can represent the object by using his body to represent the sound and movement of the object. Children also represent common situations in their lives by acting them out (dramatic play).	
Index Part of the actual object represents the whole object	**Part of the object** The child is able to mentally construct the missing part and recognize the object: He produces a mental image of the object by seeing some tracks or traces caused by the object.	

Language develops as part of a larger system of representation. It is only one way of representing the world.

The Relation Between Logic and Language

Logic Precedes Language—Logic Is Deeper than Language

Children demonstrate their logical thinking in problems concerning physical materials prior to dealing with similar problems at the verbal propositional level. Logic can precede language by several years. Children can seriate lengths and colors about five years prior to solving verbal seriation problems.[7]

Piaget points out an earlier example of this gap between logic and language. The young child demonstrated an intelligence, a kind of "logic of actions," in the sensori-motor stage prior to the emergence of observable language. Piaget believes language has roots in the child's coordination of actions, which are deeper than language itself. During the sensori-motor period the child discovers and coordinates his actions to achieve goals of increasing complexity. These group action patterns and the general pattern of discovery not only precede but also seem to underly the child's acquisition of language.[1,3,5]

The lag between logic and language continues throughout the stages even though the child begins to acquire language. Piaget explains that action patterns effective for intelligent action on the physical level need to be restructured before they are internalized at a representational level; in other words, they can't be translated immediately to the level of thought, but must be relearned. This is a gradual process and thereby accounts for the lag between physical and verbal understanding.[7]

Logic Patterns Language Usage

Until about age seven, it is a logic of actions (sensori-motor stage) which prepares a foundation for the emergence of language and a semi-logic (preoperational stage) that influences the child's construction of language. Once the child enters the concrete operational stage, by definition, the child's thinking becomes truly operational (logical). This emergence of logical thought further influences the development of language and is accompanied by related changes in language usage.

Piaget's co-workers have compared the language usage of groups of conservers and preconservers of amount.[8] The children were asked to compare pairs of objects after they were each given two dolls.

Are the
dolls happy?
Is it fair?

	PRECONSERVERS	CONSERVERS
⬭ ⬭	"The boy has the big one, the girl has the little one."	"The boy has a bigger one than the girl."
○○○ ○ ○○ ○ ○○ ○	"The girl has a lot and the boy a little."	"The girl has more."
✏️✏️	"This pencil is long, that one is short." (one variable) or "This pencil is long, that one is short. This one is thick, that one is thin." (two variables)	"This pencil is long(er) but thin(ner), the other is short but thick."

The preconservers tended to focus on one variable at a time in describing differences in objects. They were not able to apply comparative terms such as a more, bigger, longer, etc., which are associated with conservation problems. These preconservers were still in the preoperational stage and their lack of logical operations limited their language usage. By contrast, the conservers had the logical operations to consider two objects and two variables at the same time. This increased mental capacity influenced their language usage. [8]

Logic Gives Meaning to Words

Children appear to understand comparative terms such as *more* and *less* or *longer* and *shorter* in some contexts but not in others. By observing the gap between children's conservation of amount, area, weight, and volume, Piaget has demonstrated that seven-year-olds understand "more" in terms of amount but not in terms of area, weight, and volume. Although they have the appropriate vocabulary, it may be limited to specific application by their conceptual frameworks. [9]

The term *brother* is part of most children's vocabulary. The preoperational child cannot grasp the reciprocal relation involved and, therefore, cannot think of himself as a brother to Jimmy and Allan. A concrete operational boy is likely to count himself in as a brother and use the term correctly in context. Until age nine or ten, however, this boy is likely to define a brother as a boy "who lives in my house." Not until the formal operational stage does the child have a full grasp of the reciprocal relation involved in terms of kinship and interrelation. Although most children have *brother* in their vocabulary, the level of its meaning differs drastically due to differences in the extent that their conceptual frameworks have been differentiated and elaborated.[9]

Parents and teachers are often misled by taking children's verbalisms at face value. They tend to credit children with a level of understanding beyond their current capacity.

The best way to gain insight into children's true understanding is to talk to them as they interact with materials.

Language Neither Develops Logical Thinking Nor Solely Explains Thought

If language were critical to the development of logical thinking, then children who were deprived of language would be greatly impaired in logical thinking. Deaf children who are deprived of language develop comparable concrete concepts of class, serial order, and number at about the same time as non-deaf children. Forms of representation other than language must therefore play an integral part in the development of logical thinking.[8] In other words, *language is just one mode of expressing thought; it is not thinking itself.*

Language is full of expressions of logical relationships. If one were to carefully teach such logical expressions to children, would this improve their thinking ability? Piaget's colleagues have taught comparative expressions like "more than, longer than," and coordinated expressions like "longer but thinner" to preconservers. This training helped them to focus on more than one dimension of the problem, however, they failed to demonstrate a marked increase in ability to conserve amount. Ability to use precise comparative language did not improve their ability to think logically—they continued to think in their own ways. Logical thought cannot be developed solely through language instruction.[8]

Thoughts are not always accompanied by words. All of us can recall situations in which we searched for words to express our thoughts. Scientists and mathematicians working at the frontier of knowledge may change reality or make discoveries in areas beyond our reality that cannot be communicated without the invention of new terminology. Words are invented after the ideas are restructured in another symbol system. Language does not have the capacity to create new knowledge; discovery of new knowledge necessitates the invention of new language for communication.[1]

Although language alone does not explain or develop logical thought, it still remains a necessary condition for its development. Language plays an important role in refining structures of thought, particularly in the formal stage of thought development. Without language, mental frameworks would be personal and lack social regulation through interaction. In this sense, language extends logical thinking to its highest level.[10]

Formal thought is often expressed verbally, but the multiple relations possible within a total unified system of concepts go beyond the capacity of natural language. Our spoken language limits us to linear analysis of reality, to viewing only the parts, one after the other, rather than look at them simultaneously. However, particularly in the formal operational stage, we are capable of thinking beyond the linear limitations imposed by language.[11]

Teaching as Communication

Is Anybody Listening?

Each day in the classroom children are required to respond to spoken and written words. The teacher provides directions, gives explanations, and raises questions through words, but to what extent do they communicate?

Piaget's colleagues have demonstrated a limitation of words in the following examples.[8,12]

In both examples these children had relations in mind; unfortunately, they were not the relations the teacher expected in response to her questions. We hear what we are prepared to hear. If our existing framework cannot assimilate the information correctly and accommodation or restructuring is not yet possible, then we deform the information to fit the existing framework. Children's inability to follow spoken or written directions is not always due to inattention or poor memory. They see and hear what they understand. [12,13]

We hear what we are prepared to hear.

Is Telling the Same as Teaching?/To Tell or Not to Tell

A word itself has no meaning. Hearing a word evokes internal representations of meaning based on our prior interactions with the environment and with related ideas. Unless our existing framework can give meanings to words, they are a meaningless sequence of sounds.

Using telling as the main method of teaching requires that both teacher and learner have mutual frameworks to make communication possible. This means that a one-to-one correspondence would be approximated between the ideas the teacher intends and the anticipatory idea network of the learner. Since the idea network of the child is still blossoming, the chances for such a correspondence are limited. [14]

The learner may pronounce the word *photosynthesis*, but this does not reflect any understanding of the concept it represents. The learner may use the word in correct context or may repeat a textbook definition verbatim—still, this only ensures a minimal understanding of the concept. Yet children and adults are often encouraged to regurgitate ready-made definitions as indicators of their learning. This practice has led Piaget to comment on the ". . . proliferation of pseudo-ideas loosely hooked onto a string of words lacking any real meaning."[14] True assimilation of new information relates it to a network of understandings. The degree to which the learner can rephrase the concept definition and retain its meaning, or apply the concept in a different context, is a reliable indicator of his true understanding. [11,12]

Piaget recommends that prospective teachers spend considerable time interviewing children individually and questioning them to make contact with their thinking. He thinks this experience is critical to an adult appreciation of the problems of making oneself understood by children. He further recommends that such a study of children's thinking be conducted with a number of different children on the same task. This would provide experience in the range of approaches required to make contact with children's thinking. You might try using any of Piaget's tasks which have been described in detail earlier in this book. He is certain that such an experience will convince teachers that true communication with a whole class of children at any given time is not a realistic expectation. [15]

Words: Are They Merely Labels or Are They Concepts?

Since words are convenient labels for concepts, teachers are often misled to believe that a child has learned a concept, although he has only learned a label for it. Concepts cannot be transmitted through language alone. A learner who already has a rich variety of related experiences and ideas might understand from the teacher's language some loose ends and a potential connection. Even then, the learner must actively make those connections for himself. Words are merely labels for concepts—they are not the concepts themselves.[12]

Limitations of Language in the Classroom

Piaget recognized language as a valuable tool of scholars for expressing, organizing, and debating their ideas. Their experiential background assures some mutual understanding of the concepts that their precise intellectual language codifies. In the case of children, whose concepts are still being formed, Piaget cautions teachers about the limitations of language. He also provides them with some insights into a problem that all teachers have experienced: What we teach is not always what children learn.[12] He states:

> Words are probably not a short-cut to a better understanding . . . The level of understanding seems to modify the language that is used, rather than vice versa . . . Mainly, language serves to translate what is already understood; or language may even present a danger if it is used to introduce an idea which is not yet accessible.[15, p. 5]

What we teach is not always what children learn.

Putting It Together

- Construct a summary of your personal understandings of the child's acquisition of language abilities in the context of a broader, developing system of representation and reasoning.

- Given the limitations of language in the classroom which have been described in this chapter, how would you:

    give directions

    introduce a new concept

    define a new term

    give an explanation

    assess understanding of a concept

in ways which communicate and do not paralyze children's thinking? (Examples of such applications of language are illustrated at the end of Chapter 9.)

Exploring Children's Thinking and Learning Exploration 2-Length

7

A second, detailed Exploration of children's thinking and learning will open our window to children's minds a bit further. It highlights the surprising capacity of seven-year-old children for logical thinking as it focuses on their intricate mental coordinations as they construct increasingly more elaborate concepts of length. You also have a second opportunity to derive methods that facilitate children's thinking and learning as you rejoin the teacher on sabbatical leave in her Exploration. This chapter also considers how the unique sequences used in the Explorations are devised by Piaget and his colleagues and how they fit into the context of their formal research.

In the initial Exploration of the children's understanding of the conservation concept, the children are shown the following arrangement of objects (after a one-to-one correspondence had been established).

They are asked:

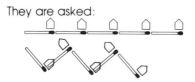

"If you walk down both roads, will you pass the same number of houses?"

"Will you have just as far to walk along each road?"

The second Exploration employs an ingenious sequence of road-building tasks designed by Magali Bovet to highlight the children's equilibration processes.[1-7] The teacher presents the children with model roads which are constructed with matchsticks arranged in different shapes. The children are given matches and are asked to construct straight roads that are equal in length to the model. The child's matches are shorter than those used by the teacher.

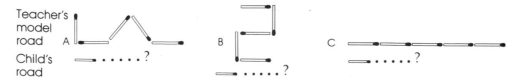

First Comes Thinking

- If the main exploration is to deal with children's understanding of length concepts, why would it begin with a conservation of number task?

- Predict how the children will do on the conservation tasks of number and length. If the children were able to conserve number, would you expect them to also conserve length in a situation where the materials had not changed? Justify your response.

- Notice that in the sequence of road building tasks (A,B,C) the tasks are presented in a reverse order of difficulty, from A (most difficult) to C (least difficult). What useful purpose might this sequence serve in this Exploration of children's thinking and learning?

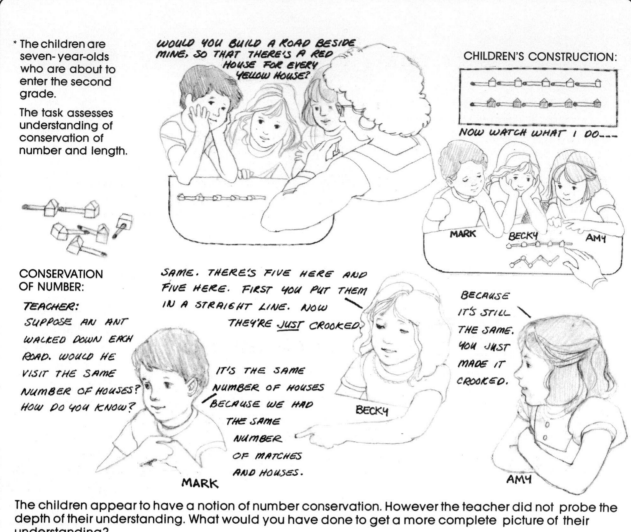

* The children are seven- year-olds who are about to enter the second grade.

The task assesses understanding of conservation of number and length.

CHILDREN'S CONSTRUCTION:

NOW WATCH WHAT I DO---

WOULD YOU BUILD A ROAD BESIDE MINE, SO THAT THERE'S A RED HOUSE FOR EVERY YELLOW HOUSE?

MARK   BECKY   AMY

CONSERVATION OF NUMBER:

TEACHER:
SUPPOSE AN ANT WALKED DOWN EACH ROAD. WOULD HE VISIT THE SAME NUMBER OF HOUSES? HOW DO YOU KNOW?

SAME. THERE'S FIVE HERE AND FIVE HERE. FIRST YOU PUT THEM IN A STRAIGHT LINE. NOW THEY'RE JUST CROOKED.

IT'S THE SAME NUMBER OF HOUSES BECAUSE WE HAD THE SAME NUMBER OF MATCHES AND HOUSES.

MARK

BECKY

BECAUSE IT'S STILL THE SAME. YOU JUST MADE IT CROOKED.

AMY

The children appear to have a notion of number conservation. However the teacher did not probe the depth of their understanding. What would you have done to get a more complete picture of their understanding?

CONSERVATION OF LENGTH:

PRETEND THAT AN ANT STARTED HERE AND WALKED TO THE END OF EACH ROAD. WOULD THE ANT HAVE JUST AS FAR TO WALK? --- HOW DO YOU KNOW?

YES, THESE HOUSES ARE THE SAME AS THOSE HOUSES.

I THINK HE WOULD HAVE TO WALK FARTHER. BECAUSE YOU BENDED THOSE.

THIS ONE'S LONGER THIS ONE IS STRAIGHT. AND THE OTHER GOES (∧∨∧).

Although the similarity of the tasks is obvious to an adult, most children at their age view them as independent encounters with the environment. They tend to look for a coincidence in the starting and ending points of a pair of lines.

*This sequence is illustrated from a videotaped exploration of children's thinking.

Exploring <u>Thinking</u> and Learning

Conservation of Number and Length

The similarity of the number and length tasks is obvious to an adult who, in thinking, almost automatically coordinates the two variables. However, most six- to seven-year-old children view them as independent encounters with the environment. They often spontaneously suggest counting the matches to justify their judgment of number conservation. But when the question on the same materials shifts to length, counting usually doesn't occur to them. Rather, they tend to look for a coincidence that indicates the starting and ending points of a pair of lines. Usually a time lag of about a year exists between the child's ability to conserve number and his ability to conserve length.

<u>Exploring</u> Thinking and Learning

In these two tasks, the teacher did not establish clearly the level of the children's understanding. She accepted the children's first responses without any attempt to probe further. Encouraging children to make additional justifications often reveals more sophisticated reasoning.* Since the teacher moved quickly through the tasks, we are left with only a vague impression of the children's competence. Generally, all the children seem to have some notion of the conservation of number; one child has a notion of the conservation of length. Without a clear indication of the depth of their understanding of these concepts, the teacher will have difficulty predicting the level of their performance on the tasks that follow. However, since Piaget considers the notion of conservation of number as a minimum prerequisite for the next activities, these children might benefit from them. In other words, developmentally, these activities appear to be close enough to the children's level for them to consider.

---

*Other, more logical reasons are also offered by children to the conservation of number question.

ROAD BUILDING (cont'd)

TASK/EXPLORATION

BUILD A STRAIGHT ROAD SO THAT
AN ANT WILL HAVE JUST AS FAR
TO WALK AS IT DOES ON THIS ROAD.

ARE THE ROADS JUST AS
LONG? HOW DO YOU KNOW?

B

BUILD ANOTHER
STRAIGHT ROAD
UNDERNEATH SO
THAT AN ANT
WOULD WALK
JUST AS FAR.
--- HOW DO
YOU KNOW THAT
THE ROADS ARE
JUST AS LONG?

C

BUILD ANOTHER
STRAIGHT ROAD
UNDERNEATH;
ONE THAT'S
JUST AS LONG.

CHILD DOES

AMY

(Notice the length difference of the child's matches.)

B1

B2

C1

AND SAYS

A2

IGNORING THE SIZE OF THE MATCHES.

YES, BECAUSE
THAT'S FIVE AND
THAT'S FIVE.

A3

YES. (AGAIN IGNORING THE
SIZE OF THE MATCHES) ---
BECAUSE THAT'S FIVE AND
THAT'S FIVE.

B3

What kinds of logical thinking will Amy need to do in order to solve all three road-building problems?

How might you learn more about Amy's thinking about the problem?

Exploring Thinking and Learning

Amy

When judging the length of two roads after one had been displaced in the pre-assessment, Amy focused on the lack of coincidence of all the ends. Since the straight road extended beyond the crooked road she decided that it was longer.

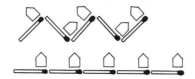

(Same number of matches of equal size)

When building roads required to be the same length as the teacher's models, she focused on another strategy—number. However, she ignored the discrepancy between the size of her matches compared to those used in the models.

Each of Amy's strategies forms part of the concept of length. As isolated strategies they are limited in their application. These strategies need to be combined, not just in a linear fashion, but integrated so that one strategy compensates for the other, for example, number and size of matches. The opportunities for action and reflection in the following sequence may provoke her to consider more than one strategy at the same time and to become aware of the discrepancies involved.

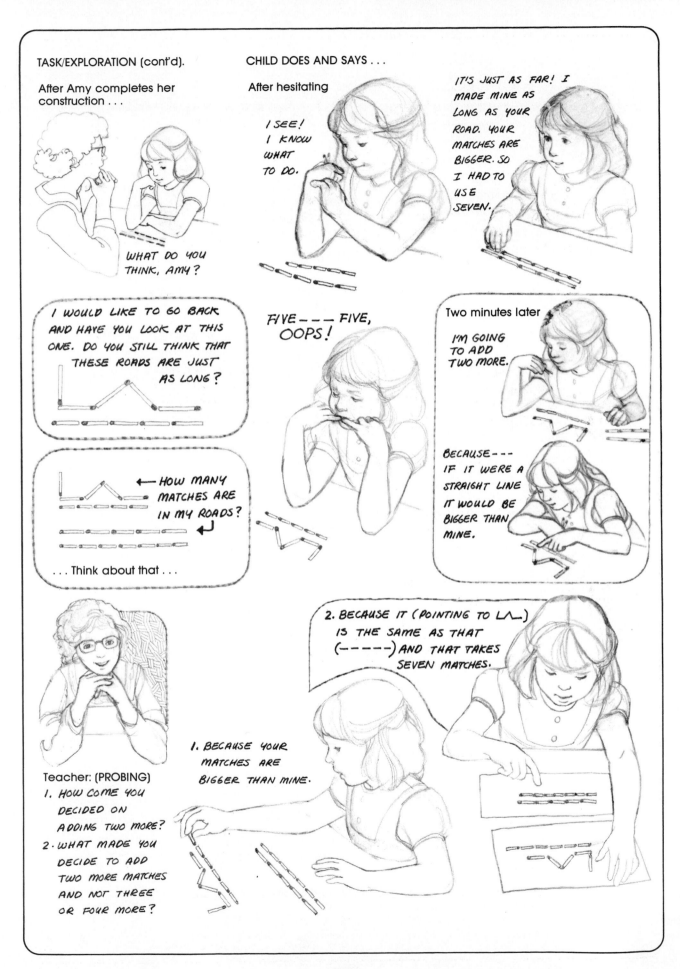

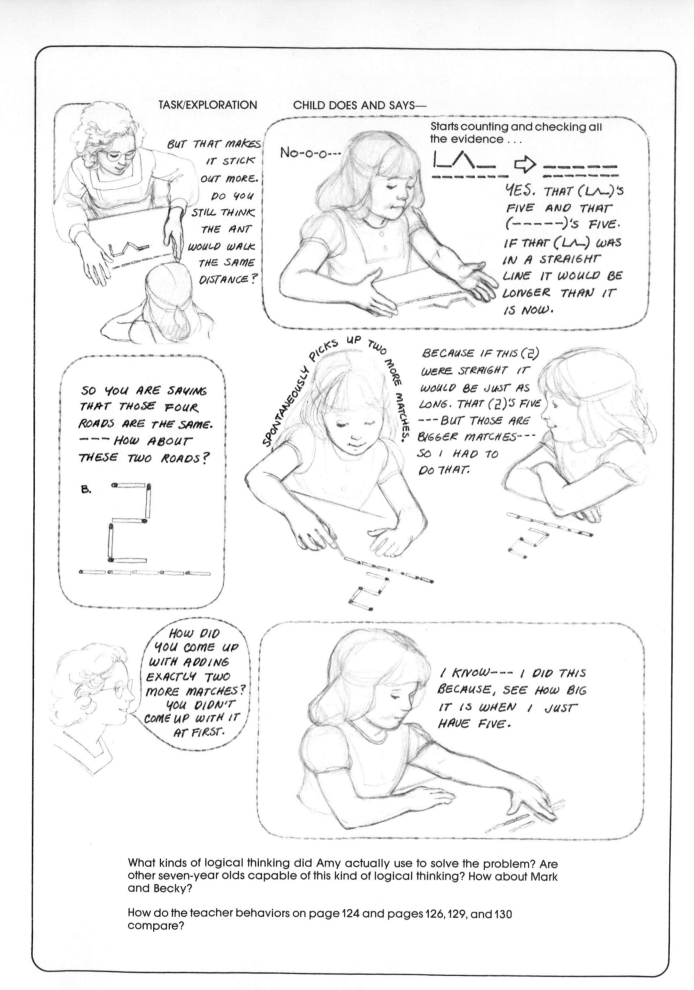

TASK/EXPLORATION

CHILD DOES AND SAYS—

BUT THAT MAKES IT STICK OUT MORE. DO YOU STILL THINK THE ANT WOULD WALK THE SAME DISTANCE?

No-o-o---

Starts counting and checking all the evidence . . .

YES. THAT (L∧_)'S FIVE AND THAT (─────)'S FIVE. IF THAT (L∧_) WAS IN A STRAIGHT LINE IT WOULD BE LONGER THAN IT IS NOW.

SO YOU ARE SAYING THAT THOSE FOUR ROADS ARE THE SAME. --- HOW ABOUT THESE TWO ROADS?

B.

SPONTANEOUSLY PICKS UP TWO MORE MATCHES.

BECAUSE IF THIS (⊇) WERE STRAIGHT IT WOULD BE JUST AS LONG. THAT (⊇)'S FIVE --- BUT THOSE ARE BIGGER MATCHES--- SO I HAD TO DO THAT.

HOW DID YOU COME UP WITH ADDING EXACTLY TWO MORE MATCHES? YOU DIDN'T COME UP WITH IT AT FIRST.

I KNOW--- I DID THIS BECAUSE, SEE HOW BIG IT IS WHEN I JUST HAVE FIVE.

What kinds of logical thinking did Amy actually use to solve the problem? Are other seven-year olds capable of this kind of logical thinking? How about Mark and Becky?

How do the teacher behaviors on page 124 and pages 126, 129, and 130 compare?

Exploring <u>Thinking and Learning</u>

Amy

In situation C Amy hesitated following her initial solution which was based on number. Although her road was constructed with the same number of matches as the model, the teacher's parallel road was longer. From Amy's actions we can infer that she

C

applied the strategy of coinciding ends simultaneously with the counting strategy. Since the strategies cannot be simply added together she experienced a conflict. Given time to reflect she volunteered a logical solution that the greater number of her matches would compensate for their smaller size. Without the capacity to consider "opposing" strategies at the same time, she would have experienced no conflict to energize the new learning.

Amy experienced further conflicts between the different strategies as she applied them simultaneously. Each strategy is itself limited in its application. The need for the road ends to coincide is enough to convince Amy on the length of roads only when they are parallel. The counting strategy is sufficient only when the matches are of equal length. The disequilibrium resulting from considering these strategies simultaneously triggers their integration into a broader framework. Amy's actions suggest that she has successfully combined a number of strategies in a compensatory manner:

coincidence of end points

size of units, and

number of units.

The organization of these strategies in relation to each other produced a stable structure at a higher level of equilibrium.*

Amy's successful application of her solution of parallel road construction to the displaced and crooked roads requires additional logic. Since the number of matches used in each of the three models was the same, Amy could extend her solution to situations A and B through *transitivity:*

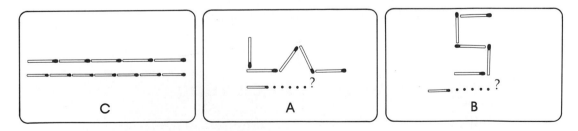

C   A   B

---

*Some educators might label the road-building tasks as "hands-on" activities. This label overlooks a critical aspect of this activity, i.e., the time available to Amy to reflect on her actions. The tasks might be more appropriately labelled as "hands-on/minds on" activities.

Things equal to the same thing are equal to each other.

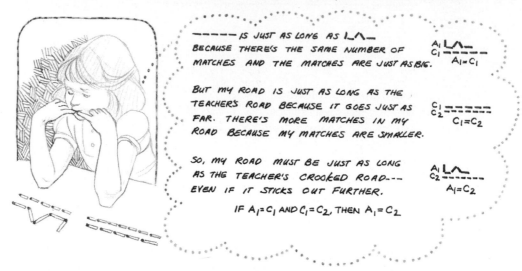

In coordinating all the strategies and transferring them to another situation, the child must not only compensate the number of matches for the size, but also realize the limitation of the strategy of coinciding ends. In addition, the child must apply the logical operation of transitivity. Although Amy's logical operation was not observed directly, it can be inferred from her successful solution.

In her stage of intellectual development, the concrete operational stage, Amy is able to reflect on her actions and mentally coordinate the similarities in length of the roads despite apparent differences. At the same time, she does not have full awareness of her thinking. Although, upon close examination, her statements and actions reflect considerable logic, Amy is unable to elaborate verbally on the logic of her thinking in adult terms. It is not until the next stage, the formal operational stage, that children have the potential to gain full awareness of their thinking as they progress from "thinking about actions" to "thinking about thinking." Despite Amy's logical capacities for dealing with concepts of length, she will need a variety of further physical experiences and social interactions in different situations over an extended period of time before demonstrating similar capacities in dealing with concepts of area, weight, and displacement volume.

At the same time that a child's development limits his ability to learn, it unfolds surprising capacities for learning.

Exploring Thinking and Learning

During this sequence the teacher kept Amy's constructions in front of her and encouraged her to make comparisons. Her questions shifted Amy's attention from one problem situation to the next. This comparison of problems and prior solutions helped to generate the conflicts in Amy's mind. The teacher's successive questions on length and number may lead her to question her own exclusive use of isolated strategies.

Unlike the conservation tasks in the pre-assessment when the teacher appeared rushed and her questions were superficial, the teacher later demonstrated a variety of appropriate applications of questioning:

She asked questions to clarify a child's response when it was not clear to her.

She probed the depth of the child's understanding by encouraging more than a single justification.

She allowed the child time to think through her responses.

She challenged the child's response even though it was correct.

The teacher's challenge of Amy's response caused the child to review and restate her evidence; this strategy often causes further justification by the child. An indirect method of questioning a response is to say, "Yesterday, another girl told me that this one had to be longer because it stuck out so much further. What do you think about that?" However, if we only question children's responses when they are "wrong" then the question becomes a threat rather than an interesting challenge.

> If we only question children's responses when they are "wrong," the children soon catch on.[8]

Exploring <u>Thinking and Learning</u>

Becky and Mark

Mark and Becky also experienced the road building sequence of activities . . .

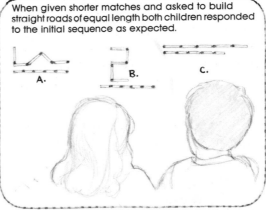

When given shorter matches and asked to build straight roads of equal length both children responded to the initial sequence as expected.

A. B. C.

The initial responses of these children to the three road building situations were based on the number strategy. However, prior to building a road of five matches below one model, both children initially built one using only four matches. This behavior suggests that the perceptual pull of the coincidence strategy may have interfered with their implementing the number strategy in full. At this point it seems that some interplay exists between "opposing" strategies.

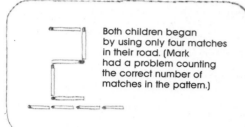

Both children began by using only four matches in their road. (Mark had a problem counting the correct number of matches in the pattern.)

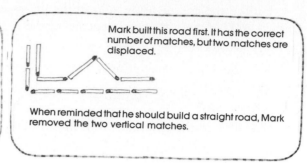

Mark built this road first. It has the correct number of matches, but two matches are displaced.

When reminded that he should build a straight road, Mark removed the two vertical matches.

Similarly, Mark attempted to correct his construction in situation A by using seven small matches. The idea of lack of coincidence meaning unequal length seemed to conflict with his number strategy. The first strategy seemed to be so overpowering that he invented another *compromise solution*. Rather than simply adding two more matches to his horizontal road, he placed them vertically. In his compromise solution he arranged the correct number of matches in a way that did not protrude beyond the model. When reminded of the requirement for building a straight road, he withdrew the two matches.

For most adults these compromise solutions are errors in need of correction. For Piaget these highly original responses are incomplete coordinations of appropriate strategies. Although they are not yet complete solutions, they are certainly indicative of progress towards that end. Mark's compromise solution provides convincing evidence of his active construction of his personal framework of knowledge.

AND—

THERE'S FIVE MATCHES IN BOTH ROADS.

IT GOES TO THERE AND YOUR MATCHES ARE BIGGER THAN MINE --- SO I PUT MORE.

The children made no further progress in spite of many attempts by the teacher to clarify the children's thinking. Many comparisons between children's roads and the teacher's models had been made during this time.

Becky was initialy convinced that roads of equal length must have the same number of matches. She repeated this strategy in all three road-building situations. However, in situation C, she eventually was able to coordinate the size and number of the matches with the coincidence of the roads ends. In this situation, in which the roads are parallel, the conflict between the strategies is most readily resolved. However, this new realization can't be extended to the other situations unless there is further competence in comparison of strategies and results—transitivity. Becky did not appear to have the competence at this time. The teacher encouraged her to compare her solutions and reminded her of her earlier conviction that roads constructed with small matches required a greater number. However, Becky could not progress beyond her initial insight.

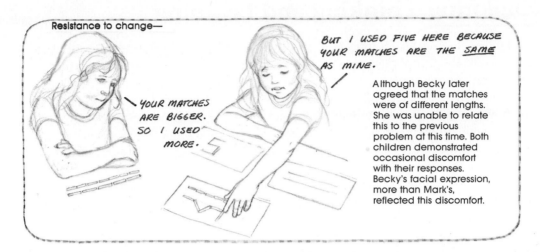

At one point, Becky showed great resistance to further change. She denied the difference in size of her matches when compared to those in the teacher's model. However, she was uncomfortable with the response and did not stick to it.

Becky's response in this situation illustrates Piaget's view of how we process information. When new information is introduced that cannot fit our existing framework, we either change our framework or we change our perception of that information to maintain our existing framework. Becky's response was the latter. Had Becky been in a state of equilibrium, she wouldn't need to distort her sensory input to assimilate it. Similarly, she wouldn't need to change the organization of her ideas very much to accommodate the difference of length in the matches.

We only see what we understand.

We need change to grow; we resist change.

What might you have done differently to —

Explore the children's thinking further?

Facilitate their recognition of the problem?

If you decided to provide the children with additional experiences,

Would you do it on the next day?

Would you postpone it to a later time?

Why?

Exploring Thinking and Learning

The teacher's decision to work with Becky and Mark again, two and a half weeks later, was based on their awareness of the problem. Both, to different degrees had demonstrated some evidence of intellectual conflict in their solutions and their facial expressions. The teacher's task was to help the children compare their strategies in ways which would sharpen the intellectual conflict.

The adaptations, that were introduced in the original sequence were both planned and spontaneous. Since the activities were no longer new, the order of presentation was altered. Another planned change was to reduce the amount of information that the child would be required to consider at one time; cards covered extraneous information, revealing only the minimum considerations for a transitivity solution.

PLANNED: (ACTIVITIES WERE DONE BY INDIVIDUAL CHILDREN.)
After the child constructed his roads for tasks B + C, the teacher covered the child's roads with cards. The cards encouraged the children to compare the teacher's model roads and to coordinate their similarities with his own roads as they were unconvered. (The dots indicate the covered matches.)

Mark's solution for Task "C" was accurate.

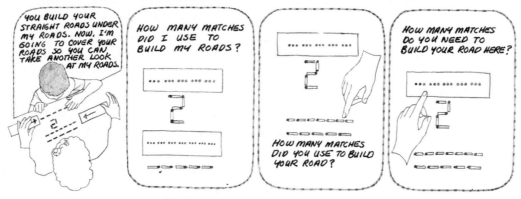

Although the teacher's initial questions focused on the number strategy, she followed up by questioning the child's response in terms of another strategy, such as coincidence of ends. Once the first transitivity comparison was successful, she presented the most difficult problem (situation A) without masking. Mark successfully coordinated his strategies throughout the sequence.

The teacher spontaneously adopted an unplanned procedure for Becky when the child became uncomfortable with her responses in the masked situation but was unable to coordinate them. The teacher decided to have her do more manipulation of materials. The teacher masked all Becky's original constructions and the child duplicated the model roads using the large matches. She build two versions of B, one duplicate and one extended. Following this additional experience, she could coordinate her strategies and answer correctly all the ensuing questions.

SPONTANEOUS:
The use of masks did not help Becky immediately. She was then given direct experience in reproducing the original patterns. This additional experience with materials facilitated the invention of a correct solution for "B."

Becky then solved without help from the masks. (c)

*Covered matches

In addition to the adaptations of the original sequence, questions and discussion at crucial points induced Becky's awareness of the contradictions, providing impetus for higher-level coordinations.

How did the teacher know whether to stop or to continue?

Since intellectual conflict provides the essential impetus for higher-level coordination of strategies the teacher was continually searching for clues to its presence. Evidence of intellectual conflict occurred in the following child behaviors:

- the amount of hesitation at crucial points in the sequence,
- the invention of compromise solutions,
- facial expressions and body language, and
- intonation of responses.

The teacher's awareness of these clues helped her make the following decisions:

- whether the children were aware of the problem,
- when to ask crucial questions,
- when to start/stop the probing,
- whether to continue the activities, and
- whether to allow the children more time to think or to move on to another activity or exploration strategy.

Her sensitivity to the behavioral indicators of disequilibrium, that is, the child's growing awareness that his solution doesn't seem quite right to him, enabled the teacher to maximize the children's interactions with the materials and with their isolated strategies.

Although many writers popularize the picture of classrooms filled with smiling faces, Piaget's view indicates that higher-order learning can only take place after some frustration has been experienced. However, once the higher-order concepts have been attained, the satisfaction is unmistakably reflected in the children's faces. The teacher's awareness of these indicators of learning in progress can facilitate the process.

Exploring Thinking and Learning

Levels of Competence in Thinking

The thinking-learning behavior of children involved in such activities is grouped by Piaget's colleagues into four categories. These levels of competence have been illustrated by the children in different parts of the explorations of displacement volume (Exploration 1) and length (Exploration 2).

1. At the lowest level, children are not aware of the problem. They react to number and length problems as being totally independent. For example, when building roads, they use number or length strategies in isolation. Despite often comparing their different solutions, they do not experience any contradictions among them.
2. Children at the next level are aware that a conflict exists between their answers in the different situations, however, they are unable to resolve the contradiction.
3. At this level, children can partially resolve the conflict by inventing compromise solutions. Although these compromises are inadequate in terms of adult logic, they are intermediate steps in the children's construction of knowledge.
4. Children at the highest level grasp the various aspects of the problem and make the coordinations necessary to solve it completely.

Piaget has identified a similar developmental order to solutions in many problem-solving situations. He sees the child's active recombination of strategies in constructing new knowledge as characteristic of not just these episodes, but fundamental to learning in real life.

Progress in Levels of Thinking

The progress that a child makes in such encounters is largely dependent on his entry level. If he understands number conservation, the conservation of length task is developmentally close enough for him to consider. Since the coincidence of end points is already a primitive approach to any conservation task, adding the number strategy opens up possibilities for coordination. If the child understands both strategies but does not experience any contradiction in their separate application, he can make no progress. Once the child is alerted to this contradiction, the intellectual discomfort will drive him actively to seek a solution. However, Piaget's colleagues have observed that children sometimes make delayed progress without any further stimulation. Such progress supports the existence of internal processes of coordination.

The children who progress the furthest are often those who appear most confused during the sequence—experiencing conflict and hesitation, struggling to coordinate the various aspects of the problem. At one point, Amy reflected for nearly two minutes before responding to a question. Meanwhile, the children who feel no need to integrate their isolated approaches into the different situations require little time to reach their lower-level solutions. Thinking through a solution takes time. Answers to real problems are not pre-formed in the children's minds. Rather, they are constructed by the children through active involvement with a problem. Yet, classroom research indicates that teachers allow children less than one second to respond to a question.

Thinking takes time . . . Children who progress the furthest are often those who were most confused initially.[1]

Can you infer one of the four levels of involvement and understanding (previous face) from each facial expression? Perhaps you can associate some expressions with specific tasks in the sequence.

Exploring Thinking and Learning in a Research Context and Some Implications for Education

This Exploration of children's Thinking and Learning of length concepts and its discussion was adapted from the work of Piaget's colleagues, Barbel Inhelder, Hermine Sinclair and Magali Bovet. [1-7] The exploration sequence was designed by the Bovet and employed by the group as part of a broader research into what children know and how they construct their knowledge. Their procedures for studying children's thinking and for provoking higher-order thinking may have implications for the areas of teaching and curriculum development, and may even serve these areas as a process model. For these reasons, their approach to studying children's thinking will be detailed in the context of formal research.

Observation of Children: A Study of UnADULTerated Thinking

First, the researcher spends a considerable period of time in a given concept area on preliminary observation of children's interaction with a variety of materials. He accepts the children's responses to his questions, to ensure that he can observe their spontaneous approaches to the problems. He carefully attends their natural, prelogical solutions and compromise solutions as indicators of their underlying thinking processes. If he focused on the details of successful solutions alone, he would overlook the intricate difficulties experienced by the children who construct compromise solutions. From these preliminary trials and observations, the researcher chooses those materials and activities that are most likely to incite children to integrate their natural strategies towards higher-level constructions.

Development of a Thinking and Learning Exploration Sequence

After learning how children naturally approach related problems, Piaget and his colleagues provided them with a range of related encounters, each eliciting a different strategy. The level of difficulty in the sequence of encounters was controlled to maximize the interaction between the child's existing low-level approaches and to incite intellectual conflict.

Contrary to expectations, the task sequences are often reversed. The first task in Episode 2 is the most difficult; the last one is the least difficult. In the pictured conservation of length sequence, situation A is the most difficult. Here the child must construct a straight road of equal length below a zigzag model, using different-size matches. Situation B, although similar, does not require the road to be constructed directly underneath. This slight alteration reduces the pull of the coinciding ends strategy. Situation C is the least difficult since the model road is straight and the child's construction runs parallel.

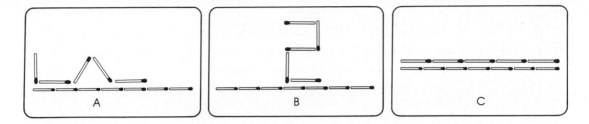

Here, since coinciding ends are "built into" the task, it becomes easier for the child to compensate number of matches for size. Placing the easiest task at the end of the introductory sequence is critical to the child's integration of all aspects of the problem. The sequence encourages children to get an overall view of the problem, then make adjustments in their thinking.

Although the introduction to the sequence is structured towards the goal of integrated strategies, it cannot be regarded as programed instruction in the usual sense. Programed instruction might have isolated one strategy — counting the matches — and proceeded from the least difficult (C) to the most difficult (A), using matches of equal size. The end result would have been a very superficial concept of length conservation. Obtaining the solution by this approach would not require the children to attempt to integrate all aspects of the problem; number of units, size of units, and coincidence of ends. By contrast, the Piagetian sequence of encounters encourages children's active construction of more elaborate concepts through the creative coordination and integration of existing concepts. A detailed comparison of both approaches is made in Chapter 8.

Pre-Assessment

Once the sequence is developed, its effectiveness with children is determined. First, a group of children is given a pre-assessment of their understanding. They are exposed then to several sessions in the sequence over a three-week period. This is followed by a post-assessment to determine the progress made by children.

In a pre-assessment of the children's understanding in a given area, they are presented with problems employing concrete objects. Close attention is paid to how the children justify their responses. This pre-assessment may determine which of the children are developmentally close enough to consider the new problems.

Post-Assessment

Following the involvement of children in thinking and learning sequences over a number of days, Piaget and his colleagues assess the depth, stability, and durability of children's understanding. They are not interested in assessing only a limited, practiced strategy but rather a system of possibilities opened up by the encounters. The following steps ensure valid information on the effectiveness of their sequence.

Include Different Materials

Rather than assess the child's understanding with only materials which have been used in the pre-assessment or used in the sequence, they also include similar tasks presented with different materials.

Include Novel Tasks

The stability of a child's learning is assessed by presenting another related problem in a different way. If the learning is unstable the child is likely to revert to the isolated, primitive approaches which had appeared to be integrated in the simpler tasks.

Question the Child's Responses and Give Counter-Arguments

To ensure a valid assessment of the sequence, the researcher challenges children's actions and justifications. Children who are in a transitional stage in their thinking usually revert to earlier uncoordinated or illogical responses when their responses are questioned. Both stability and consistency among multiple arguments can be checked in this way.

Provide for a Second, Delayed Post-Assessment

The researcher checks the stability of children's learnings over time by doing a second post-assessment within seven weeks. Only stable learnings can survive beyond the immediate period of the initial encounter.

Although these steps were taken as a stringent measure of children's learning progress in researching the effectiveness of a thinking and learning sequence, they also have implications for assessing and provoking learning in the classroom.

What additional task/activity would you use to —

- stabilize the children's understanding?

- find out if the children can transfer their understanding to a task using different materials?

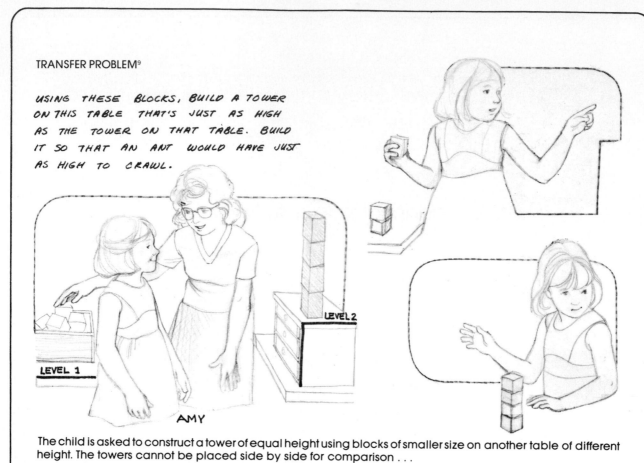

The child is asked to construct a tower of equal height using blocks of smaller size on another table of different height. The towers cannot be placed side by side for comparison . . .

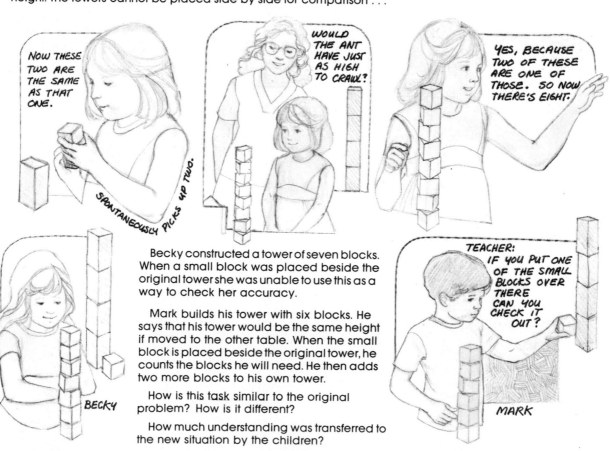

Becky constructed a tower of seven blocks. When a small block was placed beside the original tower she was unable to use this as a way to check her accuracy.

Mark builds his tower with six blocks. He says that his tower would be the same height if moved to the other table. When the small block is placed beside the original tower, he counts the blocks he will need. He then adds two more blocks to his own tower.

How is this task similar to the original problem? How is it different?

How much understanding was transferred to the new situation by the children?

Putting It Together

- Reflect back on your understanding of the equilibration process and on methods to explore and facilitate children's thinking and record a summary of these understandings.

- What are some implications of children's thinking processes and methods of exploration and facilitation for your work with children?

Piaget's Orientation to Development and Learning

8

Piaget's unique orientation to development and learning will be discussed and clarified in contrast with the opposing behaviorist position. It will also be placed in the context of his broader, interdisciplinary concerns which extend beyond psychology. Some problems and potential for applying Piaget's ideas and methods to the classroom will also be examined.

First Comes Thinking

From your understanding of how knowledge is constructed, consider the following question:

> If psychologists are trained to be objective in their scientific study of children's thinking and learning, how can they arrive at such basic disagreements as illustrated below?

Behaviorist Position

There are no stages of intellectual development.

A lack of understanding is due only to a lack of related experiences.

The law of flotation can be taught successfully to five-year olds if the environment is logically structured.

Piaget's Developmental Position

There are four major stages of intellectual development.

A child's lack of understanding may be due to lack of availability of necessary logical capacities.

The law of flotation cannot be taught successfully to five-year olds. The lack of formal operations necessary for thinking about such abstractions as density would not permit the child to construct a formal understanding of flotation regardless of his experiences A consideration of the child's inner structures must precede the consideration of external structure.

Piaget's position in developmental psychology is unique in its orientation and in direct opposition to the behaviorist position upon which much of American psychology is based. In order for you to understand Piaget's theory, you must be able to recognize negative instances of its application. For this reason, it may be profitable for us not only to describe Piaget's theory further, but also to contrast it with the behaviorist theory. First, we will consider how such opposing positions might have originated.

How Opposing Theories Can Originate

Although Piaget's theory is in direct opposition to the behaviorist theory, both theories, surprisingly have some roots in biology. Traditional behaviorists, in their laboratory studies of laboratory animals, found that a stimulus from the external environment produced a predictable immediate response in the animal. Many of their experiments involved predicting and controlling the behavior of these animals. Following successful application of their approach to other animals, behaviorists applied it to human subjects. Piaget was trained as a biologist prior to studying psychology. He observed that man's responses to stimuli are much less predictable than those of lower animals. From this he reasoned that unlike lower animals reacting passively to stimuli from the environment, man has both the ability to choose his responses and to initiate changes in the environment. Piaget, therefore, focused on the intermediary processes between stimulus and response, which could explain man's behavior.[1]

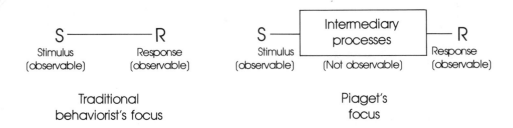

Psychologists develop conceptual frameworks from their experiences just as other individuals do. Their organization of ideas provides an expectancy through which incoming information is filtered and selected for focus. Thus certain behaviors can be anticipated and not others. Once the expected behaviors are observed, they are in turn interpreted by the selecting framework. Similar to the information processing of other individuals, psychologists revise or restructure their conceptual frameworks to accommodate discrepant information. To continue the parallel, psychologists also attempt to balance the processes which resist change to provide stability and those which produce change. Their conceptual frameworks differ from those of other individuals as a result of having been tested systematically, critiqued, and refined through interaction with other psychologists at professional conferences, and through journal articles and correspondence.[2]

The traditional behaviorist focused only on the externally observable. Piaget not only focused on observable behaviors but also on possible internal workings of the mind that would explain those behaviors. When Piaget observed children in learning situations, his expanded framework was prepared to see what went unnoticed by the behavioral psychologists. Our personal frameworks direct us to see what we are prepared to see and filter out the things that don't fit. Psychologists are also human. Their science is man-made. Despite their attempts at objectivity in explaining reality, their explanations of science reflect their limitations of humans.

A group of five knowledgeable psychologists came to see an elephant. All of them were blind in their own way. One, a Freudian, went immediately to the rear of the elephant and explained its behavior from this chosen view. The behaviorist struck the elephant on the kneecap and was kicked across the courtyard. There she sat planning a positive reinforcement program for young elephants. The cognitive psychologist began to coax the elephant into doing things so that its stage of development could be determined. The humanist felt its ears and tried to convince the elephant that it could fly. [3,p.24]

In turn some critics of Piaget would say that he is blind to behaviors other than logical thinking. He has written of the integral part that affect plays in learning but his studies are generally limited to logical behavior.

Opposing Frameworks—Opposing Methods

With the behaviorist emphasis solely on the observable externals of learning, a method evolved that attempted to reproduce the stimulus (treatment) precisely, that is, standardize it, and count the number of responses produced. A controlled experimental approach which was successful in the physical sciences was now applied to study the behavior of animals and human beings. At the same time that the experimental method rigorously controlled the treatment and focused on a narrow set of behaviors of interest, it reduced the chance of other behaviors occurring or being noticed. The relative simplicity of the subject s expected behaviors allowed the behaviorist to study a large number of subjects in a short amount of time. On the other hand, Piaget generated a contrasting method by emphasizing processes that are internal and intermediary to observable behaviors.

Piaget's clinical method with individual children involved using a series of the similar tasks, as in Explorations 1 and 2, but adapting the questions to the kind (or level) of response each child makes. His procedure, technically, could be said to vary from child to child, although his focus was always on how the child arrived at a conclusion. In other words, the treatment or stimulus was not standardized. Some behaviorists immediately rejected his work for this reason. Piaget changed his questions in an attempt to communicate to the child and to follow the spontaneous direction of the child's thinking. His emphasis was on the quality and the process of the child's thinking, whereas the behaviorist was interested in the end product and an analysis of the number of responses. The behaviorists seemed satisfied in counting right answers—Piaget became fascinated with patterns of children's "wrong" answers and their underlying processes.[4]

Piaget's method was both subtle and very time consuming. His clinical interviews could not be readily applied to large numbers of subjects. His results were reported as detailed diaries of children's thinking behaviors. The following example is his report of a child's responses on a series of tasks related to conservation of liquid amount.

Mus (5;0). This child, like those quoted earlier, relied on the number of glasses or the level, but in her case as in several others there was also a new factor, the size of the glasses. Nevertheless she followed three successive lines of thought:

I. Size of the containers. —She was given A1 and A2, ¾ full: 'Is there the same amount in both of them? —Yes. —Olga pours hers out like this (A2 into B1 and B2, almost full). Has she still the same amount? —No. —Who has more to drink? —Gertrude (A1). —Why? —Because she has a bigger glass. —How is it that Olga has less? — . . . —And if I pour these (B1 and B2) back into that one (A2) how will it be? —The same amount (as in A1). —(I did so.) And if Olga pours it back again like this (A2 into B1 and B2, almost full) is it the same? —No. — Why? —It makes less.'

II. Level. —'Now Gertrude pours hers like this (A1 into C1 and C2, almost filling C1 and C2 and leaving A1 ⅓ full). Who has more, Gertrude with those (A1 + C1 + C2), or Olga with those (B1 and B2)? —(She looked at the levels, which were about equal) Both the same. —Olga pours some of hers into another glass (B3, thus lowering the general level in her glasses). —Gertrude will have more. Olga will have less. —Olga pours again into these glasses (B1 and B2 into C3 and C4, which were then full). —She will have more (level). —But before she had less; has she more now? —Yes. —Why? —Because we put back here (C3 and C4) what was in the big glasses (B1 and B2).' The reasoning here was thus just the opposite of what it was in I.

III. Number of glasses and level. —'If I give you some coffee in one cup, will it still be the same if you pour it into two glasses? —I'll have a little more. —Where? —In the two glasses of course. —Mummy gives you two glasses of coffee (B1 and B2). Then you pour that one (B2) into those (C1 and C2) — There's more there (C1 and C2): there are two glasses quite full. There, there's only one. —And of those (B1 and the 4 C) which would you rather have, that one (B1) or all those (4 C)? —The big one (B1). —Why? —Because there's more: the glass is big.[5,p.8]

Since his questions varied from child to child these diaries were not readily compared. His studies also did not reflect the size of samples or the statistical treatment expected within a behaviorist's framework. Many behaviorists, however, continued to read reports of Piaget's studies because of their surprising outcomes and were motivated to do similar experiments of their own. Since their experiments were conducted within a behaviorist framework, the results must be examined critically.* In order to maintain the ability to rigorously control, predict, and quantify, the focus must be limited to simple behaviors, often isolated out of context. The experimental method is a powerful tool in physical science but can only study higher-order thinking processes in a limited way. When Piaget's tasks were standardized in rigorously designed experiments, the gain in quantification was accompanied by a corresponding loss in the quality of thinking being measured.[4]

For the behaviorist the treatment and quantification are standard. For Piaget, making contact with the child's thinking is standard.[6]

Contrasting Two Opposing Theories

In order to highlight and clarify the unique features of Piaget's interactionist/constructivist position in developmental psychology it will continue to be contrasted with the behaviorist position. Because of necessity, equal space has not been devoted to a comprehensive presentation of the behaviorist position(s); a simplified view will be presented here. Firstly, there is no single behaviorist position, e.g., some behaviorists now acknowledge the existence of forms of intermediary processes. What is described here is a generalized and simplified position based on the independent work of three behaviorists, B. F. Skinner, Robert Gagné and S. Engelmann, who have influenced classroom practice.

Effect of the Stimulus

Behaviorists represent the effect of an external stimulus on the organism to produce a response with the symbols $S \rightarrow R$. First comes the observable stimulus and then the observable response, with little or no mental processing intervening. Piaget by contrast, infers the existence of mediating mental processes. He states that it is the sensitivity of the child's mental framework to the stimulus which determines whether the stimulus is effective in triggering a response (assimilation). Since assimilation and accommodation act simultaneously, some modification of the framework also takes place in the process. Piaget suggests an alternative representation of this process with a second arrow, $S \rightleftharpoons R$. The double arrow indicates how the learner acts on the stimulus (assimilation) and how the stimulus acts on the learner (accommodation).[7,8]

---

*One behaviorist approach to conservation tasks might be to focus on the yes or no response because it is easily categorized. At the same time the child's justification would be ignored because it is sometimes difficult to categorize. Its omission from experiments would produce results that obviously disagree with those of Piaget, that is, the conclusions would state that children are capable of conservation at a much earlier age than indicated by Piaget.

Knowledge: Copy or Construction? Kinds?

For the behaviorist, knowledge originates outside the learner and is acquired as a copy of reality. Knowledge can be transmitted to the learner verbally or through other sensory input. Repeated exposures to these examples of knowledge improve the clarity of the copy. The learner is relatively passive while acquiring knowledge, since he merely has to receive knowledge existing externally. Any manipulation of objects is simply a means for sensory input. For Piaget, knowledge is an interpretation of reality that the learner actively and internally constructs by interacting with it. The extent of internal activity varies with the form of knowledge being acquired. Verbal transmission is limited to forms of knowledge that can't be obtained in any other way—*social, arbitrary knowledge*, e.g., labels for objects and concepts. External sensory input is important in acquiring *physical knowledge*. These forms involve some personal activity since they are interpreted within the structures of *logical mathematical knowledge*, which is constructed internally by the learner. The child's coordinated actions on external objects involve reasoning processes. He constructs internal relationships among external objects based on these interactions. Since Piaget's theory gives such an active role to the child it is known both as a *constructivist* and *interactionist* position.[9]

Knowledge: Linear-Cumulative or Reorganized?

Behaviorists view learning experiences as linear, and building upon each other in a cumulative way. An adult has more knowledge than a child because he has accumulated more experiences and therefore more copies of knowledge. Somehow, these bits of knowledge are added to the already accumulated mass in storage.

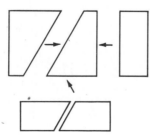

For the behaviorist, stages of development do not exist. Characteristic behaviors of a stage are explained as being a lack of understanding due to a lack of relevant experiences. By contrast, Piaget believes learning takes place within the broader process of development that entails a series of progressive intellectual reorganizations. During these reorganizations a child's partial understandings are revised, expanded and interrelated to interact more effectively with the environment. At each successive level or stage the child's potential for reacting to an identical stimulus changes. That same stimulus has a different meaning for a child at each stage of development, since the framework of related ideas undergoes a major reorganization.[9]

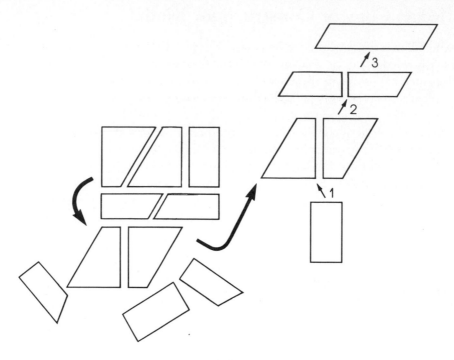

As the models below suggest, each stage incorporates structures from the preceding stage in each major reorganization. For Piaget, learning is not a simple cumulative process. Adults not only have more knowledge, but a knowledge which has undergone reorganizations and is qualitatively different from the knowledge of a child. For Piaget, learning involves changes in organization of knowledge which take place within larger reorganizations at each stage of intellectual development.

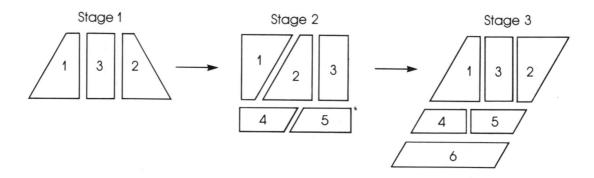

Structure: Internal or External?

The behaviorist does not recognize stages of development but does recognize levels of complexity in the structure of external knowledge. A child can learn best if experiences are carefully structured from simple to complex.

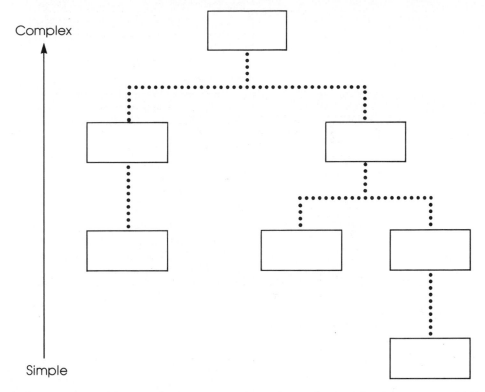

The behaviorist would state that conservation tasks or the law for flotation could be taught to any four- to five-year-old. All that would be needed are relevant experiences such as demonstrations and verbal rules.[10,11] Relevant experiences could also involve exposure to a series of experiences or bits of information which lead progressively to a cumulative understanding.

Piaget would agree that the method of presentation (external structure) could help a child learn, but his method of structuring the presentation would differ. He would emphasize, however, that elaborate attempts to teach any subject do not guarantee that a child can assimilate it. He states that conservation can be taught only when the child is already in a transitional stage.[1] In this case, the presentation can trigger a reconstruction of ideas that the child has already begun. Piaget is more concerned with the child's internal structures than he is with structure of subject matter. The behaviorists emphasize direct methods of teaching; Piaget stresses indirect methods that provide children with occasions for learning.

Teaching: Direct or Indirect Methods?

Although Piaget generally advocates indirect methods of teaching, his colleagues in recent studies have used structured introductions as illustrated in the Thinking and Learning Explorations. Although structured approaches are used there, they are still in direct contrast to a form of teaching employed by behaviorists—programed instruction. A detailed comparison will point out some important differences in their approaches.

PROGRAMED INSTRUCTION	PIAGETIAN EXPLORING—THINKING AND LEARNING SEQUENCES[12]
The sequence is usually based solely on the logical thinking of the adult developers.	The sequence is based on the natural, "illogical" strategies children have been observed to employ while approaching such problems.
One-exposure learning: a single strategy is artificially isolated and practiced. Children's creative capacities are suppressed.	One-exposure learning is avoided by using a range of related problems. Different strategies are not suppressed. Rather, they are highlighted so that children become aware of the contradictions in their isolated applications and can integrate them into a higher-order strategy. Creative capacities are encouraged.
The instructional sequence moves from the least difficult to the most difficult examples. The steps are often so small that it is not possible to get an overall view.	The level of difficulty in the introductory sequence is often reversed. This encourages children to consider and integrate all aspects of the problem and apply logical operations in its solution. The sequence encourages them to first get an overall view, then adjust their thinking. The steps vary in size.
The direction is linear. New information is simply added to the existing information.	Beyond the introductory sequence, the activity's direction is determined by the children's active construction. It cannot be linear since strategies are not simply additive; it is nonlinear since compensation and coordination are involved.
Intellectual conflict is discouraged. The steps are so small that success is guaranteed and the responses are almost automatic.	The dynamics of intellectual conflict are encouraged by shifting focus among different strategies and solutions until children can consider them simultaneously.
Immediate feedback is given to the children's responses. The evaluation is external.	Feedback is received from the materials and the logical consistency of the children's internal constructions.
The child is a passenger on a train travelling up a smooth and gentle grade, never clearly seeing where he is headed.	*The child is in the driver's seat on a roller coaster ride of discovery having multiple overlapping tracks. The disequilibrium energizes his drive to reach the goal at a higher level.*

Is There a Right Theory?

Piaget's theory is a most comprehensive one and has received research support for its main ideas. Yet no theory is ever complete, having all the answers. All theories undergo revision through the process of continuous testing, and Piaget's theory is no exception. It has undergone some shifts in emphasis within the original framework during the past 50 years, e.g., a shift from an emphasis of stages of development to an emphasis on the mechanisms that underly all stage development.[12]* When comparing theories,

*Accompanying the shift in focus in Piaget's theory is a shift in method. Recent experiments in learning reported by Inhelder et al.[12] have incorporated more control as in the experimental method while retaining some of the flexibility of the clinical method.

asking which is the "right" one is not a proper question.[13] A theory's value is reflected in its explanatory and predictive power : some theories explain certain behaviors better than do others. No theory can be applied universally. A better question, therefore, is to ask which is the best theory for a certain application. The behaviorist theory is powerful in explaining lower-level learning—memory learning. Piaget's theory is powerful in explaining higher-level learning, such as understanding relations as in logical-mathematical knowledge.

Piaget believes that the universal application of the behaviorist theory to all thinking is an error of reduction. In explaining-higher-order thinking the traditional behaviorist tends to reduce all the complexities and possibilities of inner mental processes to observable experience. He argues against this "superstition of the observable" and argues for a "conquest of what is possible."

> **If every action is a transformation of reality, it thus constitutes by its very nature a constant sampling of what is observable, and constant conquest of what is possible—which is still unobservable.**[8,p.35]

At the same time, Piaget recognizes the potential of the behaviorist theory for explaining lower-level learning. He agrees that programmed instruction might be an efficient means of transmitting certain kinds of information. Every subject area has a certain amount of arbitrary information arrived at by social consensus which could efficiently be transmitted in this manner. Some subjects such as language, have more arbitrary information than others to transmit. Other subject areas, such as mathematics and science, require more understanding of relations. Understanding relationships, a higher-level thinking process, is best explained by Piaget's theory. Since each theory best explains different aspects of learning, both theories could be considered for the totality of school learning. Piaget has written, "It is possible to envisage a balance being struck, varying from subject to subject, between different parts to be played by memorizing and free activity."[14,p.78]

On the occasion of his eightieth birthday, Piaget reflected on the theory which he has developed and refined over a fifty year period.

> **I have the conviction . . . that I have laid bare a more or less evident general skeleton which remains full of gaps so that when these gaps will be filled the articulations will have to be differentiated but the general lines of the system will not be changed.** [15,p.1]

Currently there are many developmental psychologists who are doing research along the strict lines of Piaget's theory, while others are developing variations within broad outlines of his theory. Piaget's conviction is that with time, though there will be revisions in his theory and variations of it, much of it will be retained to become part of the most generally accepted theory, years hence.

The Broad Context of Piaget's Concerns

From his early background in biology Piaget developed a conceptual framework which allowed him to integrate his later concerns of intellectual development within the broad context of organic life. One concept that links the understanding of all forms of life is that of adaptation. For Piaget, intellectual development is part of man's adaptation to his environment. Processes of intellectual development are viewed as specialized ones related to processes of total organic functioning. Since organic systems are self-regulatory, it is not surprising that within this broader biological context, intellectual (cognitive) systems would be expected to be self-regulatory, i.e., tending toward equilibrium. [16]

Piaget's theory also evolved from within the broader context of epistemology. Epistemology is a branch of philosophy which is concerned with the formation and meaning of knowledge. One approach to studying the development of knowledge is to focus on the historical development of ideas among peoples over the centuries. Since for Piaget knowledge is constructed by and exists in the knower, he chose to study children at different ages to learn about the development of knowledge. Part of Piaget's contribution to epistemology is his use of logic to analyze the meaning and validity of the content of children's knowledge in the different stages of development.

Some acquaintance with the breadth of Piaget's concerns in the contexts of biology and epistemology, as well as the depth of his studies of children's thinking processes, is essential to appreciate two aspects of Piaget's work which frustrate beginning students. First, Piaget's vocabulary is not the standard working vocabulary of American psychologists. It is unfamiliar because it not only reflects origins from other areas but also reflects broader or deeper meanings than other common terminology. In choosing to remove this barrier by limiting unfamiliar vocabulary in the writing of this book, some precision of meaning has been lost. Hopefully the general notions and the spirit of Piaget's work have been retained. Another frustration expressed by teachers is that Piaget's work says so much about children but so little about the specifics of teaching children in the classroom. Each scholar must narrow his field of study in order to pursue it in some depth. Realizing that Piaget's concerns are already amazingly broad and, indeed, monumental, it is now easier to appreciate the fact that educational applications of his theory are related to Piaget's concerns but are not his primary focus.

Piaget's Position on Education

Statements on education made by Piaget and his colleagues are both cautionary and optimistic. First, we will examine some of the cautions which have been communicated about applying Piaget's work in the classroom.

What Piaget Did Not Intend[17]

On several occasions, Piaget has expressed considerable concern about the American emphasis on accelerating children's intellectual development as opposed to facilitating the natural process. He believes that an optimum rate of development does exist but cautions that more research is needed to clarify its details and limits. He regards as potentially harmful any blind attempt to accelerate the development of all five-year-olds so that they all reach the concrete operational stage two years in advance of normal development. This acceleration attempt would probably be less effective than doing nothing at all, that is, less effective than the spontaneous process of natural development.[18]

A complete contradiction to Piaget's theory would be a school curriculum consisting entirely of Piaget's tasks, in which children were instructed directly by teacher demonstration and recitation of verbal rules. Such instruction might provide quick but superficial results whose stability and transferability beyond a specific task would be in question. Piaget's colleagues have likened such a total emphasis on conservation tasks to an attempt at fertilizing an entire field by concentrating the fertilizer in isolated soil samples. After being planted, the seeds would only grow where the fertilizer had been concentrated. The emphasis on teaching specific tasks provides the child with specific answers to specific, isolated questions that sample only a portion of the intellectual development.[19]

The Thinking and Learning Explorations illustrated in Chapter I and VII demonstrate a method of facilitating learning through equilibration that Piaget and his colleagues have found to be effective when working with individual children in research settings. The learning studies employed in research differ from the illustrated Explorations in that they provide for the child a long-term exposure (several sessions) to a richer variety of thought-provoking materials.[12] Whether the children learned from these experiences depended upon what mental structures they brought to them. In these studies the methods were found to be most effective with children who were transitional in their thinking—i.e., already in the process of reorganizing their thinking. In normal development these transitions are gradual, so we could say that these more intense encounters accelerated the transition stage.

The methods for exploring and provoking children's thinking that were employed in these learning studies differ from the classical tasks Piaget used in determining the stages in children's thinking (Chapter 4). The methods in the learning studies require considerably more skill and sensitivity to be implemented effectively. Since Piaget's earlier tasks have been misapplied in many acceleration research studies and classroom practices, a greater danger exists for mindless application of these more sophisticated equilibration tasks. At this point some cautionary notes are necessary to alert you to possible misapplications. The conflict involved during disequilibrium is between the child's framework of ideas and the feedback received is from his actions on the materials. The teacher's questions help the child to sharpen the discrepancy. Please note that the relations between the teacher and the child should be friendly—there is no conflict between them. The teacher is not attempting to intimidate the child into stating the expected answer. It is for these reasons that administering equilibration tasks to children requires unusual skill and sensitivity. Piaget recommends that teachers be required to work with individual children under supervision for at least a year to acquire the necessary skills. Since these are individual methods requiring highly-trained personnel and considerable time, the costs and practicality of these methods must be weighed against their potential benefits.

Piaget wonders about a potential cumulative effect which might arise from attempting to accelerate children's acquisition of a number of conservation concepts through the guided sequences that provoke equilibration. Even though these children would be actively engaged in constructing their understandings, Piaget is concerned that such structured guidance could create a dependence which interferes with their independent intellectual functioning. He therefore recommends an investigation of such potential long-term effects in future research.[12]

Although Piaget's colleagues state that their learning studies give some direction for the application of developmental theory in education, they also indicate the existence of a gap between the two areas:

> Although learning studies certainly do not close the gap between cognitive psychology and classroom practice, they constitute a link in the chain that may eventually unite the two. [12,p.30]

What Piaget Does Intend

In discussing his concerns about acceleration Piaget points out that there is a significance to the slower early development of humans as compared to animals. The more gradual development is a necessity for approaching the full intellectual capacity of humans.[18] Rather than focus on acceleration, he is more concerned with a natural holistic development which can be facilitated by rich and varied experiences over an extended period of time. Here the understanding of conservation, classification, ordering, etc., will develop not as specific answers to isolated tasks but as a part of a coordinated network of ideas. Other ideas gained from living and experiencing would be interwoven in this flexible network.[19]

> Rather than accelerate blindly to advanced stages, Piaget intends that teachers provide children with the opportunities to explore to its fullest the range of thought at a given stage and to build the strongest possible foundation for succeeding stages.

It is this kind of active exploration which makes children aware of the limitations of a particular kind of thinking and to initiate the construction of more effective ways.

Piaget has also made many statements about the classroom which reflect an optimism regarding the applicability of his theory to education. His statements usually contain references to such pertinent aspects of his theory as stages of development and the factors which influence development: maturation, physical experiences, social interaction, and equilibration. In discussing the teacher's role he assigns many of the attributes that are also critical in exploring and facilitating children's thinking. In other words, he advocates aspects of his clinical method for application in the classroom, though not for direct teaching of the conservation concepts that are closely tied to development. He advocates this method to facilitate the learning which takes place within the constraints of development.

> For Piaget, attributes which are critical in exploring and facilitating children's thinking are also critical to good teaching.

The application of Piaget's theory to the classroom has face validity. In other words, a preliminary subjective evaluation indicates that it is not only reasonable to think of applying it in the classroom, but that the theory appears to have a great potential for improving education. The research that supports Piaget's theory is largely based on his work with individual children. A direct transfer to the classroom must also consider a number of variables which were not previously important. For this reason, there is need of comprehensive research to evaluate the effectiveness of Piaget's theory in the classroom. Some reasons why little supportive classroom research is available are given in Chapter 11. Meanwhile, there is a growing number of committed teachers who through their personal experience find that applications of Piaget's theory to their teaching are quite fruitful. There is also a growing body of classroom research that was done independently of Piaget's theory, but provides support for classroom practices consistent with those he recommends.

Piaget has described his views on education. Since he is not an educator, he has not concerned himself with all the details of classroom application of his theory. In the next two chapters Piaget's statements on classroom practice will be placed alongside classroom examples selected by the author, an educator, to illustrate his viewpoint. This will allow you to judge the appropriateness of both Piaget's views on education and an educator's interpretation of his views.

The Thinking and Learning Explorations were illustrated in this book to demonstrate the intricacies of the equilibration processes that form the cornerstone of Piaget's theory. Also, they were included because of the questions on current methods of teaching they raise and the alternative methods for facilitating thinking and learning that they demonstrate. Classroom examples will now be illustrated in a further attempt to bridge the gap between Piaget's theory and research methods and classroom practice.

Putting It Together

- Reflect on the new understandings which you have constructed and summarize them in your own words.

- Phrase a clarifying question which you would like to ask your instructor.

Teaching Towards a Congruence with Children's Natural Capacities and Constraints
9

By observing and interviewing children within Piaget's framework, teachers gain empathy and respect for children's developing intellectual capacities. Such an understanding of their intellectual processes prevents the teacher from teaching children concepts they are not prepared to learn. In other words, this teacher is aware of the natural constraints of the child's stage of development. At the same time, the teacher has a respect for the child's current capacity for learning and is aware of the multiplicity of new capacities that become available at each new level of development. This level of awareness alerts the teacher to curriculum materials that place artificial constraints on the children's natural capacities and provides her with a basis for making on-the-spot curriculum decisions in the classroom. An examination of children's natural capacities and constraints in the first three years of schooling (K – 2) provides a basis for restructuring children's introduction to formal schooling. Alternative approaches to teaching math, reading, science, and social studies are described in this chapter. Methods of providing for a range of children's capacities and constraints within a classroom are also illustrated. This chapter also provides classroom examples of effective language usage within the limitations of language described in Chapter 6.

First Comes Thinking

Reflect on your knowledge of the natural intellectual capacities and constraints of two groups of children: five-year olds and seven-year olds. Also reflect on the demands that are placed on these children in their introduction to formal schooling.

Now, for each age-level, try to identify:

- natural intellectual capacities which go unrecognized;
- natural constraints that are ignored;
- artificial constraints placed on children's natural capacities.

Also, try to identify alternative methods of teaching that are more congruent with children's natural intellectual capacities and constraints.

Some General Considerations for Teaching

Observation of Children's Intellectual Capacities and Constraints

Through extended experiences of interviewing individual children as a preparation for teaching, the teacher has expanded her awareness of children's thinking and can apply it to the classroom, even when a multitude of children are present. She can give the same classical tasks more informally to small groups of children since numbers and time limit their extensive use with individual children. The teacher can also observe children in a variety of classroom situations and recognize the kinds of thinking demonstrated in the Piagetian tasks.

By providing for activities with physical materials the teacher can free herself to observe individuals and small groups of children. Their spontaneous comments and actions are illustrative of the capacities and constraints of their thinking processes. These opportunities for observation contribute to a growing bank of informal indicators of children's thinking levels that can supplement the information gained from Piaget's tasks or, in some cases, substitute for them. The teacher will also appreciate the need for looking at children in a variety of situations before undertaking any extended learning program. At the outset then, and at periodic intervals, the role of the teacher becomes that of observer-planner in contrast to the traditional role of planner-instructor.

Observation of Children's Thinking Level for Concept of Amount

HOW DO THEY THINK?[1, pp.4–5]

As part of a unit about sand, second graders were asked to put an assortment of empty containers in order from largest to smallest. The containers varied in size and were of regular and irregular shapes. After much argument as to which container was bigger, most agreed that height (tallness) could be used to establish an order.

They then were asked whether or not there was a good way to order them when the containers were turned on their sides. The children thought that now they would have to change the order.

Then the class looked for ways to make an order for biggest that would work standing up or lying down. A few thought the biggest container would hold the most sand. How to find out which this was and which was next biggest and so on was a problem.

Each youngster's approach was quite individual. One child started filling containers and overturning the contents on trays to compare the size of the piles. Another youngster measured how many handsful of sand were in a container. Another took a tiny cap and found out how many capsful it took to fill a small cup.

Then a girl thought of pouring the sand from one container to another. Her enthusiasm was contagious, but most of the others could not follow her idea because it was so different from their own thinking. A few children did follow her example. They would pour the sand confidently from one container to another, but with no regard for the overflow of sand. When asked which of two containers held more sand, sometimes one was singled out, sometimes another.

From an adult's standpoint it would seem that pouring sand from one container to another would be the easiest way to compare volumes. However, it appeared that unless children have had a great deal of experience —through water play, balancing volumes of materials, or other activities —this is an unknown strategy to them.

It took the children a long time to sort out what mattered, and in what way it mattered. In trying to solve the problem children said things like:

"I poured sand into the jar from the full vase and it didn't come up to the top. Does that mean the vase is bigger because it was full? Or, is the jar bigger, because I could put more sand in it?"

"If the sand flows over, that means there is lots of sand, so maybe that container is the big one. If the sand doesn't fill the jar, the amount of sand looks smaller, so maybe that jar is smaller."

"If I pour sand from one container to another and some sand spills, I don't know whether or not I did it right or whether the spilled sand means these are different-sized containers."

"I poured all the sand from this tall one into the pail and didn't even cover the bottom."

When pouring from container to container it appeared to the children that the volume of sand changed as well as the size of the container. They observed the sand and the container as a single thing; when the sand looked too small, that meant the container was too small; when there was a lot of sand that implied that the container was big. The notion of too much was not available to them because everything was changing.

It took a great deal of practice, talking, and thinking before the children realized that in each case of pouring, the amount of sand remained the same. What looked like less sand meant really that there was more container space.

These opportunities to observe children in spontaneous activity can often reveal some surprises. Most primary teachers would suggest that sand play is only appropriate for four- to five-year-old children. The direct observation of the seven-year-olds (second-graders) discussed above indicates that such expectations of children are misleading. Sand play is an appropriate medium for engaging children's minds in the construction of their understanding of the physical world.

Observation of Children's Choice of Games and Mode of Play to Infer Thinking Levels

A teacher can also plan to learn about children by noting their choices from the physical and printed materials available to them. David Elkind writes that children will repeatedly select materials that nourish their intellectual development. The games they choose to play can be used as an approximation of their level of thinking.[2] Using such informal indicators can be misleading unless the teacher checks for repetition and quality of performance. Sometimes emotionally upset children may temporarily revert to an unchallenging level that is comforting, for a time. Some games can be enjoyed at more than one level.

GAMES	CHARACTERISTICS	LEVEL OF THINKING
Hide-and-seek Marbles Tic-Tac-Toe (two-dimensional)	Hider is often visible as he is unable to take perspective of seeker. Parallel play of aiming and shooting with no specific rules. Plays a single strategy; unable to consider offensive and defensive moves at the same time.	Preoperational
Hide-and-seek Marbles Tic-Tac-Toe (two-dimensional) Checkers	Hider avoids being obvious by taking perspective of seeker. Cooperative play with specific rules. Offensive and defensive strategies are played at the same time.	Concrete operational
Tic-Tac-Toe (three-dimensional) Monopoly Mastermind Chess	Multiple variables and number of combinations considered. Use complex multiple strategies involving anticipation, i.e., hypothetical (if . . . then) statements.	Advanced concrete operational to Formal operational

Piaget's framework requires looking first to children for guidelines.

Piaget not only provides ingenious physical tasks for assessing children's levels of thinking in specific areas, but also a general framework for determining a child's intellectual capacities and constraints at a particular level. The teacher may utilize this framework and opportunities to observe children engaged in a diversity of involvements and interests, as illustrated here, to arrive at an estimate of their level of thinking in specific areas.

Reflections on Some Limitations of Textbook Guides

Piaget's theory also provides teachers with valuable guidelines for the selection of activities that are within the intellectual capacities of individual children. Any attempts to teach formal operational concepts such as the law of flotation or molecular theory to children who have just entered the concrete operational stage would be quite inappropriate. It is possible to provide related experiences using concrete materials that are challenging to children at their current level of development. These experiences serve to develop a foundation for transition to the next stage. Piaget's studies provide specific descriptions of levels of children's understanding in a variety of areas. The areas he has selected for study are limited in that they represent only a portion of knowledge and, sometimes, do not coincide with the knowledge emphasized by the schools. For other areas of knowledge which he has not studied in depth, he provides the teacher with general guidelines about the levels of thinking available to children at that stage.

The scope-and-sequence charts accompanying most textbooks have certain shortcomings when viewed from Piaget's framework, which requires looking first to children for guidelines. Many textbooks for children are prepared by people who are now formal thinkers and have difficulty identifying with earlier ways of thinking. These textbooks often appear to be prepared to impress the adult decision-makers with how much their children will be learning and do not reflect the needs of children. Piaget's framework allows teachers to examine critically these printed materials. When they first look to children for their guidelines, three problems with math textbooks become immediately apparent: inappropriate content level, lack of manipulative provisions, and an over-reliance on pictorial and abstract exercises. Similarly, in beginning reading texts, premature perceptual requirements of the materials come into focus.

Math: Inappropriate Content Level

Piaget's studies of how children develop logical thinking and an understanding of number reveal that most six-year-olds lack the logical operations (reversibility, conservation, ordering, classifying) that are necessary to construct a concept of number. Most mathematics textbook authors, however, show little awareness of this natural constraint in children's thinking. They will include problems such as $4+\square=7$ in the first-grade textbook. Many teachers are aware of these textbook limitations but don't know what to do about it. They teach such missing-addend problems despite children's inability to cope with them because the problems are dictated by the scope-and-sequence chart. These teachers and authors are imposing an artificial constraint on children's existing capacities and inviting inevitable failure. Other teachers, guided by Piaget or their own awareness of children, refuse to teach the topic until such time that children have the necessary capacity for reversibility. Piaget says,

> It is essential for teachers to know why particular operations are difficult for children, and to understand that these difficulties must be surmounted by each child in passing from one level to the next . . . Teachers must understand . . .what changes take place from one level to the next, and why does it take so much time.[3,p.25]

Math: A Lack of Manipulative Provision

Most textbooks introduce another artificial constraint on children's natural capacities by ignoring their need to actively manipulate concrete objects in constructing their meaning of number. They present number exercises through pictorial representations immediately followed by abstract symbolism. Since the children have not constructed the underlying concepts, their learning is reduced to sheer memory. Rather than constructing their own understanding through active learning, they are exposed to ready-made statements about mathematics, which they must regurgitate on request.

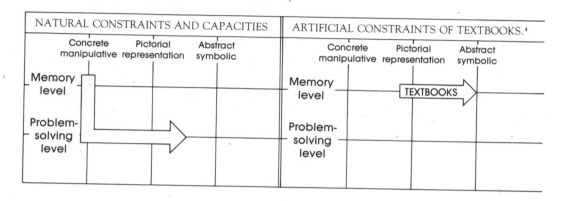

Regarding children's introduction to formal instruction in mathematics, Piaget writes,

> **Mathematics is taught as if there were only a question of truths that are accessible exclusively through an abstract language, and even of that special language which consists of working symbols. Mathematics is, first of all and most importantly, actions exercised on things.**[5,p.103]

Current teaching of mathematics, particularly in the primary grades, contradicts Piaget's observations of how children develop their understanding of number. It seems that what we do as teachers often has little relation to what is known about how children learn.

Math: An Over-Reliance on Pictorial and Symbolic Representation

A significant number of six-year-old children have demonstrated the ability to classify three-dimensional objects, yet they are incapable of comparable classification when presented with two-dimensional photographs of the same objects.[6] Some textbook authors have incorrectly assumed an equivalence between objects and their pictorial representation that would allow children to make an instant translation. From Piaget's theory, however, we see that only a rich variety of experiences with objects leads to mental construction of the object and its relationships. Later, these mental constructions can be triggered by pictorial representations. Piaget pinpoints the early emphasis on pictorial representations and abstract symbolism as the major failure in mathematics teaching:

The true cause of failures in formal education is therefore essentially the fact that one begins with language (accompanied by drawings, fictional or narrated actions, etc.) instead of beginning with material action.[5,pp.103-104]

Beginning Reading: Mismatch of Methods and Child's Perceptual and Logical Constraints

In addition to first-grade children having a limited capacity to learn arithmetic operations directly through pictorial representation and abstract symbols, there is also increasing evidence that limitations, similar to those just stated, of the ways children look at their world affect their ability to learn to read. Piaget reports systematic differences between six-year-olds and older subjects in the systematic eye movements required for reading. The young child's fixation tends to be global. He will get only an overall impression of a complex configuration and not the details. Also, his eye movements are somewhat random, rather than demonstrating any systematic scanning. Around age seven, the child's tendency to look at things globally declines rapidly and his eye movements reflect better control. Piaget suggests that these newly acquired concrete operations begin to direct perceptual activity, that is, indicating where attention should be concentrated.[7]

Most beginning reading programs with phonics approaches place five- to six-year-olds under considerable pressure to make fine discriminations when comparing words and their components, and to consider multiple sounds for letters or letter combinations. These demands are made with no apparent awareness of children's capacities and constraints at that age. Supporting perceptual and logical capacities for making fine discriminations are still being developed at this age. Teaching reading by this method at such an early age is based also on a questionable assumption that children have the knowledge to give meaning to those marks on paper—to reconstruct the writer's ideas. Although Piaget has not spoken out on the teaching of reading, his work allows teachers to be aware of children's developing perceptual and logical abilities. Teachers now have greater sensitivity in detecting programs that violate the natural development of children's capacities by imposing artificial constraints.

Placing artificial constraints on children's existing capacities is inviting inevitable failure.

Observation of Children's Thinking Levels — A Basis for On-the-Spot Curriculum Decisions

A teacher's knowledge of Piaget's observations and theory not only prepares her to plan and select curriculum materials appropriate to the children's developmental level, but also to undertake on-the-spot curriculum development when school is in session. Many decisions must be made spontaneously in response to children's comments and actions reflecting their level of thinking. Prior administration of Piagetian tasks under clinical conditions, rather than in a fixed format, as part of the teachers' training , provides her with valuable experience in listening to children and reacting to their responses. By then observing children in classroom activities, the teacher uses this experience to gather insight into each child's thought processes, and to consider questions and activities that might extend their thinking. Piaget writes,

> **It is not the stages that are important. It is rather what happens in the transition.**[3,p.25]

Personal meanings of Piaget's work are reflected in the statement of two teachers who write:

It leads me to realize that, in every matter, every day, every child will have a point of view different from my own. And, to him his point of view will be the interesting one, the precious one and, if he is very young, the only one. I still have the advantage, of course, for given patience and perceptiveness, I can understand his point of view as well as mine while he does not even know that mine exists . . . Whoever I am, whatever my relationship to him may be, I owe it to him to seek to understand his point of view so that I may diagnose his needs. Then I can wisely enrich his environment while he will enjoy learning and developing intellectual skills.[8,p.113]

— Mary Sime

If a method isn't teaching a child—try something different. Look to the child and change how you teach until you find something that works.[9,p.1]

— Mary Baratta-Lorton

These teachers have incorporated their understandings of Piaget's work into a personal working framework in their classrooms.

In order to select activities or questions that not only match a child's thinking but also extend it at that teachable moment, the teacher must be aware of the child's thinking patterns—their capacities and constraints. What is a discrepancy for one child presents no problem for another. The assimilation process requires that any new learning experience must match the existing thinking patterns. However, if the match is exact, then no accommodation will take place. As previously stated, the balancing of the complementary processes of assimilation and accommodation is equilibration, the essential mechanism of learning and development. The teacher should plan experiences to aim for a degree of novelty or discrepancy requiring some accommodation or restructuring of thinking patterns to take place.* In this regard Piaget says

> **If the teacher discretely changes the situation slightly, thereby preventing the child from succeeding immediately, in the next step, the child will wonder why he was successful the first time and not the second. So now it becomes a question of understanding.**[3,p.25]

---

*Examples of this teaching process will be illustrated in the next chapter. Also, see the funnel activity on page 172 of this chapter. Also in Chapter 10, there will be illustrations of Learning Cycles for approaching a balance in Activities emphasizing Accommodation and those emphasizing assimilation.

If the teacher's question or activity requires too much restructuring, the child is either not aware that a problem exists or is overwhelmed by its demands. The active nature of equilibration ensures that a child will learn when engaged in situations having an optimum degree of cognitive match and moderate novelty or discrepancy, without the need for external rewards. Certainly the teacher's on-the-spot decisions are only educated guesses. Their potential effectiveness increases with the awareness she gains from observing the outcomes of her attempts to enter the child's world.

Restructuring a Child's Introduction to Formal Schooling

According to what we know about how children learn, the demands placed on kindergartners and first graders to learn mathematical operations through abstract symbols and to learn to read through a focus on fine discrimination and analysis (as in phonics) do violence to their natural capacities. At this age, children have a limited capacity for the logical operations and perceptual skills that would support such formal approaches. Forcing children to attempt what they are incapable of doing reduces learning to rote, perhaps initiating a growing spiral of academic failure. Although children are required to attend school until they are sixteen, many have dropped out mentally by the first grade. Millions of dollars are being spent on reading and mathematics textbooks, although they impose artificial constraints on children's natural capacities, which limits their contribution to early education. Piaget's framework can provide guidelines for restructuring children's introduction to formal schooling.

Foundations for Learning in Spontaneous Play

Formal instruction in math and reading should be postponed until children's perceptual and logical thought processes are developed to support it. This means a postponement of at least two to three years (K−2) for most children. In place of formal instruction, children would have ample opportunity to play and work with a variety of material in activities that stimulate the development of thinking processes. Piaget writes,

> We need pupils who are active, who learn early to find out for themselves, partly through their own spontaneous activity and partly through materials we set up for them. [3,p.5]

Elsewhere, Piaget states,

> Mathematical training should be prepared, starting at nursery school, by a series of exercises related to logic and numbers, lengths and surfaces, etc. And this type of concrete activity must be developed and enriched constantly in a very systematic way during the entire elementary

education. On these terms, strictly mathematical education is grounded in its natural surroundings of equivalency of objects, and will give full scope to the intelligence which would have remained purely verbal or graphic.[5,p.124]

The more meaningful and varied the child's encounters with the real world are in these early years, the stronger his foundation for logical thinking and his receptivity to mathematics instruction will be.[5]

Although Piaget calls for a gradual and systematic development of ordering, classifying activities, etcetera, he also supports spontaneous play. Spontaneous play not only develops the child's capacities for representation, but also provides him with opportunities for developing physical and logical knowledge and perceptual abilities.

Block-Building

Constance Kamii and Rheta DeVries describe what an alert observer can notice in children's play and interaction with materials.[10] Block-building allows children to develop physical knowledge about the properties of the blocks. Furthemore, opportunities to classify arise spontaneously during building and children may discover that "the large blocks don't fall down as easily when at the bottom." Subsequently, they might begin by grouping blocks according to size prior to construction. Similarly, an opportunity for serial ordering might arise when a child needs a specific size block to complete the construction. The first block is too short and the second too long, so the child compares the other blocks to the first two to find one that is a "between" length. In block-building, the child constructs space and experiences a variety of configurations, patterns, and part—whole relationships that are important precursors to reading. Furthermore, when the child is constructing his castle or house with blocks, he is representing his knowledge symbolically. The child who looks for a flag for every castle turret or a cup for every saucer in the doll house is experiencing one-to-one correspondence.

During block-building play, children use language as part of their representation, either talking to themselves or communicating to others. Here the teacher can provide the children with names for objects or events in context. She can even provide written labels for their constructions on request. After the play, as children put away the blocks, they classify them according to shape. They find the right place for each block as they match it to a two-dimensional representation or a written label. Throughout the block-building, the alert teacher will recognize opportunities for entering the activity to extend the child's thinking.

Work Versus Play

In the following excerpt, George Hein discusses work and play in light of Piaget's work.[11,p.9-10]

A third major insight we can gain from looking at the work of Piaget is about the kind of distinctions we make between play and work. What we immediately realize when we perform the Piaget tasks with children, or read his accounts of them, is that this distinction is an adult one and does not exist for children. A little reflection will make us realize that this is a very obvious and straightforward point and needs little elaboration. It does however have to be stated, because it has some significant consequences for education.

If we look at children before they start school we note that they do not play or work, they simply *do*: they experience and learn. They interact with the world, explore it, and learn from those interactions. At some point in school (and in society), they are taught a distinction. This distinction between work and play is not always dramatic, but schools essentially tell children that one can learn from certain kinds of activities (work) and not from others (play). Worse, the distinctions are arbitrary and become classified by stereotypes. Everyone knows, for example, that fifth graders are too old to play with blocks although blocks can pose geometric problems that puzzle adults.

Piaget's theory gives criteria for the types of experiences which are likely to be rewarding and to lead to learning and to the development of intelligence. But the classification cuts across our whole work-play distinction. It deals with such questions as: is there active involvement for the child (rather than just passive acceptance)?; is the child led to question his own views?; and do the kinds of experiences offered lead to disequilibrium or cognitive dissonance? By these kinds of criteria—involvement, enthusiasm, questioning, and puzzlement—most of the things that we call work (writing papers, doing math problems, and taking school tests) would be ruled out, while many of the things we call play (exploring new materials, interacting with peers, testing oneself against others) would qualify as learning experiences.

This discussion becomes particularly significant when we remember that we are talking not just about learning particular things but about learning how to learn, developing intelligence. The adverse consequences of insisting on "work" in school is that we are actually depriving the children of the opportunity to develop intelligence. We say that some kinds of things are not worth learning, and, worse yet, that some kinds of ways of learning are not worth as much as others, or even that they are worthless. The kinds of approaches to learning that are downgraded usually cover the whole range of activities that include manipulation of the world with the hands as well as with the head; the free, explorative, imaginative ways of dealing with the world, as well as the simply playful. By insisting on a rather narrow intellectual method of learning, memory, repetition, and drill, we restrict what is learned in school and make it especially difficult for children to accept alternative styles of learning.

Anyone who makes the attempt to expose children (or adults) to the kinds of situations where alternative modes of learning are legitimate, will soon see that different individuals learn in a surprising number of ways and that the distinctions between work and play will simply vanish in the wealth of activity.

On the place of self-directed activity in education, Piaget says,

> The goal of intellectual education is not to know how to repeat or retain ready-made truths. (A truth that is parroted is only a half-truth.) It is learning to master the truth by oneself at the risk of losing a lot of time and going through all the roundabout ways that are inherent in real activity.[5,p.103]

Sand Play

In a child-oriented introduction to schooling, opportunities for sand and water play would be ample for all ages. The introduction of four different grades of sand, each a different color, can extend the sand play activity for older children by providing interesting effects and new challenges. This excerpt from the Elementary Science Study unit, *Sand,* describes a number of possible activities and outcomes:

> *In addition to enjoying SAND, children explore major concepts about what sand is; they examine subtle properties of color, size, weight, structure, and material. They try to decide whether it is a liquid (it pours), or whether it is a solid (it is hard to crush). They see how sand acts in different conditions: wet, dry, mixed, sorted, massed and dispersed. They may see that a material which seems simple reveals considerable complexity. There are many attributes to be considered.*
>
> *Artistic and mathematical explorations are an intrinsic part of SAND. The children's impulse to feel the sand and watch it flow seems never to be satisfied. Colored sand is dribbled into patterns through fingers, cups, sieves, and straws. Sand pendulums make patterns which can be predicted with a little experience. Glue fixes sand paintings onto paper and wood. Paste and sand make a fine substance for sculpting.*
>
> *Children of all ages seem to find SAND appealing. It has been most successful in the second and third grade classes. They find the sorting and volume work a little difficult but a manageable challenge, and making sand from rocks a satisfying accomplishment. Older children become adept at measuring, weighing and making pendulum patterns and timers.* [12,p.8]

Many questions arise directly from the children's explorations with sand. The teacher can observe their actions and discussions and intervene when there are opportunities to guide them without directly answering their questions. Similarly, the teacher can suggest specific tasks of manageable complexity that spin off from the children's present activity.

George Forman and David Kuschner suggest the following activities as potential challenges for young children, who are fascinated by the act of pouring. Introducing funnels of varying stem diameters allows the teacher to enter the child's activity when he is pouring sand into a funnel. The teacher chooses a different size funnel and challenges the child to a race, and asks him to predict which funnel will empty the fastest. The race may be run a few times until the child associates the diameter of the stem with rate of emptying. The two funnels can now be combined so that one funnel empties into the other. The child will discover that it makes a difference which funnel is on top. The teacher can also suggest comparing a third funnel with a different stem size (one of the original funnels is set aside). If funnel A overflowed funnel B and now funnel C overflows funnel B, what will happen when funnels A and C are combined? These problems should be introduced when children are pouring water or sand (the sand grade should be the same for all the funnel problems). [13] Since the grain size of sand also affects the rate of flow, comparisons of rates from different combinations of funnel and grain size would quickly complicate the problem beyond the level of young children. The concepts developed through direct experience are relationships between speed, space, and time; and, in particular, the transitivity relation.

Cooperative Games

Cooperative activities with physical materials can be devised to help children decenter from their egocentric viewpoint in order to achieve a goal. Forman and Kuschner suggest a "Cones Through the Hole" activity, which is played by two children who must cooperate in order to get both cones through the hole, since both cones can't pass through at the

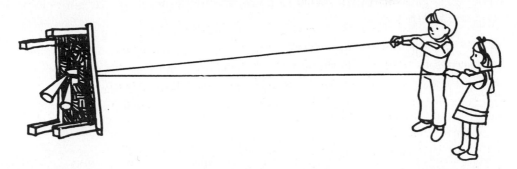

same time.[13] Kamii and DeVries describe a "Driving a Truck with Ropes" activity in which a child's pull produces two contrasting motions on a toy truck. Successfully driving the truck requires the child to decenter from his egocentric view to consider that the pulling action required to move the truck backwards is inversely related to the pull towards his body. Some disequilibrium usually precedes the child's mental coordination of body action and truck movements.[10] On another day, changing the direction of the rope to pass around a table leg will produce a variation that requires the child to do some rethinking before resuming driving.

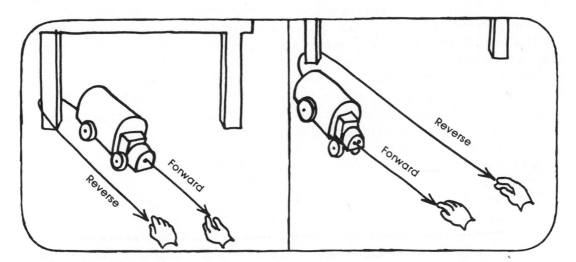

Observing and Describing Change

Preoperational children tend to focus on beginning and ending states rather than on actual transformations. As a result, they report incomplete observations of change or approximations influenced by their expectations. Piaget suggests the inclusion of activities that "exercise the powers of observation" and representation:

It can be seen that the practice in observation could be very useful; the phenomena to be described would be simple everyday examples of causality, the descriptions themselves of various kinds: imitation of the action (easiest), its verbal description, a graphic representation, (with the help of an adult, etc.).[5,p.26]

Examples of causality might include a range of activities from the categories identified by Kamii and DeVries.[10]

Direct action	Body movement
Direct action on objects	Pushing, pulling, squeezing, blowing, throwing, rolling
Actions involving interactions of objects resulting from a child's actions	Pouring, sifting, sawing, sanding, and related actions of joining, counting, and separating
Actions involving interactions of objects independent of a child's actions	Interaction of magnets and objects, interaction of objects that make up a flashlight, interaction of animals and their environment, interaction of sunlight and plants as well as chemically treated paper.

These categories begin with activities that focus on the child's body and readily observable actions and extend to those that are no longer the direct result of a child's actions but involve complex interactions encouraging inferences. Piaget recommends the inclusion of additional activities that involve two observers. These encourage comparison of observations from differing perspectives, thus encouraging the children to decenter from their egocentric focus and thereby to appreciate the relativity of observation.[5]

These two record sheets are from the Science Curriculum Improvement Study unit *Interaction and Systems.*[14] Children record their observations and inferences after completing the physical activities.

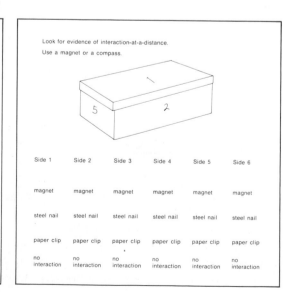

These two worksheets are from the SCIS unit *Relativity*.[15] Children are required to record observations from the perspective of other observers, such as Mr. O.

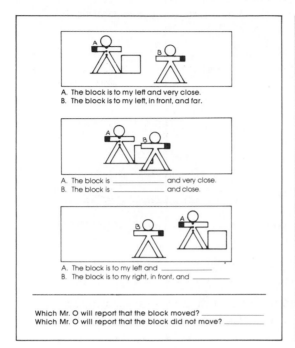

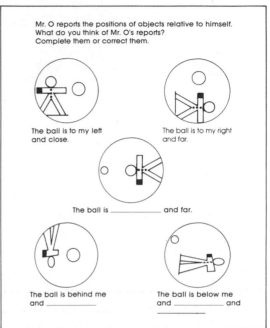

Transitions to Reading: Language Experience

Piaget's recommendations for observational activities include a variety of representations of the events. His list suggests that other representations are possible, but stops short of stating that an adult should record the child's oral descriptions and read them back to him. Since the child has had the experience that is being described in his own words, his ability to read the content is enhanced. As he sees his own words in written form, he is motivated to read. As the child becomes exposed to his words in print he soon gains a sight vocabulary that is personally tailored. Soon he is able to read his own descriptions of events. Many such experiences build a natural connection between reading and oral language. Roach Van Allen's language experience approach to reading is built within the natural relationship of all the communication skills: reading, listening, speaking, and writing.[16] This allows the development of a working sight vocabulary without specific instruction. The reading materials do not come from textbooks, but are developed directly from the child's own thoughts. His oral and written expression has its basis in his physical and social environment. Through this natural transition to reading, the child gains the impression that his own thoughts are worth expressing. Once he begins to see himself as an author he becomes interested in reading materials written by other authors in the class and, later, in the world.[16]

Although Piaget has made no direct reference to methods of teaching reading, his educational focus is on natural, holistic methods of learning such as the language experience approach described above or the psycholinguistic approach.[17] At the same time,

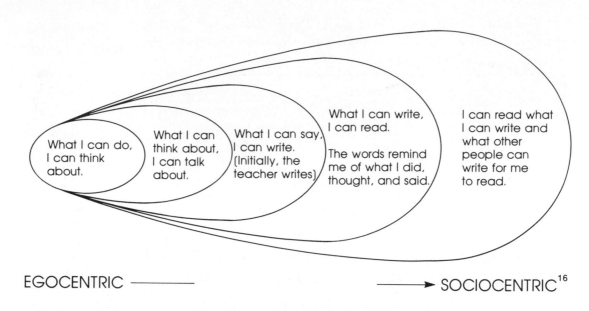

What I can do, I can think about.

What I can think about, I can talk about.

What I can say, I can write. (Initially, the teacher writes)

What I can write, I can read.

The words remind me of what I did, thought, and said.

I can read what I can write and what other people can write for me to read.

EGOCENTRIC ————————————→ SOCIOCENTRIC[16]

Piaget's work does not support any methods of introducing reading which exercise certain skills apart from the meaning of words, as in the phonics approach to reading. Once children have been introduced to the reading process and their perceptual and logical systems allow more systematic searches (age seven) children naturally expand their capacity to analyze components of words.

Beginnings of Mathematics

Constructing and Representing Patterns

Children can view mathematics as a way of thinking by building and searching for patterns in activities at their level. Mary Baratta-Lorton has developed many such activities in *Mathematics* Their *Way*, a K−2 program.[9] Children study, duplicate, extend, or represent patterns in a variety of ways. Once they are introduced to the activity they will volunteer more complex patterns for other children to develop and represent. Sequencing and constructing patterns in a wide variety of modes contributes to their understanding of mathematics as a search for patterns. It also develops a foundation for reading.

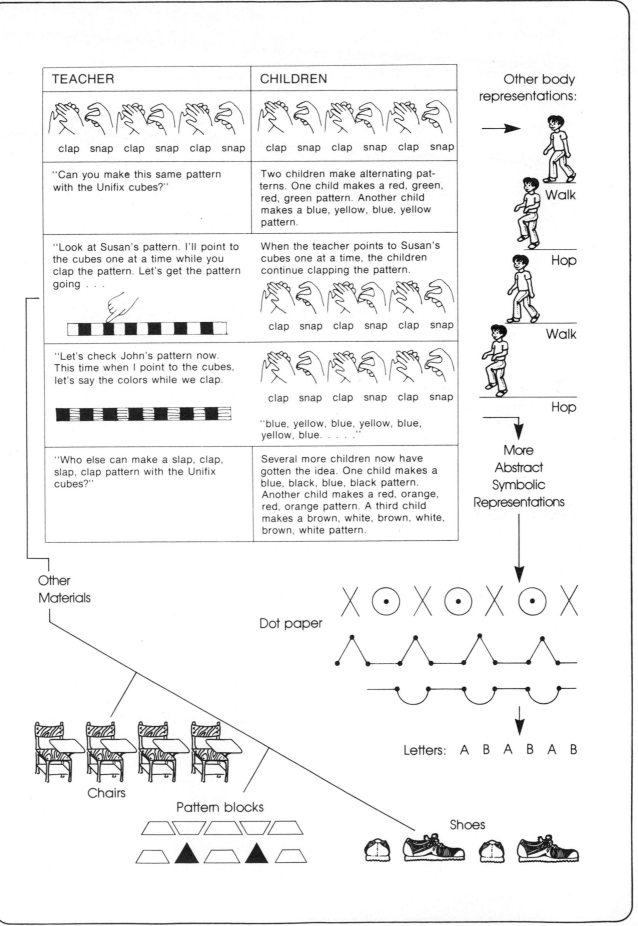

TEACHER	CHILDREN
clap snap clap snap clap snap	clap snap clap snap clap snap
"Can you make this same pattern with the Unifix cubes?"	Two children make alternating patterns. One child makes a red, green, red, green pattern. Another child makes a blue, yellow, blue, yellow pattern.
"Look at Susan's pattern. I'll point to the cubes one at a time while you clap the pattern. Let's get the pattern going . . .	When the teacher points to Susan's cubes one at a time, the children continue clapping the pattern. clap snap clap snap clap snap
"Let's check John's pattern now. This time when I point to the cubes, let's say the colors while we clap.	clap snap clap snap clap snap "blue, yellow, blue, yellow, blue, yellow, blue. . . . ."
"Who else can make a slap, clap, slap, clap pattern with the Unifix cubes?"	Several more children now have gotten the idea. One child makes a blue, black, blue, black pattern. Another child makes a red, orange, red, orange pattern. A third child makes a brown, white, brown, white, brown, white pattern.

Other body representations:

Walk

Hop

Walk

Hop

More Abstract Symbolic Representations

Other Materials

Dot paper

Letters: A B A B A B

Chairs

Pattern blocks

Shoes

Math as Action on Things; The Gradual Evolution of Math Ideas

Baratta-Lorton introduces the number operations as action on things. Children are involved in a variety of activities which focus on the process rather than on the answer. Preoperational children have rich and varied experiences with numbers up to eight. (Piaget's studies indicate that understanding of conservation of numbers smaller than eight develops before age seven with the aid of perception. Beyond eight, a logical foundation is essential for understanding of conservation, etc.) In *Mathematics* Their *Way*, children are only asked to work only with the quantity of objects that they can count, or one beyond, to provide a manageable complexity. They construct a variety of arrangements of numbers of objects using a range of materials from their environment over an extended period of time. The patterns of five below are constructed with toothpicks and tiles.

This experience contributes to the concept of "fiveness," independent of pattern of arrangement or kind of material. The concept of conservation is implicit in these activities. At the same time, the arrangements of the materials reveal combinations of smaller numbers that make up five. As well as counting objects forward, as in addition, the children also count backwards as in subtraction. Similarly, using objects, they count by twos as in multiplication. In describing children's development of mathematical understanding, Piaget writes,

> **Mathematics is, first of all and most importantly, actions exercised on things, and the operations themselves are more actions, . . .**[5, p.103]

Furthermore, he assigns importance to actions at all levels of learners.

> **. . . At all levels, including adolescence and in a systematic manner at the more elementary levels, the pupil will be far more capable of "doing" and "understanding in actions" than of expressing himself verbally . . . "Awareness" occurs long after the action.**[18, p.731]

A striking aspect of these levels of thinking is the extended time required for gradual reorganization to more efficient levels. (See Chapter 4, pages 88~90.) The design of *Mathematics* Their *Way*[9] provides for this gradual evolution of ideas.

NUMBER AT THE IN-TUITIVE CONCEPT LEVEL

Children actively construct different combinations of a set of objects and orally describe that combination, "three and two." The emphasis is on the process and not on the answer. There is no recording.

NUMBER AT THE CONNECTING LEVEL

Mathematical symbols are linked to familiar activities with materials. One child completes the physical process and the other records the process on a pictorial representation of the activity using printed numeral cards.

NUMBER AT THE SYMBOLIC LEVEL

Written symbols are used to record the process and the answer. One child demonstrates the physical activity and the other records the numerical relationship on worksheets having a pictorial representation of the materials.

PEEK THROUGH THE WALL

LIFT THE BOWL

THE HAND GAME

One group of Baratta-Lorton's activities for children demonstrates a developmental sequence of activities which is particularly sensitive to the intellectual capacities and constraints of six-year-old children. This sequence recognizes the existence of a major gap between the child's ability to act out mathematical operations on objects and his ability to symbolize these actions in traditional mathematical terms. Not only is considerable time provided for the gradual development of these abilities, but an intermediate level of activities is provided to help the child bridge the gap between understanding in action and mathematical formulation. First of all, children explore number relationships in natural ways without the imposition of adult approaches or symbols, at an *intuitive Concept Level*. Children's intuitive approaches are respected and given opportunity to flourish since they form the foundation for adult understanding. They actively construct different combinations and orally describe them. The children first play the games with the materials and focus on the process rather than on the answer. The total mathematical relationship remains intuitive at this level. Once the three games have been played at different times, the children play all three games in the same session to help them abstract the common process from the different activities at an intuitive level. In her *Workjobs II* Baratta-Lorton provides other supplementary activities which require different actions that also translate into the addition operation. These activities are also played at the intuitive concept level in a wide variety of contexts using different materials before returning to the original games at another level. [19] The provision for exploration of number relationships at this level with unhurried time over a number of weeks is supported by Piaget's statement:

> **Freed from the necessity of computation, the child enjoys building actively all the logical relations in play and arrives thus at the elaboration of procedural operations that are flexible and precise, often even subtle. Once these mechanisms are accomplished it becomes possible to introduce the numerical data which take on a totally new significance from what they would have if presented at the beginning. It seems that a lot of time is lost in this way, but in the end much is gained, and, above all, an enrichment of personal activity is achieved.** [5, p. 101]

At the *Connecting Level* children return to familiar activities and begin to represent their actions in terms of traditional math symbols. The children work in pairs, with one child demonstrating a combination with objects and the other child recording by placing printed numeral cards on a pictorial representation of the materials. The situation can also be reversed, with one child constructing a symbolic representation from which the second child constructs the combination. Again, the focus is on the process and its representation, rather than on the answer or the total numerical relationship. The latter is provided additional time for continued development at an intuitive level. Once these three games have been played at the connecting level, the children will continue to establish links between familiar games and mathematical symbolism through the supplementary activities from *Workjobs II*.

Again, after several weeks of involvement and other intervening activities, the children return to the familiar games at a higher level of abstraction. The games are replayed and now the entire numerical relationship is represented in terms of mathematical symbols in the child's own handwriting. The supplementary games are also replayed at this *Symbolic Level*. At this point it is important to note a number of features of this sequence of activities.

- Children act out the physical process with materials even at the highest level.
- Children focus on the process and intuitive relationships before focusing on the answer or symbolization of the total numerical relationship in mathematical terms.
- It is only after considerable experience at a given level that a child is exposed to familiar activities at another level of representation.
- At any one time in the classroom, different children can be playing the same game at different levels. Teachers look to children in scheduling activities at the next level.
- The children have opportunities to be in the driver's seat and to generate their own problems and represent the operations.

By contrast, introductory math textbooks often neglect extended experience with materials and impose mathematical symbols before any relationships have been developed by the children. If there is provision for concrete experiences, it is usually in terms of "concrete to abstract" in a single lesson. However, the level of abstraction demanded by textbooks would be achieved in Baratta-Lorton's developmental sequence only after months of relevant experiences in exploring number relationships.* According to the work of Piaget and Baratta-Lorton, the old educational slogan, "teaching from concrete to abstract" must be interpreted as a long-range goal in order to make abstractions meaningful to children in the classroom. In support of this idea, Piaget writes,

> **Without a doubt it is necessary to reach abstraction, and this is even natural in all areas during mental development of adolescence, but abstraction is only a kind of trickery and deflection of the mind if it doesn't constitute the crowning stage of a series of previously uninterrupted concrete actions.**[5,p.103]

"Concrete to abstract" is not a lesson objective but, rather, a long-range goal.

Evolution of Math Ideas:
Early Accessibility of Operations and Ideas at a Concrete Level

Piaget's studies of how children develop number concepts not only reveal some limitations of preoperational children, they also reveal some surprising capacities of children entering the concrete operational stage. Traditional scope-and-sequence charts indicate the order of teaching addition, subtraction, multiplication, and division in an isolated sequence, with the latter two operations postponed until the first two are "mastered." Piaget's work has demonstrated that beginning notions of these four operations develop

---

*By spring of the first grade, *Mathematics Their Way—Workjobs II* children would be ready to meet the intellectual demands that are prematurely required of beginning first graders in September by textbooks.

simultaneously and are available at about age seven. In Mary Baratta-Lorton's number activities for six-to seven-year olds, addition and subtraction are frequently alternated from day to day to build relationships between the operations. The inclusion of parallel activities with a related operation further enhances the breadth of experience at each level of abstraction. One such subtraction activity from *Workjobs II* is illustrated at each of the three levels. The resulting visual display of the child's work provides the teacher with feedback on the child's progress.

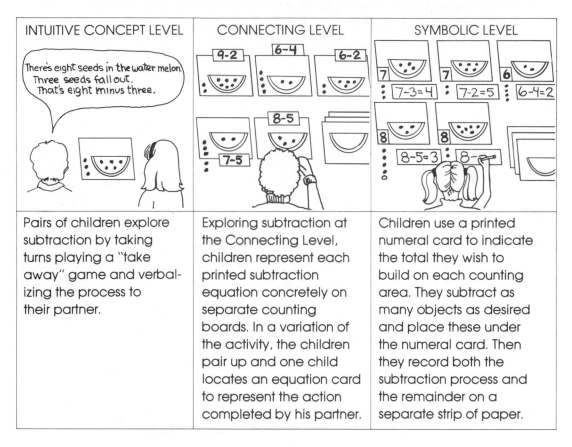

INTUITIVE CONCEPT LEVEL	CONNECTING LEVEL	SYMBOLIC LEVEL
Pairs of children explore subtraction by taking turns playing a "take away" game and verbalizing the process to their partner.	Exploring subtraction at the Connecting Level, children represent each printed subtraction equation concretely on separate counting boards. In a variation of the activity, the children pair up and one child locates an equation card to represent the action completed by his partner.	Children use a printed numeral card to indicate the total they wish to build on each counting area. They subtract as many objects as desired and place these under the numeral card. Then they record both the subtraction process and the remainder on a separate strip of paper.

Another surprise to teachers is that word problems which upper graders find most difficult, are also accessible to many seven-year-olds. Piaget writes,

> . . . A student's incapacity in a particular subject is owing to a too rapid passage from the qualitative structure of the problems (by simple logical reasoning but without the immediate introduction of numerical relations . . .) To the quantitative or mathematical formulation . . .[5,pp.14–15]

In *Mathematics Their Way*, six- to seven-year olds solve problems involving all four number operations. Some of the activities place the operations side by side to help children construct their relationships. These children also act out word problems for each operation or demonstrate it with physical materials. Again, the emphasis is on the physical operation with no rush to focus either on the answer or on abstract representation.

"Jack built five buildings. Each building has three stories."

"Carla has six cans. She put them in two different cupboards. She put the same number in each cupboard."

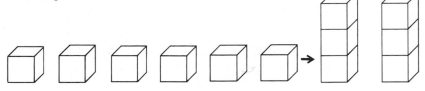

The children gain an intuitive awareness that in all situations they are either combining or separating objects. This is an early construction of the relationship between all four operations that many adults don't possess.

The previous example demonstrates a surprising capacity of children to solve verbal problems when concrete objects are available for manipulation and the content is familiar. Piaget points out the difficulties older children (nine–ten) have when problems are presented verbally in either oral or written form. (See Chapter 4, page 77, for a specific example of ordering lengths of objects and ordering hair darkness of hypothetical individuals from a verbal description.)

> **If a child at this level is asked to reason about simple hypotheses, presented verbally, he immediately loses ground and falls back on the prelogical intuition of the preschool child . . . That is why in school they have such difficulty in resolving arithmetic problems, even though such problems involve operations well known to them. If children were able to manipulate objects, they would be able to reason without difficulty, whereas apparently the same reasoning on the plane of language and verbal statements actually constitutes other reasoning that is more difficult because it is linked to pure hypotheses without effective reality.**[20,p.62]

Piaget's work has demonstrated that a child's knowledge passes through stages of creation and re-creation at different levels and that the passage through stages is very gradual. The evolution of mathematical ideas begins with a qualitative construction with materials, before a quantitative construction. To Piaget, these levels are not just limitations, but indicators of new possibilities. To respect the child's thinking is to dwell on activities at his level and to allow him time to explore those new possibilities to their fullest; it is *not* to be seduced by empty symbolism at a level only superficially higher. Piaget describes an example of an abstract idea difficult for algebra students that is yet one of the surprising possibilities for a seven-year-old, if presented with the problem at his level.

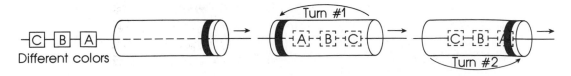

When the hidden beads are rotated with the tunnel the first time, the child understands that the order *ABC* changes to *CBA*. After the second turn of the tunnel, the child will predict that the beads will come out in the order *ABC* again. After the third turn, the prediction will be *CBA* again, and so on. Piaget relates this concrete operational activity to a formal operational idea of algebra:

> **In this way he discovers, without knowing it, the rule of composition that states that two inversions in direction cancel each other. In other words "minus times minus equals plus." But when he reaches fifteen to sixteen years of age, he will not understand the algebraic computations, of which he will learn the existence, unless they appear to him as a continuation of actions of this type![5,p.105]**

The apparent loss of time in dwelling on a variety of physical activities for children is, in actuality, developing a logical foundation for understanding later abstractions. The end result is a net gain.

To respect a child's thinking is to dwell on activities at his level and to allow him time to explore these new possibilities to their fullest: It is _not_ to be seduced by empty symbolism at a level only superficially higher.

The Gradual Evolution of the Place Value Concept and the Role of Materials in Its Development

At a time when most children are just grasping the concept of number, the scope-and-sequence chart requires that they tackle exercises in addition and subtraction that require an understanding of place value concepts. Usually this expectation includes dealing with problems at an abstract, symbolic level with only a short exposure at a pictorial level, and with no experience with related materials. The children are given little opportunity to construct their place value relations before applying them. Those who begin to develop their own methods find that the teacher's method cannot be superimposed on their's, consequently, they give in to authority and memorize and follow blindly a set of rules.

When numerals are written in combination, such as 27, not only does each represent a number itself, but their positions also take on a value that is some multiple of ten. This coding system is very efficient for communication among mathematicians, but most confusing to children in initial stages of understanding.

$$\begin{array}{r} {\scriptstyle 1} \\ 27 \\ +\ 19 \\ \hline 46 \end{array} \qquad \begin{array}{r} {\scriptstyle 1}\ {\scriptstyle 17} \\ \cancel{2}\cancel{7} \\ -\ \ 9 \\ \hline 1\,8 \end{array}$$

Teachers can recall having traumatic experiences with new math when required to calculate in bases other than ten using in abstract symbols. The topic of bases other than ten no longer appears in most elementary school texts. Yet, in *Mathematics Their Way*, Baratta-Lorton uses bases other than ten to introduce seven-year-olds to the decimal system. By now, this should be no surprise in light of Piaget's statements, as the children experience the activities at their level of thinking, with physical materials. Most teachers have only experienced bases other than ten at an abstract level, without a foundation of relevant physical activity.

In Baratta-Lorton's place value games, children form their own groupings of objects according to the game being played. Each different grouping is given a nonsense name (zurkle = 4, bosco = 5, etcetera) with the exception of the ten grouping (see page 186). Each counting game is played both forward (addition) and backwards (subtraction). The games are repeated at the concept level with different materials and increasingly large groupings. After some time and experience at this level, the children play the games again and keep a record of objects and groups with flip cards. Again, after some time and further experience, a child's game board is removed by the teacher after each count and a visual display is formed. The display is used to construct a connection between the activity and the more symbolic recording at the next level. The teacher now does the recording as the children continue to play. They are encouraged to notice patterns in the arrangement of numerals. Finally, a number of different activities are possible with little teacher-involvement:

Children record on their own as they count and group objects.

Counting by ones is replaced by counting by twos or threes or is randomized with a spinner.

Children are provided with many situations in which counting and grouping are needed to solve a problem, such as estimating the number of objects in containers.

As children gain experience in these activities they begin to anticipate the next move(s). This is evidence that they are constructing flexible place value concepts through their own activity. Piaget comments on the value of such an approach,

> **In most mathematical lessons the whole difference lies in the fact that the student is asked to accept from outside an already entirely organized intellectual discipline which he may or may not understand, while in the context of autonomous activity he is called upon to discover relationships and ideas by himself, and to re-create them until the time when he will be happy to be guided and taught.**[5,p.99]

The place value activities in *Mathematics Their Way* are carefully attuned to children's natural approaches to learning and to their level of thinking. Children are provided varied

---

*The children's introductions to these place value games are highly structured and behavioristic in approach. Unlike many other activities in the program there are no opportunities for spontaneous exploration during these introductions. Yet, at the advanced stages of the activities, e.g., the search for patterns and the problem solving which follows appear to be supported by Piaget's statement, "Teaching means creating situations where structures can be discovered; it does not mean transmitting structures which cannot be assimilated at nothing other than a verbal level.[21,p.3] The activities were organized so that the external structure brought the child to situations in which he could construct internal structures. Here is an example of behavioristic methods being used in support of active learning.

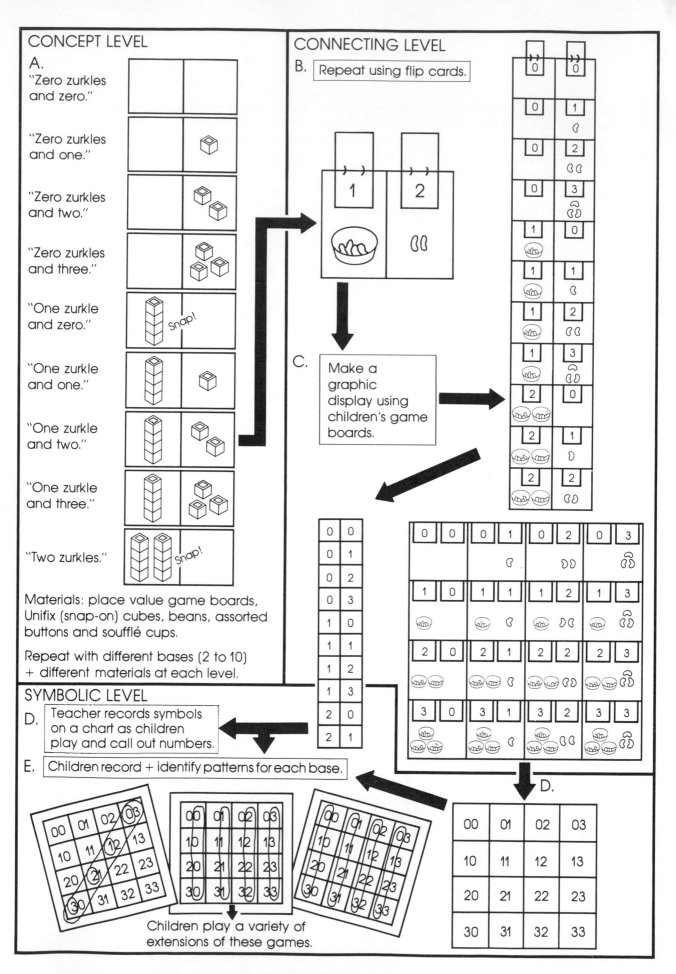

CONCEPT LEVEL

A.
"Zero zurkles and zero."

"Zero zurkles and one."

"Zero zurkles and two."

"Zero zurkles and three."

"One zurkle and zero."   Snap!

"One zurkle and one."

"One zurkle and two."

"One zurkle and three."

"Two zurkles."   Snap!

Materials: place value game boards, Unifix (snap-on) cubes, beans, assorted buttons and soufflé cups.

Repeat with different bases (2 to 10) + different materials at each level.

CONNECTING LEVEL

B.   Repeat using flip cards.

C.   Make a graphic display using children's game boards.

SYMBOLIC LEVEL

D.   Teacher records symbols on a chart as children play and call out numbers.

E.   Children record + identify patterns for each base.

Children play a variety of extensions of these games.

D.

00	01	02	03
10	11	12	13
20	21	22	23
30	31	32	33

opportunities to construct their own place value relationships through active grouping of materials and a search for patterns.* Baratta-Lorton's gradual and systematic approach is sensitive to levels of development through which children's ideas are created and recreated. She writes,

> Because mathematics is made by human beings and exists only in their minds, it must be made and remade in the mind of each person who learns it. In this sense mathematics can only be learned by being created. [22,p.12]

Baratta-Lorton's gradual and systematic development of place value activities also avoids the problem of children moving too quickly into numbers that are beyond their understanding. Although most children at age seven can conserve quantities as large as eight or ten, their conservation of numbers to infinity develops more gradually. As a result, children who are regrouping 25 beans prior to removing six beans may believe that there are more beans after regrouping.

Mary Baratta-Lorton, who dedicates her book to "children lost in a world of adult symbols which they cannot fathom or begin to understand," has, indeed, developed a program for helping children to learn mathematics in their own way.

A Cautionary Note on the Use of Place Value Materials

Number relationships are a child's mental constructions. When an adult already understands these relationships, he believes they exist in the objects themselves, since

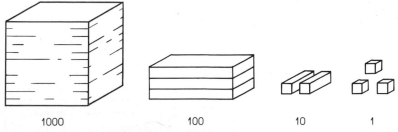

1000	100	10	1

these objects trigger a recall of the relationships in his mind. This adult is likely to demonstrate the numerical relationship between objects to children as if, during the brief exposure, the child could make a mental copy of it. Human minds do not work like cameras copying reality. Rather, human minds interpret reality, that is, construct their own understanding of it. Whereas the adult may "see" 1,323 represented by the place-value materials, a young child may only see 11 blocks of varying size. On the construction of knowledge, Piaget writes,

> Knowledge is not a copy of reality. To know an object, to know an event, is not simply to look at it and make a mental copy, or image of it. To know is to modify, to transform the object, and to understand the process of transformation, and as a consequence to understand the way the object is constructed. An operation is thus the essence of knowledge; it is an interiorised action, which modifies the object of knowledge.[23,p.8]

For this reason, Piaget cautions teachers about the misuse of concrete materials for brief demonstrations before moving quickly into more symbolic abstractions.[24] To use these materials effectively, children must manipulate them extensively in situations that engage their minds. Children also need to be given time to reflect on their emerging ideas and relations. Piaget believes active learning does not involve mindless manipulation of physical materials. Rather, he emphasizes the interaction between mind and materials—a coordination between physical and mental activity—as essential for constructing logical knowledge.

Mathematical relationships are constructed by people and exist only in their minds. Interaction between mind and materials are necessary for constructing these logical relationships.

A variety of materials is available for engaging the child's mind in constructing place value relationships. Each material can contribute to the child's understanding, yet it may be limited in its application. Although the materials are all physical, there is a range in the levels of representation involved.[25] On page 189, these materials have been ordered along a scale of approximate difficulty for children at the concrete operational stage. Exposure to a variety of materials in meaningful situations, however, encourages the child to detach the relationship from any particular material, basing it solely on relative position in which it is expressed in abstract symbolism.

When regrouping and renaming are needed, rather than blindly follow a rule for subtraction, children can complete these operations with understanding while using place-value materials. Some materials have greater potential for contributing to the child's construction of initial understandings than have others.

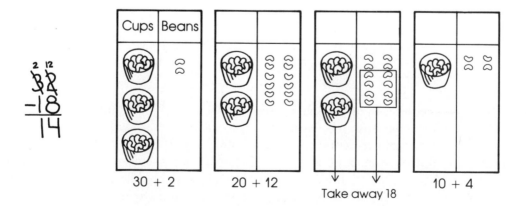

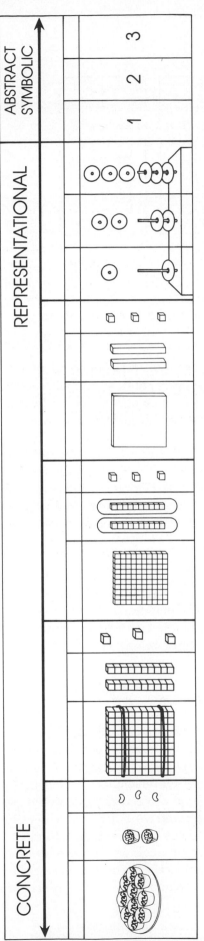

	CONCRETE			REPRESENTATIONAL		ABSTRACT SYMBOLIC

Beans grouped in soufflé cups and then in dishes are natural/familiar materials that are readily available.

These materials are in one-to-one correspondence with the number represented. There are actually 123 beans that can be counted.

The children construct the groupings of beans.

Unifix cubes are commercial materials, initially not part of a child's environment.

The interlocking property of the cubes allows children to snap them together in groups of ten.

These materials are in one-to-one correspondence with the number represented.

Beans and tiles can be grouped on sticks and rafts (arrays) in a fixed arrangement. These materials are part of children's natural environment.

Since the groupings are fixed on the materials themselves, these materials impose a structure on the child (unless the child actually constructs the "sticks" and "rafts").

There is a one-to-one correspondence.

There are cubes, rods, and squares that are commercially available.

These materials are already constructed. The child can neither construct nor decompose them. Although constructed to scale in a 10-to-1 relationship, the child cannot "see" the relationship of the dimensions. It is only through considerable experience that the child constructs the relationship. Initially, he may only see six objects of differing size, without realizing the one-to-one correspondence to 123 small cubes is based on physical dimensions.

These commercial materials differ only in color (a kind of structure). When arranged on pegs they form an abacus.

These chips are arbitrarily assigned different values, which may differ from one situation to the next.

There is no one-to-one correspondence to 123 as only six chips are visible.

Although the materials are concrete in nature, their use is highly representational. Teachers are often impressed with their flexibility (switching bases) and easy storage and too often overlook their limitation.

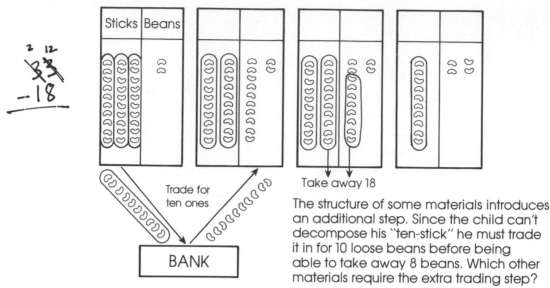

The structure of some materials introduces an additional step. Since the child can't decompose his "ten-stick" he must trade it in for 10 loose beans before being able to take away 8 beans. Which other materials require the extra trading step?

Concrete operational children require experiences with materials to do relational thinking. This does not mean, however, that they can never think logically in the absence of materials. When a third grader was asked why he no longer uses beansticks in solving numerical problems of subtraction requiring regrouping, he replied, "I close my eyes and see the beansticks. Then I move them around in my head to figure it out. Children cannot develop such mental images during a teacher's brief demonstration with materials—they must have extensive experience with them. The third grader developed vivid mental images of the materials and the regrouping/subtraction operation through such experience. At this point, pictorial representations can substitute for material. In learning a new topic such as long multiplication, this child would need to manipulate the materials again. Piaget writes,

> Up to this age (eleven-twelve) the operations of intelligence are solely "concrete," i.e., they are concerned only with reality itself, and in particular, with tangible objects that can be manipulated and subjected to real action. When at the concrete level, thinking moves away from tangible reality, absent objects are replaced by more or less vivid representations, which are tantamount to reality.[20,p.62]

A discussion of Materials as part of the classroom environment will be further discussed in Chapter 10.

The examples of block-building, sand play, cooperative games, and the introductions to mathematics and reading discussed in this chapter are only samples of a rich variety of activities that should be available to children. These activities would be of manageable complexity, i.e., sensitive to children's ways of thinking, yet sufficiently challenging for them. Through coordinated physical and mental action on objects, children would not only be exploring their environment in ways which are natural at their level of development, they would also be constructing a logical foundation for more formal (abstract, paper-and-pencil) approaches to learning. The apparent time lost would be an ultimate gain in the child's competence, curiosity, and confidence as a self-directed learner. Piaget's framework does provide a basis for generating a viable alternative to today's primary education of children. Although Piaget recommends the continuation of such methods throughout the elementary school, a reorganization at the primary grade levels is most critical.

The ideal of education is not to teach the maximum, to maximize the results, but above all to learn to learn, to learn to develop, and to learn to continue to develop after leaving school.[26,p.30]

Providing for a Range of Capacities and Constraints in a Classroom

Within any classroom children will function at different stages of development. Different examples of coping with this range of intellectual abilities in a classroom are described on the following pages. One example of children working on different levels of similar activities has already been given in Baratta-Lorton's beginning number sequence. Although the examples are taken from elementary school classrooms, the approaches can apply equally well to classes at any educational level, through university.

Beginning Measurement Activities Coded to Children's Level of Thinking

All the children in the classroom may be involved in related activities, but at different intellectual levels. For example, *Measure Matters*, a commercial learning center unit on measurement, provides a range of activities for measurement of length, area, weight, volume, etcetera.[27] The teacher's guide identifies specific activities for each general topic appropriate for preconservers, transitionals, and conservers. The teacher aware of the child's present understanding of each conservation concept can suggest specific activity cards consistent with the child's intellectual level. The illustrated cards sample a range of length measurement activities from the introductory unit, *Measure Matters A.*

Teaching Suggestions Nonconservers should be in involved in pre-measurement activities of direct matching, comparing, and ordering of height, length, and width.
Suggested Cards: Level A L-1 — 12
(Suggestions for Parts B and C have not been included in this sample.)

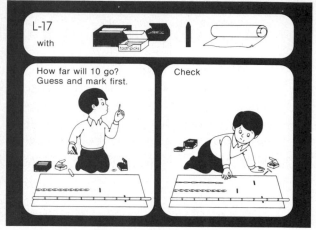

Transitional conservers still need to be involved in premeasurement activities.
Suggested Cards:
    Level A L-1—12
They may also benefit from measuring activities using nonstandard linear units.
Suggested Cards:
    Level A L-13—18
    Level B L-5, 6, 7, 8
    Level C L-1, 2, 3

Conservers should be involved in the following activities:
    measuring with nonstandard linear units;
Suggested Cards:
    Level A L-13—18
measuring with standard metric linear units.
Suggested Cards:
    Level A L-19—23

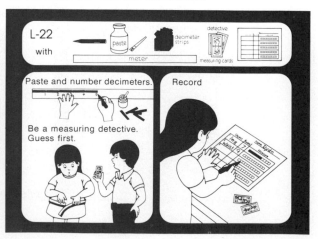

Tailoring Worksheets to the Problem-Solving Capacity of Each Child

Robert Wirtz, in his program *CDA Math,* has developed mathematical activities that provide children with necessary practice and at the same time reflect the quality of thinking available to children at the concrete operational level.[4] There are some introductory worksheets based on activities with materials. These are to be followed with blank worksheets with no numbers filled in. The teacher is invited to tailor these to the intellectual abilities of individual children. This is possible on the same worksheet by

varying the size of the numbers involved,

varying the location of the information,

varying the amount of information,

having children generate their own problems.

Thus Wirtz provides teachers with an "unfinished curriculum" in which activities are based on experiences with materials and can be variously modified to provide for a range of needs and interests. The teacher has control over the content as he plans for the child who appears to need specific practice and the one who needs to be challenged. Furthermore, the child is provided with opportunities to be in the driver's seat and construct his own problems for study.

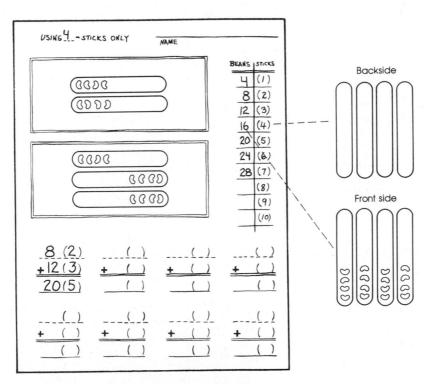

A. Children are introduced to the activity by recording the number of beans with increasing numbers of sticks. The children then make combinations of sticks and record both operation and answer. The answer can be obtained by counting the beans or referring to their own record ("X" table). The sheets are used again with different number sticks.

B. The prepared worksheet at right has a single focus. The number of sticks is given and the child "experiments" to find the missing information. The next worksheet gives only information on the number of beans. The blank worksheet can be used by the teacher to provide children with additional practice. Children can also develop sets of problems for each other.

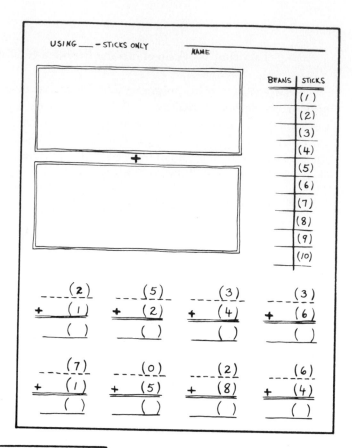

USING ____ - STICKS ONLY   NAME _____

	BEANS	STICKS
		(1)
		(2)
		(3)
+		(4)
		(5)
		(6)
		(7)
		(8)
		(9)
		(10)

```
   __(2)      __(5)      __(3)      __(3)
+   (1)    +   (2)    +   (4)    +   (6)
    ( )        ( )        ( )        ( )

   __(7)      __(0)      __(2)      __(6)
+   (1)    +   (5)    +   (8)    +   (4)
    ( )        ( )        ( )        ( )
```

USING 5 - STICKS ONLY   NAME _____

	BEANS	STICKS
		(1)
		(2)
		(3)
		(4)
+		(5)
		(6)
		(7)
		(8)
		(9)
		(10)

```
  15( )      __(9)     30( )      __(7)
+   (5)   +   ( )   +   ( )   +   ( )
    ( )      (10)     45( )     40( )

   __( )     __( )    25( )      __(8)
+   (4)   +35( )   +   ( )   +   ( )
    (9)     50( )      (8)      (10)
```

C. Another prepared worksheet varies on the focus as well as the level of difficulty. Varying the location of the information brings all four operations into play in solving the problems on the sheet. Furthermore, different approaches to solving a problem become possible. The teacher could use the blank worksheet to develop more challenging problems for children who are capable of meeting the challenge. She may choose to reduce the variety of problems on a given page. Children can also become involved in developing sets of problems for themselves or for others. The same worksheet can provide for a range of abilities within a classroom.

A Search for Patterns: Multiple Methods

Another example of children working similar problems at different levels is illustrated by the following problem:[28]

> "If each of four people shakes hands once with each of the other three, how many handshakes will there be? How many will there be for five people?"

> "In what different ways can we find out?"

> "How can knowing the number of handshakes for three, four, and five people help you to predict the number of handshakes for six or seven people?"

With a variety of materials available, children can be encouraged to tackle the problem at their levels of competence. Children who are intellectually advanced can be asked, "Is there an easy way to find out how many handshakes there would be for any number of people?" They can also be encouraged to generate a number of different methods. If the classroom atmosphere allows an appreciation of unique solutions, the children will focus on the process as well as specific answers. Some approaches are illustrated on the following page that range from concrete operational to formal operational solutions. Most upper-elementary school children could arrive at some basis for predicting the number of handshakes for one or two more people than actually studied. Very few of these children could extrapolate to hypothetical numbers by developing a formal rule. Nonetheless, this activity could tap the range of children's capacities available in the classroom.

ROLE PLAYING

REPRESENTATION WITH OBJECTS

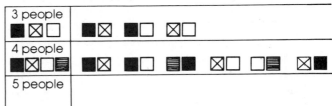

3 people		
4 people		
5 people		

DRAWINGS

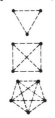

TABLES

People	Shakes
1	0
2	1
3	3
4	6
5	10
6	15
7	

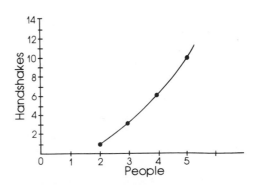

CALCULATION

$$\frac{4 \times 3}{2} = 6 \text{ handshakes (for 4 people)}$$

others

don't shake twice

$$\frac{5 \times 4}{2} = 10 \text{ handshakes (for 5 people)}$$

FORMAL RULE:

$$\text{number of handshakes} = \frac{n(n-1)}{2}$$

Additional Alternatives
in Teaching Elementary School

Science as Action on Objects

For many areas of knowledge, Piaget has identified levels of understanding that develop prior to a comprehensive and formalized understanding at the final stage. On this gradual development of knowledge, Piaget writes,

> **"The child must pass through a certain number of stages characterized by ideas which will later be judged erroneous but which appear necessary in order to reach the final correct solution."**[5,p.21]

Respect for children's thinking is reflected in allowing them to experience these erroneous views and providing them with a wide range of experiences through which they begin to reorganize the limitations of these views.

Floating and Sinking

As we have said, any attempts to teach the law of flotation to children who have just entered the concrete operational stage would be quite inappropriate. It is possible, however, to provide to them related experiences with concrete materials that are challenging at their current level of development. These experiences develop a foundation for transition to the next stage. Since development of knowledge is such a gradual process, it is appropriate that children be exposed to water play and floating and sinking activities prior to beginning their formal education. This encourages development of their observational powers of physical knowledge, and classifying abilities that help them, around age twelve, understand floating and sinking in terms of relative densities.

Balancing Activities

Similarly, balancing activities can be appropriate for preschool children. A teeter-totter is good experience in physical balancing. Many activities with two-pan balances motivate primary-grade children to plan their own activities for comparison of weights of objects. By the middle-elementary grades, the two-pan balance activities can lead them to ordering of objects by weight. Children working with graduated balance beams at this level can partially understand the effects of weight and distance from the center, prior to coordinating relationships on both sides of the beam at about age twelve.

The Pendulum

Teachers might introduce the pendulum in kindergarten for these activities: to count events, to isolate its regular swinging action from the child's actions, to aim and control the direction of its swing to knock over a target with the return swing, or to control and predict the patterns made by a sand pendulum.

Controlling Variables

Piaget's emphasis on isolating and controlling variables in the classic pendulum task can be integrated into children's play in the early grades through easily manipulated materials. Children at this age already have an intuitive awareness of the fairness of any contest.[29] By rolling balls down a ramp at a target, children can isolate variables such as height of ramp, which affects the distance that the target was pushed. Other materials can increase the number of variables children must control, for example, size and weight of balls, length of ramp, weight and size of target object, surface on which target rests. As more variables are included in the activities the level of difficulty increases. These children will develop their awareness of what is fair or how to make it fair, although they will be unable to state the rule in advance of their experiments. Similar experiences with increasingly remote aspects of their environment exercise the children's thinking to its full capacity and prepare them to construct a formal rule applying to all such problems. Although teachers can introduce activities for isolating and controlling variables to concrete operational children, they should not be accompanied by unrealistic expectations of the children's performance or by undue pressures to verbalize a formal rule.

Matter as Particles

Piaget has reported that children have a limited capacity to explain phenomena that are removed from their everyday experience of concrete reality — particularly astronomical and submicroscopic phenomena (see page 80). Yet scope-and-sequence charts for elementary science textbooks often place a study of molecular theory at about the fourth grade, with a study of atomic theory soon to follow. It is quite unreasonable to expect children to reason about submicroscopic particles without having rich prior experiences with tangible materials. Although no English translation of Piaget's work documents the growth of children's understanding of molecular phenomena, it appears reasonable to expect that a range of enriching experiences with concrete reality helps children to construct a foundation of understandings on which they can develop a formal molecular model for explaining physical behaviors of materials.

The following activities are taken from extensive lists suggested by Verne Rockcastle,[30] and Larry Lowery.[31]

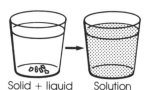
BB's

Marbles

In a container "full" of a substance there may still be room for other substances.

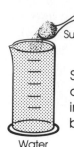
Sugar

Water

Some substances can be added to water without increasing the volume by the amount added.

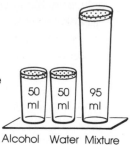
| 50 ml | 50 ml | 95 ml |
Alcohol   Water   Mixture

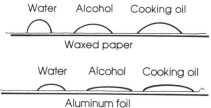
Solid + liquid   Solution

Soluble materials can spread through a liquid even though the liquid is neither stirred nor heated.

Moth balls

Days

Some substances lose weight and get smaller with time. Although part of the substance has disappeared, it can still be detected.

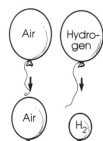
Air   Hydro-gen

Air   H₂

Some substances may pass through objects that do not appear to have holes.

A material that will not permit one substance to pass through it may permit another to do so.

The Elementary Science Study unit, *Kitchen Physics,* suggests a rich variety of activities with readily available materials.[32]

Water   Alcohol   Cooking oil
Waxed paper

Drops of different liquids are different in size and shape.

Water   Alcohol   Cooking oil
Aluminum foil

Different surfaces influence the size and shapes of drops.

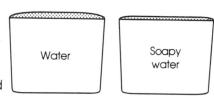
Water   Soapy water

There is a relationship between drop size and the "heaping" in cups of various liquids.

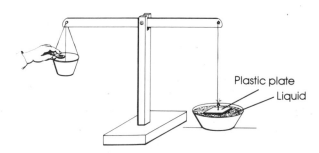
Plastic plate
Liquid

Different liquids have different "stickiness" and "grabbiness" properties.

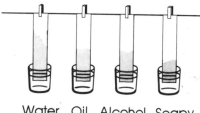
Water   Oil   Alcohol   Soapy water

Different liquids have different rates of evaporation and rates of climb in absorbent materials. (Liquids rise in narrow spaces.)

Children can experience most of the above phenomena directly through personal activity. Other phenomena can be demonstrated by the teacher. Children are encouraged to focus on the regularities that emerge from the *Kitchen Physics* activities and to speculate on explanations. At no time are authoritative statements imposed on them for regurgitation upon request. Together, all of these activities form a concrete base from which the children can later reconstruct an abstract model for molecules. From such a concrete base, inferences about existence of molecules, the spaces between, their relative size and attraction, their movement, etc., can be inferred. To help children bridge the gap from behavior of concrete materials to making inferences about unseen particles Lowery suggests comparable experiences in which characteristics of hidden objects in sealed containers are inferred.[31] Wooden blocks can be placed in a sealed container with a marble. By rolling the marble and observing its deflection from the block the shape of the block can be inferred, even though it was not seen.

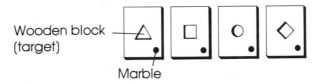

Wooden block (target)

Marble

Many other areas of the elementary school science curriculum, as reflected in textbooks, violate the level of children's intellectual development by placing unrealistic demands on them for abstract understanding while, at the same time, robbing the children of essential physical experiences with their environment. A number of such violations have been documented by Ron Good.[33]

Social Studies

In comparison with mathematics and science, the social studies have not been carefully analyzed for their intellectual demands in relation to children's natural capacities and constraints. The study of mapping skills will be discussed in terms of these capacities and constraints and leading alternatives will be described.

Mapping

One of the more abstract demands placed on the elementary school child is asking him to relate cities, states, and countries to their spatial representation on maps (see pages 75 and 79). Children have not directly experienced regions beyond the immediate neighborhood as physical realities, so their geographic relationships develop gradually. For most children these regions are only "things they see on the map." The map itself becomes an abstract representation of something they have never seen before, so children are asked to learn about geographic features of countries from symbols on maps, which teachers then attempt to explain. David Welton and John Mallan point out other reasons why the map is such an abstract representation.[34] The reading of maps requires a bird's eye perspective of spatial relations. Children's spatial relations are coordinated gradually and their experience doesn't include many opportunities to consider this unusual perspective. Maps contain fewer recognizable details than photographs and lack a one-to-one correspondence with reality. In a map of a neighborhood, familiar landmarks such as trees are the first details to go and the remaining landmarks represented by color-coded dots and squares are no longer recognizable as churches and schools. Maps also contain abstract reference systems such as grids which are not part of concrete reality.

By looking back at Piaget's explorations of children's thinking we are reminded of ways in which mapping activities can be challenging but not unrealistic in their demands on children's natural capacities. Rather than beginning with map symbols and attempting to explain their meaning to children, it is possible to give children opportunities to explore actual objects which are represented by symbols on maps. The E.S.S. unit, *Mapping*, suggests a number of ways in which children can move back and forth between three-dimensional objects and their representation of these objects on maps.[35]

Making and Mapping Patterns   Tangrams, Pattern Blocks, etc., can be used to construct patterns and a representation can be drawn. Children can exchange their "maps" and construct a matching three-dimensional pattern from its two-dimensionsl representation.

Taking a Bird's-Eye View of Things   Children begin by examining objects and drawing them from different perspectives, before focusing on a bird's eye view of common objects. (The use of a ladder can expand the possibilities.) Again the children can exchange drawings and identify the three-dimensional objects they represent. This experience can be expanded to mapping bird's-eye views of arrangements of three-dimensional objects.

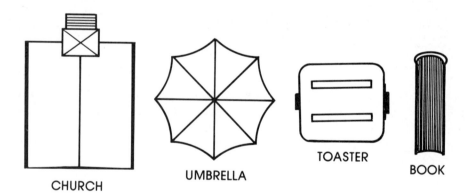

CHURCH   UMBRELLA   TOASTER   BOOK

Mapping the Room, School, and Neighborhood   The children can construct three-dimensional models of familiar objects in space before drawing a pictorial map in one-to-one correspondence with the objects. Finally, they can invent their own codes and draw more abstract representations of the same objects.

These are only some of the mapping experiences that are appropriate challenges for primary grade children and that help to bridge the gap between concrete reality and abstract representation. Older children will require further concrete experience to deal with the complexities of scaling and the abstraction of longitude and latitude lines found on geographer's maps.

Effective Language Usage

The constraints of language were described earlier in Chapter 6. The following classroom examples illustrate effective use of language within its built-in constraints.

Words as Pseudo-Explanations[36]

To a second-grade child, "static electricity" is verbal nonsense, out of touch with her reality. The teacher's use of this label does not serve as an explanation for the child, rather, it may only cut off her curiosity. It may also tell the child that the answer comes from the teacher's head. By focusing on the "why" of the child's question, the teacher is lead to the realm of abstract theory, beyond the child's reach.

The teacher's response did not cut off the child's curiosity, but encouraged her to observe carefully, to speculate, and to construct an explanation that made sense to her. The child did construct a model of the force consistent with her own experience with reality. The teacher also could have converted the "why" focus of the question to a focus on "how" the phenomenon could be studied further with other materials.

Victor Perkes, writing in *Science and Children*, says,

> By word and deed we must convey the message that the unknown
> is a challenge not to vanish with the utterance of a word. [36]

Using Technical Language with Young Children

FIND OUT IF THE SET OF COOKIES IS EQUAL IN NUMBER TO THE SET OF CHILDREN.

Piaget has expressed serious concern about how some teachers tend to impose overly abstract technical terms on children without first communicating to children in their own language:

FIND OUT IF THERE ARE JUST ENOUGH COOKIES FOR ALL THE CHILDREN.

. . . when you teach set theory you should use the child's actual vocabulary along with the activity — make the child do natural things. [37]

Words as Veneer that Distracts Teachers[38, 39]

One of Piaget's early insights was that adults should not take a child's verbalism at face value. Even though the word *metal* was used correctly in the context of the initial question, further inquiry revealed that the child only had a surface understanding of the concept. This example and the one that follows illustrate the importance of going beyond the child's initial response.

Definitions as Ready-Made Truths[40]

"A leaf is a projected growth from a stem which functions in food manufacture by photosynthesis."

The first definition would have to be passively accepted by fourth-grade children on the authority of the teacher or the textbook. This formal definition contains reference to concepts outside the children's experience.

"A leaf is a part of a plant that is seen above the ground, is usually attached by a stem, is flat or needlelike and many of them make shade from sunlight."

The second definition could be actively constructed by children. When fourth graders are allowed to study leaves from different plants and encouraged to verbalize and generalize their findings based on what they had experienced, their kind of definition can be a consensus of different group definitions.

Introducing Lessons with Labels and Definitions[41]

An Alternative

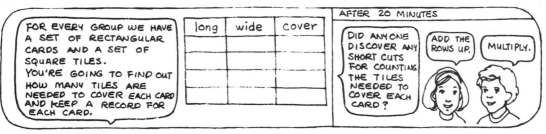

THE NUMBER OF SQUARE TILES THAT ARE NEEDED TO COVER A CARD IS CALLED ITS AREA. YOU WERE ABLE TO FIND IT IN DIFFERENT WAYS — COUNTING OR CALCULATING THE AREA.

In the second example, children are provided with relevant experience prior to labelling or defining. The definition given by the teacher is based on what they already know — it is based on their actions. A variety of other activities can follow that refine the concept of area. One will include finding the area of irregular shapes by covering them with a transparent grid and counting fractions of units.

Sometimes the labelling can be done after reminding the children of what they already know. This is illustrated by the introduction to a grammar lesson on the use of prepositions.

"All of your ideas that I've written down in this way are phrases. You suggested a number of different words for starting each phrase. Since they come before the other words in the phrase, they are called prepositions."

By involving the children and acknowledging what they already know, the teacher avoided prematurely closing their interest with a formal definition or label.

Avoiding Labels as Curiosity Killer[42]

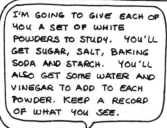

The introduction of the label encourages premature closure to any inquiry. Some teachers report that the Mystery Powders activity is completed in a single session. Others report that it goes on for weeks.[42]

AN ALTERNATIVE

Avoiding the use of labels for powders adds to the children's motivation. Inquiry and language development are encouraged in the process. The need for careful record keeping is introduced and reinforced by the activity itself. *Tasting chemicals should be discouraged at all times. In this activity, no access to the sense of taste sustains the inquiry, as any apparent familiarity would prematurely close the investigation..

Artificial Constraints on Natural Capacities

Piaget, in his writings, continually refers to examples from mathematics or science as having the greatest potential for intellectual development:

> **We have stressed this example of mathematics somewhat since there is no field where the "full development of the human personality" and the mastery of the tools of logic and reason which insure full intellectual independence are more capable of realization, . . .**[5, p.105]

Piaget also views the controlled experiment as an index of overall intellectual development. The ability to isolate and control variables in search of the cause for a given effect is essential to understanding one's world. Although he is aware of the intellectual potential in mathematics and science, he expresses concern that, ironically, these capacities are continually hampered by the artificial constraints of traditional educational practices. He is specifically concerned with the teaching methods in mathematics and the lack of emphasis on teaching experimental methods in science.[5,37]

America's schools appear seduced by language as they look to empty verbalisms as indicators of children's understanding or of the instant success of teaching. This seduction is particularly reflected in the early immersion of children in reading and formal approaches to other subjects that depend solely on language for transmission. Such an emphasis gives the teacher a rather limited view of children's intellectual capacities.

The boys who lit the bulbs were problems in their language-oriented, inner-city classroom. They were probably not good readers and, in their frustration, became sources of classroom disruptions. Their teacher was shocked at the successful problem-solving by her "slowest" students. She didn't provide many opportunities for learning other than through language, and as a result, saw only one side of the children's capacities from her limited perspective. Children who experience difficulty with language and reading are often capable of solving complex problems with physical materials. In contrast to their classroom behavior, these boys continued to experiment with batteries and bulbs for about thirty minutes despite interruptions by adults who interviewed individual children as part of the program. The teacher did not see the children as they were but, rather, she saw them only to the extent that her methods allowed the children to reveal themselves.

The overemphasis on language as the main teaching method for young children limits our view of their level of understanding and capacity for learning. The flawless regurgitation of ready-made "answers" by some children leads teachers to overestimate their level of understanding. At the same time, nonverbal or less fluent children's capacity for logical thinking is grossly underestimated. Often such an early emphasis on language maximizes language differences among children and creates artificial problems, which must then be "remediated." The remedial programs in turn take up more school time and prevent children from succeeding in other subjects that develop logical thinking and are potential contributors to reading success. Similarly, the money required to finance such high-priority programs leaves little for physical materials that young children require for the natural development of their intellectual and linguistic capacities.[44]

Language-oriented classrooms limit the teachers' view of children and deemphasize math and science activity which Piaget identifies as basic to intellectual development. Piaget's framework expands our view of children and provides us with a basis for reexamining the curricular emphasis to remove artificial constraints and fully develop children's capacities within natural constraints.

Putting It Together

- Contrast the following statements made by two psychologists. To what extent are they similar? different?

  ". . . Any subject can be taught effectively in some intellectually honest form to any child at any stage of development."

  — Bruner[45,p.33]

  "Basic notions in these fields (physics and geometry) are perfectly accessible to children of seven to ten years of age, provided they are divorced from mathematical expression and studied through materials that children can handle themselves."

  — Inhelder[45,p.43]

- Relate these statements to the examples discussed in Chapter 9.

- What are some implications of this chapter for your own work with children?

- Select intellectual tasks that are required of children in your classroom. Compare the intellectual demands of the task to the intellectual capacities and constraints of your children.

- Did you find the author's selection of classroom activities to be congruent with Piaget's general framework established in previous chapters as well as with his statements on education in this chapter? If not, why not? What classroom activities would you have included in this chapter?

Developing a Classroom Environment for Active Learning

10

Piaget's studies of children indicate that prior to any formal instruction they have already demonstrated remarkable competence in self-directed learning. He has found that children are generally curious and that they interact readily with materials and people around them. Children construct meaning in their expanding world through this interaction. Any attempt to teach them, therefore, must be undertaken with respect for these capacities.

How can the school extend the children's environment and refine their natural, "experimental" methods without interfering with an already-successful process? If children learn in ways described by Piaget, every classroom should provide an environment that highlights the four processes responsible for transition to higher levels of intellectual development. Every classroom, therefore, should make adequate provision for children's involvement through *physical experiences*, *social interaction* and *equilibration*, with adequate *time* (maturation) to reflect on ideas and reconsider them.

First Comes Thinking

Consider the teacher's role in providing for each of the four factors that influence intellectual development in the classroom. Predict how Piaget might describe the teacher's role in the classroom in providing for each of these factors.

In Piaget's classroom the teacher's role is not one of transmitter of information, but facilitator of interaction. In communicating Piaget's concept of an "active" classroom, Eleanor Duckworth writes

> Good pedagogy must involve presenting the child with situations in which he himself experiments in the broadest sense of the term — trying things out to see what happens, manipulating things, manipulating symbols, posing questions and seeking his own answers, reconciling what he finds at one time with what he finds at another, comparing his findings with other children. [1, p.2]

Physical Experiences

Piaget indicates that children's manipulation of objects is critical to their development of logical thinking during the eleven years prior to entry into the formal operational stage.

> **Experience is always necessary for intellectual development . . . the subject must be active, must transform things, and find the structure of his own actions on objects.** [1, p.4]

A child makes sense of his world to the extent that he interacts with it, transforms it, and coordinates both mental and physical actions. In the process of transforming objects the child, himself, is transformed. Piaget defends the need for materials in elementary school classrooms by the following statement:

> **Manipulation of materials is crucial. In order to think, children in the concrete operational stage need to have objects in front of them that are easy to handle, or else to visualize objects that have been handled and that are easily imagined without any real effort.** [2, pp.22-23]

To this end, he prescribes a multitude of thought-provoking materials and defines the teacher's role in relation to them.

The Teacher's Role

Piaget envisions the teacher's role as facilitating children's discovery of knowledge through their spontaneous activity and by organizing encounters.

> **We need pupils who are active, who learn early to find out by themselves, partly by their own spontaneous activity and partly through material we set up for them.** [1, p.5]

As a facilitator of children's interaction with materials, the teacher has tasks of understanding, organizing, adapting, and creating materials. (What an assignment!) Piaget suggests that teachers should understand the materials and have some expectations for children's understandings through their encounters with children. Further, he stresses the importance of the teacher remaining open to the unexpected as new avenues for exploration. An understanding of a wide variety of materials would help the teacher organize encounters at certain stages of an activity, providing manageable complexity and promoting the child's mental engagement. Although this reduces spontaneous activity, the child is still an active participant in such encounters through manipulation of materials and reflection on his actions. However, maximum mental engagement occurs when the child asks the questions and identifies his own problem for investigation. To this end, the teacher can provide a rich variety of thought-provoking materials.

Piaget writes,

> **The teacher's role then is to make certain that the materials are rich enough to allow simple questions at the beginning, with solutions that each time open up new possibilities.**[2,p.24]

In following the direction of children's spontaneous activity, the teacher may have only a vague plan. As a result, she may have to adapt or create materials as needed. If she can focus on the properties of materials rather than their common uses, she probably can generate multiple uses for them, and encourage children to do so as well.

Organizing for Spontaneous Exploration: Selecting Materials

Nonrepresentational and primitive materials such as blocks, containers, sand, and water for construction and symbolic play invite children to be creative. Adding other basic materials—blocks and containers in a variety of shapes, tiles, rice, beans, a two-pan balance—will invite children to combine all materials and create problems and situations of increasing complexity. Such multi-relational materials as Geo Blocks, Pattern Blocks, and Attribute Blocks open up further possibilities for complex construction based on spatial relations, patterning, and classifying activities.[3] As children develop these logical abilities, they can explore these multi-relational materials at a different level of awareness.

Children can also use live materials such as seeds, plants, and insects; physical materials such as magnets, batteries, and bulbs; and materials for floating and sinking in a variety of related interactions.* A versatile insect for classroom study is the mealworm, an immature stage of the darkling beetle. Children usually observe and describe it, but the study may expand spontaneously through their questions to include explanations and experiments. A discrepant event for most children is the overnight appearance of more mature insect forms in their containers, particularly the appearance of the dark adult beetle. This experience motivates them to speculate on the explanations for such observed behavior and to test the explanations' reasonableness.

---

*The batteries and bulbs activity is described at the end of this chapter, page 240.

The following are speculations of six-and-a-half-to seven-year-old children on the appearance of the adult beetle in one of the children's containers:

BEETLE THEORIES*

John: I think the beetle just flew in the window.

Eric: I think the beetle came from a mealworm when it turned white.

Mike: I think the beetle is a mealworm because he has lines on his body.

Matt: I think the beetle came from a mealworm or just flew in.

Wesley: I think the beetle came from the mealworm as it was getting fat.

David: I think the beetle came from outside the door. Because I don't think the beetle never was a mealworm.

Larry: I think the beetle came from a mealworm of Wesley's container.

Kevin: I think the beetle crawled in the classroom and went into Wesley's dish.

Lori: I think the mealworm shed and turned into the beetle.

Robbie: I think the beetle is a mealbeetle because it was a mealworm and it turned.

Wendy: I think the beetle is something we all have to watch for.

Many possibilities for experimentation occur as a result of children's questions about mealworms:

Can a mealworm see? Does it have a favorite color?

What kind of food does it like?

Why does it hide in the cornmeal? Does it ever come to the top?

What makes a mealworm back up?

Does it prefer a wet or dry place? Hot or cold?

Does the beetle like the same things that the mealworm likes?

Children can explore answers by experimentation on a variety of levels.

Organizing for Specific Encounters

In Piaget's view, the teacher, in addition to providing a multitude of materials for spontaneous activity, also acts as an organizer/creator of encounters that engage the child's mind at specific stages in his activity. Piaget regards this role as indispensable. He describes a task to be undertaken by the organizer/creator:

> **Teachers should select materials that make the child become conscious of a problem and look for the solution himself. And, if he**

---

*The Beetle Theories were constructed by children in Elyse Johnson's suburban classroom in Thousand Oaks, California. The speculations were shared orally in a group discussion. They were then recorded by the teacher, duplicated, and distributed to the children to read as part of a language experience approach to reading. The above sample represents the range of speculations. Most of the children thought that the beetle flew in.

generalizes too broadly, then provide additional materials where counterexamples will guide him to see where he must refine his solution. It's the materials he should learn from.[2, p.23]

In the following examples, the teacher organized a specific encounter in response to the child's exploration of a variety of materials that float or sink in water.[4] In each case, the new materials presented can extend the child's understanding.

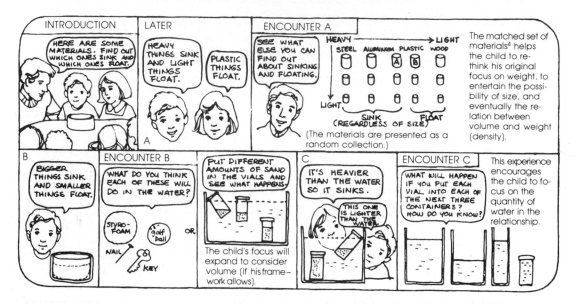

Piaget asks teachers to be alert to the unexpected and flexible in regarding those interesting sidetrips that seem to detract from the main direction of the activity:

But still you should be on the lookout for unexpected things that develop and make sure he (child) can pursue these, too.[2, p.23]

She can then use these unexpected happenings as starting points for other investigations.

As stated throughout this book, when the teacher observes children's spontaneous comments and actions during their activity, she gains insights into the level of their understanding. This preliminary observation is crucial to organizing specific encounters. The teacher can make an educated guess as to what the child already knows or how he thinks, and present him with materials that will raise the right questions in his mind at that moment. On this delicate role of the teacher as observer-planner, Piaget writes,

> **If the teacher discretely changes the situation slightly, thereby preventing the child from succeeding immediately in the next step, the child will wonder why he was successful the first time and not the second. So now it becomes a question of understanding.**[2,p.24]

Such an encounter is organized to make the child's expectations interact with reality. If the discrepancy between expectancy and reality is moderate, the disequilibrium will stimulate the child to reflect on his understandings and extend their meaning to a higher level of equilibrium. An organized encounter for creating a discrepancy is illustrated below. Once the children resolve it, they are more likely to generalize their ideas of flotation beyond a specific example of a liquid to a general class of liquids.

By identifying the key properties (variables) of materials in a certain activity, the teacher can locate substitute materials, or adapt or construct materials. The key variables for the previous activity are the relative densities of the liquids and solids in each container. If the children worked with the materials in Encounter A for some time, they would expect plastic A to sink. The introduction of a clear salt solution (with a density that allowed the plastic to float) as a substitute for water could also produce the discrepancy, perhaps when least expected. The value of understanding the properties of materials and their resulting interactions is further illustrated in the following example of changing an object's floatability.

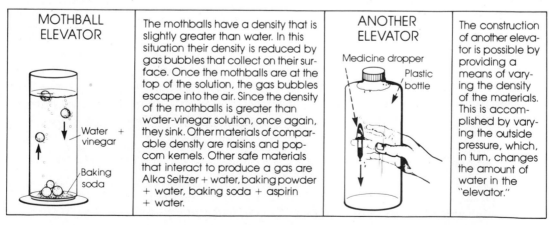

A Cautionary Note on Materials

Materials are critical to the development of children's thinking but managing them is the bane of many teachers. In addition to the above considerations, careful thought must be given to the following:

Acquiring sufficient materials: Sharing intriguing materials that are in short supply can lead to conflicts among children.

Distributing materials: Some children may complete an introductory activity before others have received the materials.

Collecting materials: Some materials are just never returned.

Timing and locating discussions: Distribution of intriguing materials prior to giving directions can sabotage your efforts with large groups.

Terminating the activity: Children can become extremely frustrated by interruption of their involvements.

All of these are potential problems that can be minimized through teacher awareness and planning with children. Although a detailed discussion of materials management is beyond the scope of this book, some possible solutions will be illustrated in the episode at the end of this chapter. A more complete discussion of the logistics of materials management is found in Mary Budd Rowe's *Teaching Science as Continuous Inquiry.*[5]

Many teachers get involved in scrounging inexpensive materials and adapting them for alternate uses in the classroom. Before long, some limitations of this approach are discovered. Firstly, scrounging for inexpensive materials can be expensive in terms of the time involved and must be weighed against the cost of commercial materials. Secondly, some specialized materials (Encounter A) are only available commercially. A valuable resource for sources of materials, *A Materials Book for the Elementary Science Study*, discusses these problems.[6]

Social Interaction

Although physical experiences engage the mind in cognitive activity, verbal interaction with peers and teachers provides additional experiences that can promote cognitive growth. Piaget's active school would provide opportunities not only for individual work but also for work in groups. The teacher would allow children to talk to each other, and organize verbal encounters so that children involved in a common activity could share their points of view. A real exchange of thoughts and discussion would inevitably lead children to justify explanations, verify facts, resolve contradictions, or adjust attitudes.[7] The awareness that other children share viewpoints different from their own plays an important role in getting children (or other learners) to rethink their ideas and adjust (accommodate) them to reach a more coherent level of understanding. Piaget states,

> When I say "active," I mean it in two senses. One is acting on material things but the other means doing things in social collaboration, in a group effort. This leads to a critical frame of mind, where children must communicate with each other. This is an essential factor in intellectual development. Cooperation is indeed co-operation.[1,p.4]

Such cooperative exchange has the potential of developing critical attitudes and "discursive reflection." As in the provision for physical experiences, there must be opportunities for spontaneous interaction as well as organized intellectual exchanges.

ENCOUNTER I — PRIMARY GRADERS[8, p.125]*

*Copied by permission from B. Lansdown, P. Blackwood, and P. Brandwein, *Teaching Elementary Science Through Investigation and Colloquism*, New York, Harcourt Brace Jovanovich, 1971.

Other girls summarize their understanding in their own words.

Brenda Lansdown and her coauthors outline potential outcomes of organized verbal encounters or "colloquia" such as those illustrated on the previous page:

1. Perception is sharpened.
2. Discrepant events result from the children's collective observations, expressed in their own language.
3. Hidden likenesses are found and stated.
4. Models are constructed.
5. New questions are raised which stimulate further investigation.
6. Potential learning is actualized. Preverbal and preconscious experience are consciously probed into awareness.
7. Learning moves dynamically from concrete towards abstract.
8. Thinking and language coalesce to enrich thought. [8, p. 138]

In such discussions, teachers probe into the children's experience with materials in search of meaning.

At the beginning of such discussions the children share observations, experiences, and reactions. At the end of twenty minutes they have moved from the immediate concrete experiences to more abstract levels such as explanations, analogies, hidden likenesses. Lansdown illustrates this movement by contrasting the remarks made by four 11-year-old girls at the beginning and end of the discussion. [8, p. 136]

These children, involved in a common activity, based their discussion on concrete experiences with sinking and floating materials. They first discussed physical knowledge because it was the result most readily available from these experiences. The logical mathematical knowledge of relationships of materials that explain floating and sinking must be constructed by coordinating mental and physical activity. Since these explanations appeared, not at the beginning of the discussion, but as it progressed, this delay is evidence of the power of such social interaction in engaging the mind to construct relationships and explanations, and to foster a cooperative growth of meaning. Although in the illustration older children advanced from physical knowledge to logical knowledge, younger children make comparable advances at their level of intellectual development. Furthermore, children who did not speak during the early part of the discussion showed evidence of mental activity when they later verbalized their thoughts, which were more highly developed than those expressed by others at the beginning of the discussion.

The Teacher's Role

Scheduling Discussions and Facilitating Exchange of Ideas

Although children benefit from small-group work with materials, a larger-group meeting is advantageous since the results of comparable activities may differ among small groups. The timing of a formal discussion, originated by the teacher, is critical. She might start it after observing conflicting results, yet she should not call it if the children are still highly involved in the activities. In the discussion, the teacher might call for observations and results from different groups then juxtapose any conflicting results. By highlighting the contradiction, she encourages controversy—an essential condition for intellectual development. The children are allowed to exchange viewpoints and justify their results. During a heated controversy, the teacher's role is important—to encourage children to listen to each other's arguments. Any contradictions arising can be resolved by further experimentation. [8]

Providing for Psychological Safety

In such open discussions, children must feel free to risk trying out their ideas. The teacher helps build an atmosphere of psychological safety by encouraging children's honest attempts, and supporting those who risk sharing tentative ideas, alternative explanations, or other speculations. In addition, she does not attempt to cover any mistakes she makes or disclose blunders that children did not observe. She communicates that it is human to make mistakes, that they are a natural and valuable part of the learning process because of the feedback they provide. Lazer Goldberg describes a view of errors that would encourage children's willingness to risk sharing their ideas:

> Errors make the heart grow fonder.
> All honest errors are respected.
> Interesting errors are admired.
> Children who are rarely wrong,
> Rarely dare ideas that are their own. [9]

At the same time, the teacher is willing to admit that she doesn't know and to accept the same answer from children. The uncertainty and errors that have accompanied scientific discovery have been edited out of journal reports and, unfortunately, this has created an unrealistic expectation for classroom exploration.

Encouraging Group Consensus

The teacher can also arrange for an Investigator's Log, which represents the children's consensus on the ideas discussed in the group. The teacher or, with older children, a group secretary can record it. In asking for class agreement on a child's summary statement, the teacher stimulates further discussion prior to consensus. The Investigator's Log can be duplicated and distributed to all the children to read. Since this record reflects the children's own language it may contain grammatical errors; some teachers choose to publish a second version called "The Scientist's Way of Writing," which restates the children's statements in standard English. The following Investigator's Log was recorded for a group of second-grade children following water play activities.[8,p.72]

INVESTIGATOR'S LOG

We pour water in a funnel and it come out.

We pour water in a strainer and it come out.

We pour water in a paper towel and it come out.

Water go through things that have holes in them.

We pour water in a bottle and it stay there.

We pour water in a can and it stay there.

Water stay in things that don't have no holes.

Water is wet. Water can be hot or cold.

Water don't have no shape. It fit all shapes of containers.

Occasionally, the children will agree on a summary statement that is in error. This statement is recorded, but the teacher plans a careful selection of materials for the next day to challenge the incorrect statement.

Some of the teacher's tasks in facilitating group interaction to stimulate intellectual development are to: call group meetings as needed, juxtapose children's statements to reveal contradictions, encourage children to listen to each other's arguments, develop an atmosphere of psychological safety, and encourage a consensus of children's ideas. A more detailed discussion of the teacher's role in conducting such organized encounters is found in *Teaching Elementary Science Through Investigation and Colloquim* by Brenda Lansdown, Paul Blackwood, and Paul Brandwein,[8] and in *Teaching Science as Continuous Inquiry* by Mary Budd Rowe.[5]

Facilitating Development of Relationships, Respect and Responsibility

Piaget advocates social interaction and collaboration as a means of advancing both intellectual and moral development as part of the total development of the child's personality:

> **Full development of the personality in its most intellectual aspects is indissoluble from the whole group of emotional, ethical, or social relationships that make up school life.**[10,p.106]
>
> **No real activity could be carried on in the form of experimental actions and spontaneous investigations without free collaboration among individuals — that is to say, among the students themselves, and not only between the teacher and student. Using the intelligence assumes not only continual mutual stimulation, but also and more importantly mutual control and exercise of the critical spirit, which alone can lead the individual to objectivity and to a need for conclusive evidence.**[10,p.108]

For Piaget, the social interaction in a classroom implies "a whole range of mutual intellectual exchanges and relationships and of both ethical and rational cooperation."

The ethical goals for the active classroom are to develop individuals with free consciences who are capable of independent decisions, who respect the freedom and rights of others. In order to encourage autonomy, the adult must reduce her power and provide the children with opportunities to decide for themselves. To communicate this balance of power between the teacher's and students' opinions, Piaget used the metaphor of two classrooms for each class—one where the teacher is and one where the teacher isn't.[1] This kind of atmosphere is essential for the child to construct his physical and social realities. By working out at least some rules for classroom operation, the children develop a sense of social obligation that substitutes for the teacher's authority. These rules are constructed as children become aware of their necessity, rather than being imposed ready-made by the teacher before their understanding develops. As children establish their own rules and begin to live with them, they will recognize transgressions and willingly undertake the agreed consequences with no loss of self-respect. Similarly, they will realize that some of the rules are in need of revision. In the process of constructing and reconstructing social reality, the children must listen to and coordinate the views of others, which leads to the development of mutual respect. Piaget writes,

> **This is why the active methods give an equally invaluable service in ethical education as in the education of the mind. They intend to lead the child to construct for himself the tools that will transform him from the inside — that is, in a real sense and not only on the surface.**[10,p.120]

He believes that without this freedom of expression and intellectual exchange, any development of human values is merely an illusion.

---

*Piaget's work on moral development has served as a basis for Kohlberg's theory of moral development and related classroom applications. Illustrations of classroom discussions of moral dilemmas would be appropriate here, but their inclusion goes beyond the scope of this book.

Conflict Resolution During the course of daily group living, many social conflicts will arise regarding encroachments on personal property rights, personal space, personal feelings, etcetera. Rather than resolving these conflicts through acts of authority such as moralizing, separation, punishment, the teacher encourages the children to interact by listening to each other's perception of what took place, and clarifying their feelings, thus resolving the conflict themselves.[11] If the class has become emotionally involved in the conflict, the teacher may suspend the current activity to take advantage of this opportunity for social learning. She may have the children role-play potential conflict situations to explore creative alternatives to spontaneous physical reactions. Role reversal provides opportunities for decentration. Since many classroom conflicts arise from children's mistaken inferences that others' behavior towards them is "wrong," the teacher provides situations in which children explore differences between observation and inference. Through such experiences they become aware that inferences can be erroneous. By discussing their inferences with the apparent offender prior to acting on them, the children learn how to avoid conflict. Although the teacher may have organized these social encounters, the children construct their own social reality from them. The teacher thus avoids making conclusions for the entire class. She also helps the children develop a framework for establishing social relationships based on independence and mutual respect. Piaget writes,

> **Only a social life among students themselves — that is, self-government taken as far as possible and parallel to the intellectual work carried out in common — will lead to this double development of personalities, masters of themselves and based on mutual respect.**[10,p.110]

Communication which Encourages Self-Responsibility It is possible for the teacher to give up much authority—except in cases of expediency during an emergency—and still gain the children's respect. An authoritarian teacher issues commands to children as the basis for classroom operation and behavior, with no recognition of their rights or capacities to participate in decision-making. An aware teacher can replace authoritarian commands with statements of his feelings or needs. By speaking in terms of himself as a person, he can shed the authoritarian role and communicate his needs in a more positive tone.

ENCOUNTER L

HEY: CUT THAT NOISE!

The teacher yells across the room.

WHEN I'M DISTRACTED BY NOISE, I KEEP LOSING MY PLACE AND I GET REALLY FRUSTRATED THAT I CAN'T TEACH.

OH!

I DIDN'T REALIZE THAT WE WERE SO NOISY.

O.K.

WE'LL SPEAK SOFTLY

The teacher walks over and makes his statement when he is at eye level.*

The teacher's "I" statement provides, factual yet personal feedback. It does not place the children on the defensive by threatening their self-respect. Rather, it provides them

---

*By getting down to the children's eye level, the teacher avoids an authoritarian posture.[5]

CONFLICT RESOLUTION*

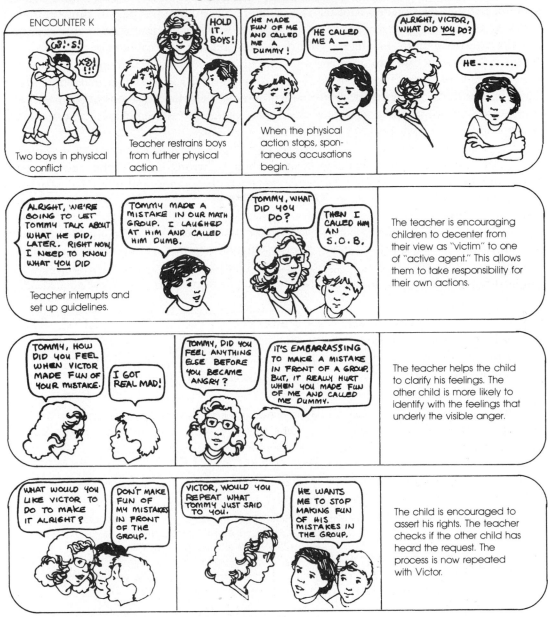

The teacher then encourages free expression. By this time, the conflict has usually been resolved. Most children can restrain themselves when aware of their effect on other children's feelings.

In working with a group of anti-social children, an insecure teacher would likely use behavioral modification methods for survival. A secure teacher would likely use logical consequences as an approach to managing a classroom of children. Once a relationship between the children and teacher has developed the teacher begins to share the power and help the children develop self- and social responsibility. Since every child might not be ready to undertake such responsibility the teacher may work with a small number of individuals at lower levels.

---

*This encounter was taken from the third-grade classroom of Shirley Labinowich.

with an option of taking responsibility for changing their behavior.[12] In an atmosphere in which a positive relationship between the teacher and children has begun, the children will have concern for the teacher's feelings and needs. They are therefore likely to respond positively to this honest encounter, gaining self-respect. As the teacher continues to model this behavior, the children begin to experiment with similar statements in their interactions with peers. They learn to give personal feedback rather than make abrasive demands of others. Awareness of personal feelings parallels the awareness of the rights and freedom of others and contributes to the development of mutual respect and social responsibility.

A Personal Interpretation

The personal meaning of Piaget's work is reflected in the following statement adapted from a conversation with the teacher, who conducted the Explorations of Thinking and Learning in Chapters 1 and 7. She finds a parallel between the cognitive learning emphasized throughout the book and the socio-emotional learning described in the preceding section.

Just as I cannot talk a child into knowing, I cannot talk him into understanding and changing his classroom behavior. Words do not automatically explain and communicate understanding.

In social learning, I can only give the child feedback on how his behavior affects me, and encourage other children to provide feedback on how his behavior affects them. In his own time, the child will recognize a discrepancy in his behavior and alter it in a way that is consistent with his own needs and the needs of others. Occasionally I can organize an experience that brings the discrepancy in his understanding or behavior into focus and, if the child is ready to recognize this discrepancy, the experience may, to an extent, speed up his social growth.

Time (Maturation)

A third process that accounts for advances in intellectual development is *maturation*. The older a child is, the more likely he will have more coordinated structures. The nervous system controls potential intellectual possibilities; it is not fully matured until about age 15 to 16. In the classroom, biological maturation is translated in terms of time. Since Piaget has demonstrated that children construct their own meanings and that their intellectual development is very gradual, the teacher's role is to develop an environment that provides them TIME:

- to pursue investigations knowing the materials will be available the next day, and that they will not interrupt without apparent reason or warning;
- to reflect on ideas, or even daydream in a quiet area;
- to let qualitative ideas "gestate" before considering their quantitative counterparts, and expressing them in abstract terms or formulas;
- to pursue interesting side trips tangential to the direction of other children, or the direction suggested by the teacher;
- to construct a response to the teacher's question and expand on or reconsider it during a group discussion;
- to compare viewpoints and try out ideas with other children apart from organized intellectual exchanges;
- (and opportunity) to plan parts of the day and decide how time should be spent; and
- to integrate and consolidate new ideas prior to the next question.

Unfortunately, most teachers' dilemma is that natural learning (within the constraints of development) requires more time than they are prepared to give. Piaget places this concern for time in an interesting perspective:

> **If you spend one year studying something verbally that requires two years of active study, then you have actually lost a year. If we were willing to lose a bit more time and let the children be active, let them use trial and error on different things, then the time we seem to have lost we may have actually gained. Children may develop a general method that they can use on other subjects.**[13,p.31]

Natural learning (within the constraints of development) requires more time than today's schools are prepared to give.

Wait Time

Mary Budd Rowe in her research reports that the teacher's willingness to give children time to think and respond during discussions greatly affects the quality of their responses. She labels the potential pause between the teacher's question and her calling on a child to respond *Wait Time 1.* Sometimes the child answers quickly and voluntarily, but the teacher attempts to wait. *Wait Time 2* is the potential pause that follows the child's response. If a child is constructing a response—an explanation—he needs time to think (Wait Time 1). Since a child's explanation or other thoughtful response comes in bursts, a teacher's pause before reacting (Wait Time 2) increases the possibility that he will expand his response or that other children will add to it. Although average teacher wait times are about one second and the quality of classroom thinking is limited, a number of positive outcomes were observed when they were extended to an average of at least three seconds:

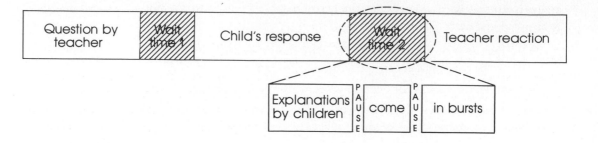

Children gave longer responses and the contributions of "slow" students increased.

Children initiated more appropriate responses and asked more questions.

Children gave more alternative explanations.

Children made more and better connections between observation and inference.

Similarly, related teacher behaviors underwent change:

The teacher's questions and responses to students became more varied.

The teacher's expectations of "slow" children improved as they began to recognize their capacities.[5]

One of the features of Piaget's clinical interview, which accounts for its remarkable ability to facilitate children's thinking, is the amount of wait time provided the child. Rowe's research, although conducted independently from Piaget's studies, supports the value of translating this aspect of his clinical techniques to classroom practice.[5]

Equilibration

Equilibration orchestrates the companion processes of physical experiences, social interaction, and maturation in advancing the child to higher levels of understanding. This cycle of repeated and expanding interactions between the child and his environment spotlights the child as the mainspring to his own intellectual development.

The Teacher's Role

Since equilibration is so closely related to the other processes, a number of examples of how a teacher can facilitate it have already been illustrated. First, there is the need to observe the children's actions and spontaneous comments. After gaining insight into the child's current level of understanding, his focus and way of thinking, it is possible to intervene and confront the child in a way that will provoke disequilibrium. If the child is already experiencing disequilibrium, a furrowed brow, related body language, and an offering of contrasting explanations at different times will appear as some observable clues to the teacher. At this point it might be possible to organize an encounter that would sharpen the discrepancy to become a springboard to the construction of a more coherent understanding at a higher level of equilibrium.

To enter the child's world with an appropriate question or object at just the appropriate moment is an unusually sensitive task requiring considerable understanding of children and materials as well as questioning skills. The task is possible under ideal conditions such as the Thinking and Learning Explorations with individual or small groups of children. Although based on an educated guess, the probability of success increases with increased teacher awareness and knowledge of children. Under conditions of crowded classrooms with 36 minds thinking in a variety of directions, the "right question" and the "right time" will vary with individual children. At this point the task approaches an impossibility. However, the child's ability to raise his own questions in the presence of thought-provoking materials and the stimulation of other children's explorations shifts some of the weight from the teacher's shoulders. This natural expansion will provide many of the "right" questions at the "right" time and still allow some opportunities for the teacher to make contact with the thinking of individual children.[14]

Planning a Learning Cycle of Expanding and Focusing Interactions

A group instructional process that provides for all four factors that influence intellectual development, including equilibration, within the confines of a crowded classroom is called the *learning cycle*. This approach was developed by Robert Karplus and used in designing and teaching activities in the Science Curriculum Improvement Study. The learning cycle consists of three phases which differ in emphasis on the kind and level of the child's activity. The phases are known as exploration, invention, and application.[15]

Exploration   In the first phase the children explore materials which have been selected to expand their awareness in a specific area of their environment. Although this activity may be highly organized by the teacher (in a manner similar to the Thinking and Learning Explorations) it usually involves free exploration or data gathering with a minimum of teacher guidance. One outcome of this exploration is an increase in the child's curiosity. In this phase, the child accommodates to new materials and his attempts at assimilation of these new experiences to existing mental organization of ideas usually result in disequilibrium.

Invention   The concrete experiences resulting from the children's exploration are used as a basis for constructing a relationship, concept, or generalization or for developing a working understanding of a particular thinking process. Here the teacher helps the children to construct the relationship, etcetera, by focusing on the relevant aspects of their experience with materials. One way of facilitating this construction or invention of a relationship is to involve children in discussion to produce a cooperative growth of meaning. A comparison of observations made by different children will contribute towards the construction of relationships consistent with the results of explorations with materials. The teacher may also introduce or invent a new term which can be applied to some aspect of the common experience in order to facilitate communication. At the end of this phase most children are still grappling with the construction of a relationship and are therefore experiencing disequilibrium.

Application   The third phase provides the children with related experiences with similar materials in different contexts or with novel materials. The children have a continued opportunity to accommodate and construct the relationship. By the end of this phase most children reach equilibrium. The variety of related experiences also contributes opportunities to stabilize the initial insights as well as to refine or to broaden their understanding through integration with other existing knowledge. Once the major accommodation of internal structures has been accomplished, additional experiences can be assimilated with only a minimum of accommodation.

Since equilibration requires time and rarely takes place as one-exposure learning, the third phase is a critical part of the learning cycle which can extend over a number class sessions.

Two nested learning cycles in an introductory sequence of activities in a unit on electricity are illustrated in the Classroom Thinking, Learning, and Teaching Episode at the end of this chapter. The sequence is outlined below in order to highlight the phases in the learning cycle.

Exploration 1:   Children explore arrangements of a single flashlight bulb, a battery (dry cell) and a wire to find different ways to light the bulb. Given pictures of different arrangements of these materials, the children predict and test the outcome of each arrangement.

Invention 1:   Referring to the exploration with materials, the children are encouraged to construct a rule for lighting a bulb. They attempt to generalize a relationship from arrangements of materials that lit the bulb. Once the relationship is under construction the teacher introduces the term *circuit*.

Application 1:   The children apply their rule to a widening context of related materials used to build circuits. They revise or extend their rule as needed. Materials are distributed in the following sequence:
        a. battery + bulb + 2 wires;
        b. same materials as in (*a*) + battery holder + bulb holder;
        c. same materials as in (*b*) + a variety of materials (conductors and nonconductors) to be placed in a gap in the circuit.

Exploration 2:   Given a variety (different types of batteries, bulbs, and wires) and increased quantity of materials, the children construct circuits of their own choosing. They explore different variables which effect the brightness of the bulb. Based on personal experience and that of other children in the class, they generate a multitude of possible variables (factors).

Invéntion 2:   The children are asked to focus on a child's hypothetical experiment to test the effect of varying one factor in the circuit on the brightness of the bulb. They identify the variables being tested as well as those that are being controlled or in need of control. In discussion they attempt to construct a generalization for isolating and controlling variables.

Application 2:   Children apply their understanding of this process by designing and conducting their own controlled experiments to test a variety of different factors of their own choosing.

A careful examination of the sequence reveals an alternating between expansion and reduction of focus as well as an alternating between activity and discussion.

Each cycle began with a *spontaneous or minimally guided activity* with materials that expanded the children's experience in a given area. This unfolding of new possibilities was followed by a *focused discussion* in which comparisons were made, relationships were constructed, or procedures were analyzed and evaluated. Once the construction of a higher order of understanding was underway the children became involved in *directed activities* and discussion, which consolidated and extended their understanding through its application to a variety of situations. As children become confident in their own understanding they begin to ask their own questions, and to combine materials in different ways to open new possibilities for extending that understanding still further. This capacity of children to raise their own questions forms a natural transition to the next learning cycle.

Phrasing Questions that Encourage Specific Mental Activity

To facilitate children's construction of reality through their own activity within the learning cycle, the teacher must learn to ask questions which encourage children to:

- generate possibilities in expanding a new area of study;
- review what information is known or readily available;
- transform this information through comparison, analysis, construction of relationship, etcetera, and test these ideas;
- evaluate ideas, results and procedures.

It is important, therefore, to be able to phrase questions that encourage the children to become engaged in the specified types of mental activity. Since the learning cycle may be viewed as a cycle of alternate broadening and narrowing of focus, these types of questions will be examined further as categories along a continuum of narrow to broad. These categories are adapted from the work of Larry Lowery.[16]

The narrow questions organize children's learning toward a specific planned direction. Broad questions encourage different interpretations or solutions, so that the outcome is less defined or predictable.

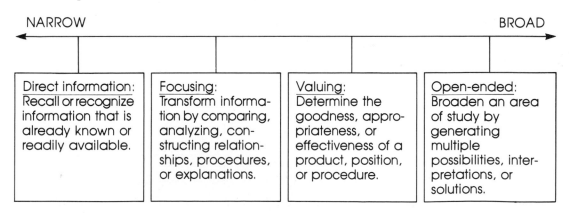

NARROW — BROAD

| Direct information: Recall or recognize information that is already known or readily available. | Focusing: Transform information by comparing, analyzing, constructing relationships, procedures, or explanations. | Valuing: Determine the goodness, appropriateness, or effectiveness of a product, position, or procedure. | Open-ended: Broaden an area of study by generating multiple possibilities, interpretations, or solutions. |

Direct Information Questions

"What is the brand name of your battery?"

"Did your bulb still light when you turned the battery upside down?"

Direct information questions ask the child to recognize information which is readily available, e.g., social and physical knowledge, or to recall information already known. A review of information can serve as a basis for constructing relationship in the invention phase. Since this type of question usually has a short, specific, and ready response, it does not require an extended wait time period.

Focusing Questions

"What is a rule for lighting the bulb that describes all the arrangements that worked?"

"What were the contact points on the bulb in all the arrangements that lit the bulb?"

"Which variable is not controlled in this test?"

Focusing questions guide the child in a given direction or help him to focus on the relevant aspects of a problem, but the child constructs the response on his own. Arriving at the response requires a comparison or analysis of the information or a reorganization of the information to construct a relationship, generalization, or explanation. Any probes or challenges that encourage the child to reconsider and restate a response to a focusing question or to provide evidence for it can also be included in this category. Although it is narrow in focus, this type of question encourages a high level of thinking. An extended wait-time period averaging at least five seconds is therefore recommended for focusing questions. Some questions will require considerably more time to construct a thoughtful response. Focusing questions are concentrated in the invention and application phases of the learning cycle.

Valuing Questions

"Which of these rules for lighting a bulb do you like best? How did you decide?"

"Which of these two experiments is the 'fairest' test of the effect of the number of batteries on the brightness of the bulb? What are your reasons?"

Valuing questions encourage children to judge the excellence, appropriateness, or effectiveness of a product, position, or procedure. They are often accompanied by a request to explain the criteria for this judgment. Valuing questions are considered as broad questions because more than one defensible position is usually possible. A thoughtful response requires a very high level of mental activity which incorporates the processes involved in the above question categories and therefore demands an extended wait-time period for its construction. Valuing questions may be asked during the invention or application phases of the learning cycle.

Open-Ended Questions

"In what different ways can you arrange a battery, a bulb, and a wire to light a bulb?"

"In what different ways can you change the brightness of a bulb?"

"In what ways can we test this variable?"

Open-ended questions can encourage children to generate possibilities that broaden a new area of study and, therefore, are usually found in the exploration phase of the learning cycle. The possibilities can be generated through direct activity or through discussion which follows activity with materials. Sometimes the discussion will have the spontaneity of a brainstorming session, while at other times it will be paced to encourage thoughtful alternatives. An important role of the teacher is to alert children to shifts in focus which accompany each type of question and, therefore, affect the time that children are given to construct a response and the time that children allow others to construct their responses.

Although questioning is certainly an important teaching skill, it must be employed with both sensitivity and flexibility. In the exploration phase of the learning cycle the asking of focusing questions prior to considerable "messing about" with materials may actually interfere with the construction of relationships. The preliminary exploration provides opportunity and time for intuitive ideas to be developed. This experience must precede attempts to reorganize this understanding at a level of action to one at a higher plane. The categorization of questions is a useful exercise in learning to phrase questions that encourage specific kinds of thinking. These questions, however, may elicit unexpected kinds and numbers of responses depending on the developmental level of the children and the timing of the questions. The child's available mental structures allow him to see only what he is prepared to see. There are times when physical knowledge is not readily available as children disagree on what they observe. This example illustrates that the outcome of a direct information question is not always predictable. Similarly, focusing questions are directed towards a specific response. If a focusing question is directed at a group of children who are at various levels of understanding in a specific area, a number of different responses are possible at different levels of completeness. Each child will interpret this "narrow question" in terms of his own understanding or may engage in a game of "what's on the teacher's mind." The above examples underscore the need to consider the question categories flexibly and ask questions with sensitivity. They also stress the importance of listening to the content of a child's response rather than listening for a category of response.

Responding Flexibly to Individual Children and Situations

Within Piaget's framework it is possible for a teacher to respond differently to *children's questions* based on a distinction between three kinds of knowledge. In the case of arbitrary social knowledge, she either responds directly or refers the child to an authoritative source. If a child is deeply involved and needs a particular label or physical fact, the teacher should respect the degree of his involvement and provide him with the necessary information. Ordinarily for questions about physical knowledge, the teacher refers him to the materials since they can provide him with direct feedback. In the case of logical mathematical knowledge, a direct response would not be appropriate. The teacher should respond with another question that encourages the child to develop his reasoning processes by thinking about certain hidden relationships between materials.[11]

The teacher can vary her responses to *children's answers* according to the kind of knowledge involved. Since social knowledge involves people and is based on arbitrary decisions of cultural authorities, a teacher's response can provide useful feedback—"Yes, the second Sunday in May is Mother's Day." Similarly, when teaching certain memory skills, for example, foreign language vocabulary, the teacher can provide feedback in a drill. On the other hand, no social feedback is necessary when the child is responding in terms of physical knowledge or logical mathematical knowledge. In the case of physical knowledge, direct feedback is available from the materials. For logical mathematical knowledge the correctness is based on the logical consistency between the environmental input and the structure of the child's framework of ideas. Although social knowledge responses are readily classified as either "right" or "wrong", children's logical-mathematical responses must be viewed from a broader, developmental perspective.[11]

In the absence of materials to work with, the child learns to accept authority as the source of knowledge and stifles his own curiosity. Even using materials, he is often unable to provide answers that are complete and logical in adult terms. Teachers who insist on "right" answers are demanding something that young children are incapable of giving.[25] When teachers regard their incomplete responses as "wrong," the children soon learn to distrust their own abilities and believe the correct answer exists only in the teacher's head. They begin to watch the teacher's eyes rather than explore the materials for the answer, responding with an inflection, as if asking, "Is this what you want?"[5]

When the children do not produce adult responses, teachers tend to impose ready-made answers on them before they are capable of asking the questions. Then, to reinforce these answers, as much as 25 percent of teacher talk becomes evaluative. Teachers often praise single-word or other automatic replies, with no encouragement to the child to think for himself. This praise usually falls into two categories: *global praise* involves the random use of stock phrases so that what is being rewarded (child, effort, or problem solution) is not clear; *pertinent praise* is distributed only in cases of "correct" responses.[5] As the children lose interest in learning for themselves, the teacher fosters competition among them. She also administers rewards for "right" answers—grades.[17]

Needless to say, the classroom atmosphere created by this barrage of sanctions is oppressive. Rather than sharing spontaneous responses in discussions, children become very guarded and risk only those that they think the teacher wants.[5] Soon, through the use of rewards, the teacher controls the children's expressed thoughts. This psychological manipulation of thought can be so subtle that many observers and participants (teachers and children) are unable to recognize it.[18] What they observe appears to them an efficient system of learning, in which quick and quantifiable evidence of "learning" is demonstrated. Since this system appears to have a quick payoff in terms of test results, alternatives without immediate payoff may not be considered.

The child, once self-directed as a learner (prior to coming to school), is dominated by other-directed activity as he becomes caught up in the competition for grades and other forms of adult approval. A common outcome of long-term exposure to manipulative praise in a concentrated form appears to be a negative spiral of attitudes that runs counter to equilibration and restricts the natural development of intelligence. The final, sad state of the spiral of other-directedness is self-alienation and a kind of trained helplessness.[5, 11]

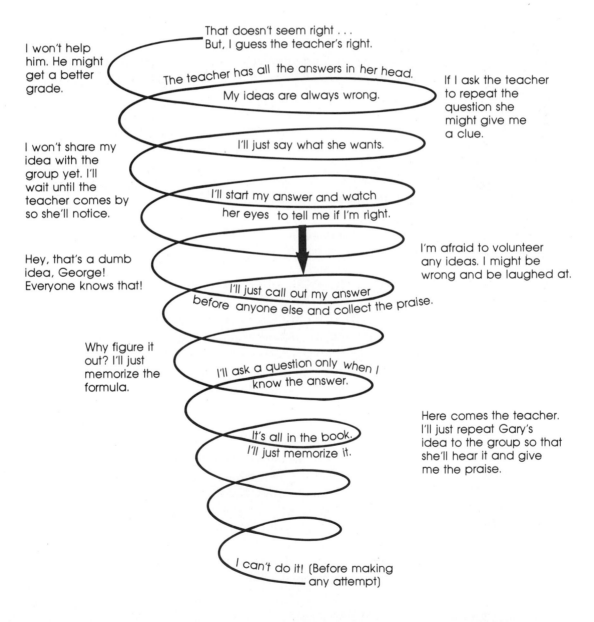

Piaget, who is interested in a deeper level of knowing, warns us against being misled by children's ability to give the "correct" answer at memorized, verbal level without internalizing that knowledge:

> **False accommodation which satisfies a child because it agrees with a verbal formula has been given. This is a false equilibrium which satisfies a child by accommodating to words—to authority and not to objects as they present themselves to him.**[1,p.4]

The result of such superficial mental activity is the application of a shiny veneer of ready-made answers over the children's true beliefs and understandings. In relation to the negative attitudes that often accompany such learning, Piaget has described similar negative attitudes initiated by inadequate teaching methods in mathematics, leading to countless emotional blocks to further learning in that area. In turn, he urges an intellectual freedom that gives the child the right to be wrong:

> **Only this activity, oriented and constantly stimulated by the teacher, but remaining free in its attempts, its tentative efforts, and even its errors, can lead to intellectual independence.**[10,p.105]

Since natural learning involves trial and error, faulty speculations, and numerous fluctuations between ignorance and insight, Piaget pleads for an atmosphere of freedom in which such natural learning can flourish.

Piaget has provided teachers with a developmental framework for looking at children's responses apart from their "correctness". On the child's right to be wrong, he states,

> **In order to understand certain basic phenomena through the combination of deductive reasoning and the data of experience, the child must pass through a certain number of ideas which will later be judged as erroneous but which appear necessary in order to reach the final correct solution.**[10,p.21]

Within Piaget's framework, it is possible to consider children's "wrong" answers as being appropriate to their current level of development. Similarly, they are often partly correct and will be reorganized and integrated into a more coherent response at a later stage (as in Exploration 2). It is also possible to learn much about a child's thinking through these apparent errors. Piaget writes,

> **Yes, I think children learn from trying to work out their own ways of doing things—even if it does not end up as we might expect. But children's errors are so instructive for teachers. Above all, teachers should be able to see the reasons behind errors. Very often a child's errors are valuable clues to his thinking. . . A child always answers his own question correctly: the cause of an apparent error is that he did not ask himself the same question that you asked him.**[2,p.24]

Without teacher acceptance, children's responses always will be ADULTerated. Without the freedom to risk an honest response, the children will never reveal their true thoughts and the teacher can never make contact with their thinking.[11, 13]

A CAUTIONARY NOTE ON FREEDOM AND DISCOVERY

When learners (children and adults) who have been exposed only to superficial methods of learning are provided with materials to explore, they are likely to feel threatened by the prospect of learning on their own. Their early attempts will appear hesitant and shallow. Many teachers have interpreted this observation as meaning that the learners are incapable of such thinking. Children and adults who experience such emotional blocks to learning need extended periods of time for exploration, tasks of manageable complexity, time to verify that their answers will be accepted. The time required to relearn how to learn and to develop self-confidence as an independent learner is more than we seem to be willing to provide.

In creating an atmosphere of psychological safety in which the quality of thinking can flourish, the teacher must accept and respect children's incorrect responses as honest attempts at learning. The potential negative effects of manipulative praise of children and their responses are illustrated below. Alternatives to manipulative praise are also described and illustrated.

Acceptance   The teacher accepts all children's responses and encourage them to express alternate views. Acceptance is not agreement; it is an acknowledgement that the child's response has been heard. Children can build on each other's views or totally reconstruct their own views. Although the teacher may not agree with their ideas, she doesn't impose her own ideas on them. Children may consider another child's view as just another opinion, but the teacher's view carries more weight and he may accept it as fact without any true understanding.

Silence   The teacher makes no comments during investigations. When children are ready to share their explanations, these are likely to be well developed and to include alternatives. Children will tend to use each other as resources, become less dependent on the teacher, and demonstrate more task persistence. Under this condition, children will share their ideas spontaneously.[5]

Specific Feedback on the Task   Rather than praise the child, the teacher praises the task. Also, rather than praise all products following a cursory glance, she examines them carefully to provide specific feedback on the task. This kind of feedback can encourage children to extend their level of performance.

Self-Evaluation   Rather than undertaking the responsibility for all evaluation, the teacher encourages the child to get increasingly involved in self-evaluation of his own product.[3] When a child brings a product to the teacher for evaluation, he can encourage the child to review the process. If the child requests a value judgment, the teacher can ask him, "How do you feel about this?" Once the child has diagnosed a problem in his work, he can be asked, "Now, what can you do about it?" These behaviors can involve the child in the process of self-evaluation and shift this responsibility from the teacher to the child.

Probe All Responses   The teacher probes right as well as wrong answers to encourage the child to rethink his response or search for more supporting evidence. Rather than reinforcing only right responses, the teacher can contribute to strengthening the child's reasoning processes. Because questioning a child's response or referring to materials is common practice, the child with a wrong response can accept further teacher guidance without any emotional blocks. The teacher's question can focus on a particular aspect of the materials, which then allows the child to clarify his understanding. Similarly, the teacher can introduce additional materials that challenge the child's original conclusion.[20]

The teacher attempts to structure further experiences based on the child's response to broaden or clarify the child's understanding. This emphasizes the value of listening to any response rather than a specific response.[21]

The preceding alternatives to manipulative praise allow the teacher to develop in the classroom that feeling of psychological safety in which both the quantity and quality of ideas can flourish. With the variety of alternatives, the teacher can respond flexibly to children's responses.

The teacher's responses may vary in relation to the specific phase of the Learning Cycle. During the Exploration phase, which is often open-ended, acceptance or silence would encourage most children to generate multiple responses. In the advanced phases of the Cycle which converge on a specific relationship or skill, a probing response would be appropriate. Yet, for some children acceptance is more facilitating of invention of relationships, unless the probing is done for a group's response. Once again, we must conclude that there are no simple formulas that apply to teaching.

From the previous discussion, it is apparent that a classroom teacher can create an environment congruent with children's natural learning processes. The child becomes engaged in an expanding environment and freely constructs his meaning through interaction with objects and persons. His intellectual development proceeds in a positive spiral and his world becomes more ordered. Equilibration, the motor behind the child's activity, is stimulated by interaction with other people. However, no direct praise is necessary to extend the spiralling development.* When the child is allowed to flourish in an accepting, supportive environment, a spiralling development of attitudes of competence accompany his intellectual development. As he learns how to learn in more refined ways, his curiosity is not dampened, nor is his willingness to take risks. He has enough confidence in his own ideas to try them out with materials or on others. Intellectual and emotional growth are mutually supportive.

---

*Research reported by Rowe[5] and others supports the need for reducing praise in the classroom to promote higher-level thinking. All conducted independently of Piaget's studies, it supports the value of translating this aspect of Piaget's clinical method, along with wait time, into classroom practice.

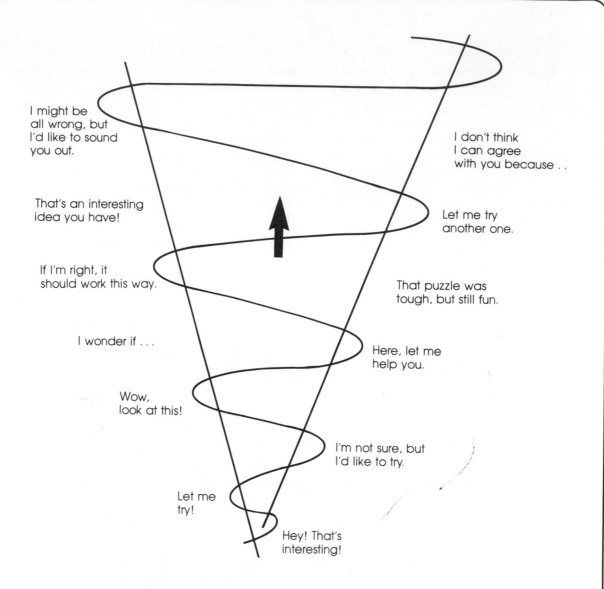

Intellectual and emotional growth are mutually supportive.

Evaluating in Terms of Long-Range Goals

The following list of evaluative questions, developed by Bill Hull for the Elementary Science Study, reflect the values of Piaget's active classroom.[22,pp.153–154]

Do the students talk with each other about their work?

Do they initiate activities which are new to the classroom?

Do they persist over a period of days, weeks or months on things which capture their interest?

Do they have real interests of their own?

Are they able to say, "I don't know," with the expectation that they are going to do something about finding out?

Do they exhibit any initiative, have they developed any skill, in finding out what they want to know?

Do they continue to wonder?

Can they deal with differences of opinion or differences in results on a reasonably objective basis, without being completely swayed by considerations of social status?

Are they capable of intense involvement? Have they ever had a passionate commitment to anything?

Do they have a sense of humor which can find expression in relation to things which are important to them?

Do they continue to explore things which are not assigned—outside of school as well as within?

Can they afford to make mistakes freely and profit from them?

Do they reflect upon their errors and learn from them?

Do they challenge ideas and interpretations with the purpose of reaching deeper understandings?

Are they charitable and open in dealing with ideas with which they do not agree?

Can they listen to each other?

Are they willing to attempt to express ideas about which they have only a vague and intuitive awareness?

Are they able to make connections between things which seem superficially unrelated?

Are they flexible in problem solving?

Are they willing to argue with others?

Can they suspend judgment?

Are they capable of experiencing freshly and vividly?

Do they know how to get help when they need it and to refuse help when appropriate?

Are they self-propelling?

Can they accept guidance without having to have things prescribed?

Are they stubborn about holding on to views which are not popular?

Are they inner-directed?

Can they deal with distractions, avoid being at the mercy of the environment?

Are they intellectually responsible?

Do they recognize conflicting evidence or conflicting points of view?

Do they recognize their own potential in growing towards competence?

The Classroom Atmosphere

Goldberg conveys the essence of the classroom environment, outlined by Piaget, in the following statement:

> *The real challenge is to cultivate an air, a climate, in which children's imagination is sensitized to conceive of what senses do not convey, to have wild, exciting ideas, the kind that cause a halt in the ongoing transactions because flights of the imagination appear unrelated, at least for a little while, to all that has gone on before. Essential ingredients for such an environment are mutual respect and patience. It is an atmosphere where the child who announces that she has built a pendulum that will swing forever is not greeted with shouts and laughter, but with serious and admiring questions. It is where a child is not compelled to witness a dissection, or where a private request for assistance does not become a public announcement. It is an environment which provides time to tinker and to fail, time to chat and to reflect, to stare vacantly while the elusive threads tangled deep below disengage themselves and find their way to consciousness.*
>
> *It is a happy place not governed by a scarcity economy of good feelings that are the rewards of pleased adults, but one filled with activity, where feelings are associated with the task and the acceptance of one's fellows. It is a place where joys and sorrows, as well as knowledge, are shared. It is a community.* [9, p.103]

Although the classroom is basically a happy place, social and intellectual conflict are not avoided; rather, they are viewed as essential conditions for intellectual development.

Despite a comfortable climate, an inescapable tension exists in learning, which may spill over from challenging tasks. During the process of equilibration, a child may pass through stages of frustration to excitement and elation, which add valleys and peaks to the emotional climate of the classroom. While experiencing disequilibration, children may not be easy to live with. The classroom atmosphere of acceptance, mutual respect, and cooperation will minimize the social conflicts that could divert their energies from the intellectual process through which they construct higher levels of understanding.

Putting It Together

In contrast to the Thinking and Learning Explorations with small groups or individual children, the Classroom Thinking, Learning and Teaching Episode that follows will illustrate activities in which an entire class is engaged over an extended period of time. In addition to providing further insights into thinking and learning, it will bring the teaching role into focus. Rather than continue discussing the ways in which a teacher might provide for each of the four factors—physical experiences, social interaction, time, and equilibration—in isolation, these factors will be illustrated in the context of a working classroom.

The Classroom Exploration will focus on the teacher's and children's activity during two units: *Batteries and Bulbs, (Elementary Science Study,*[23, 24]) and *Consumer Product Research: Product Testing* (United Science and Mathematics for Elementary Schools— U.S.M.E.S.[25]) over a period of several weeks. Unlike the Explorations which were based on videotaped interviews with children, the Classroom Episode is a hypothetical situation. It is based on a composite of personal observations of children and adults doing similar activities and reports from teachers and other observers. The setting is a sixth grade classroom.

Like the Explorations, scenes in the Classroom Episode provoke thought. Rather than being analyzed in the text like the Explorations, the Classroom Episode awaits your analysis. You are asked to analyze it for yourself and to reconstruct your ideas of thinking, learning, and teaching. It will be helpful to read the Episode and think in terms of children's intellectual capacities and constraints as well as factors influencing intellectual development.

Classroom Episode: Thinking, Learning and Teaching

EXPLORATION OF BATTERIES AND BULBS

THE TEACHER INTRODUCED THE ACTIVITY BEFORE DISTRIBUTING THE MATERIALS.

CONTINUED INVESTIGATION IS ENCOURAGED.

EACH OF YOU IS GOING TO GET ONE BATTERY, ONE BULB AND ONE WIRE.

TRY TO FIND WAYS THAT LIGHT THE BULB AND WAYS THAT DON'T LIGHT IT.

NONE OF THE MATERIALS CAN GIVE YOU A SHOCK.

DO THIS ON YOUR OWN. WE'LL SHARE YOUR FINDINGS LATER. IF YOU SHOW SOMEONE ELSE HOW YOU DID IT, YOU MIGHT BE TAKING AWAY THEIR SATISFACTION OF FINDING OUT FOR THEMSELVES.

CAN YOU FIND ANOTHER WAY TO LIGHT THE BULB?

PREDICTION SHEETS ARE DISTRIBUTED.

PREDICT AND TEST EACH OF THESE ARRANGEMENTS ONE AT A TIME. KEEP TRACK OF YOUR PREDICTIONS AND OBSERVATIONS.

PREDICTION SHEET

Some children (and adults) find the initial exploration very frustrating and can't seem to find an arrangement to light the bulb. The teacher will distribute the prediction sheet within a few minutes to avert children from reaching their frustration threshold. (Children accustomed to these methods have longer task persistence.)

INVENTION OF A CIRCUIT CONCEPT

The prediction sheet becomes a record of arrangements that light the bulb and those that don't light it.

Groups of children are encouraged to generalize a rule from their data.

SEE, THE BATTERY IS BEING TOUCHED ON THE TOP AND BOTTOM

THAT'S RIGHT. IT DOESN'T MATTER HOW YOU TURN IT AROUND. IT ALWAYS HAS TWO CONTACTS.

SUPPOSE YOU WERE TALKING TO A FRIEND ON THE PHONE WHO HAD NEVER STUDIED BATTERIES AND BULBS BUT WANTED TO KNOW WAYS TO LIGHT A BULB. WHAT COULD YOU TELL HER THAT WOULD LET HER LIGHT THE BULB REGARDLESS OF ARRANGEMENT?

LOOK AT YOUR PREDICTION SHEET AND COMPARE ALL THE WAYS THAT LIGHT THE BULB AND ALL THOSE WAYS THAT DIDN'T.

WHICH PARTS OF THE BATTERY ARE ALWAYS IN CONTACT WITH A WIRE OR BULB? WHICH PARTS OF THE BULB ARE TOUCHING?

In the process of comparing results and generalizing a rule through small group discussion, children went back to the materials several times to verify their observations or to facilitate communication.

A GROUP DISCUSSION IS HELD FOR SHARING IDEAS.

Materials were returned to the bags at the children's table before children reassembled at the front of the room. Some materials for demonstration were available in the center of the circle.

A RELATIONSHIP OF GROUP CONCENSUS:

Rule for lighting the bulb
    Just as long as the bulb is touching the top and bottom of the battery and the wire connects the bulb to the other end of the battery, it will light up. The position of the battery doesn't matter.

(The two contact points on the bulb are seldom noticed and incorporated in the rule after exploring the first set of materials.)

THE TEACHER INVENTS A LABEL.

THE WAY IT'S CONNECTED, THE "JUICE" KIND OF GOES ROUND IN A CIRCLE TO THE BULB AND BACK TO THE BATTERY.

LOOK ON YOUR SHEET TO SEE IF THE CIRCLE IDEA IS TRUE FOR ALL THE WAYS THAT LIT THE BULB.

THE KIND OF ARRANGEMENT THAT HAS A COMPLETE PATHWAY MAKES CONTACT WITH ALL THE NEEDED POINTS ON THE BATTERY AND BULB AND LIGHTS THE BULB. THIS KIND OF ARRANGEMENT IS CALLED A COMPLETE CIRCUIT.

The label is introduced after the children have constructed their own relationship of the materials.

FEELINGS ARE SHARED.

Awareness of feelings contributes to development of mutual respect.

> HOW DID YOU FEEL WHEN YOU WERE TRYING TO LIGHT THE BULB BY YOURSELF IN THE FIRST FEW MINUTES?

> IT WAS REALLY EXCITING TO FIND OUT HOW TO DO IT BY MYSELF.

> I REALLY FELT GOOD WHEN I PUT IT TOGETHER AND THE BULB LIT UP.

> I WAS ALL THUMBS AT THE BEGINNING AND COULDN'T GET STARTED. THE PREDICTION SHEET HELPED ME A LOT, BUT IT SEEMED FOREVER BEFORE THE SHEET CAME.

> WHEN I SAW THAT OTHER PEOPLE HAD LIT THEIR'S I GOT NERVOUS AND STARTED TO THINK HOW DUMB I MUST LOOK.

APPLICATIONS AND EXTENSIONS OF THE CIRCUIT CONCEPT

Batteries and Bulbs

① Try to light the bulb with a battery and two wires in your circuit.

Joining two wires into a single, long wire is not a fair solution.

Review your rule for a complete circuit to see if it needs any revising.

Try #② when you are finished.

> WE'RE GOING TO HAVE "BATTERIES AND BULBS" MATERIALS AVAILABLE IN THE ROOM FOR A LONG TIME. I KNOW THAT SOME OF YOU HAVE SOME GREAT IDEAS THAT YOU'D LIKE TO TRY OUT.
>
> SINCE ITS IMPORTANT THAT YOU HAVE A SOLID UNDERSTANDING OF CIRCUITS BEFORE BRANCHING OUT, I NEED TO ASK YOU TO WAIT A COUPLE OF DAYS. FIRST, I'D LIKE YOU TO TEST OUT YOUR CIRCUIT RULE WITH NEW MATERIALS.

APPLICATIONS AND EXTENSIONS (CONT'D)

Before arriving at a solution that extends the circuit rule, groups of children grapple with the problem. Some signs of disequilibration are evident as they revert back to the "unfair" solution. A solution often requires checking of earlier findings as it brings the importance of all four contact points into clearer focus.

Working together, the children help each other to focus on all four contact points and to juggle the materials.

MORE MATERIALS

Bags of new materials are dropped off as each group solves the previous problem. The children's attention is directed to the board.

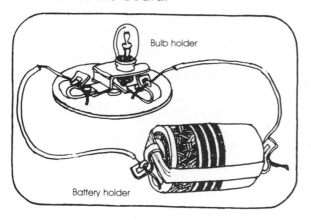

Bulb holder

Battery holder

② Light the bulb by adding a bulb holder and battery holder to your circuit. How do the new materials take the contact points into account? Will you need to change your rule?

Children are left to their own devices with the materials, experiencing most difficulty in "threading" the wire through the clips.

TESTING PATHWAYS

With the addition of a third wire the circuit is opened up to become a "pathway tester." Children are encouraged to empty pockets and purses to find materials for testing as electrical pathways.

Once they have developed an expectancy for the kinds of materials that are electrical pathways they usually generalize to include all metals, now, the teacher introduces other materials to refine their understanding.

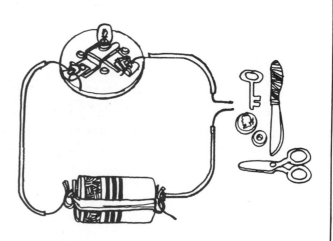

Nichrome wire

APPLICATIONS AND EXTENSIONS (cont'd)

The children are given a five-minute warning to wind up what they are doing and to bag the materials. They congregate at the front of the room. Here, the group focuses on their original rule and how the new materials might alter that rule. During the discussion the teacher introduces the term <u>electrical conductor</u>. The children decide to replace the term wire with electrical conductor in the consensus rule for a complete circuit.

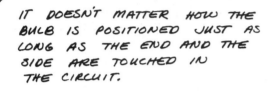

EXPLORATION OF CIRCUIT VARIABLES

DAY THREE-EXPLORATION

The teacher was satisfied that an important foundation had been built during the first three hours. More of the same materials were made available and children were encouraged to construct their own circuits, with a partner. Children who were slow to start, picked up ideas from others. Most children became fascinated by the increased bulb brightness produced by more batteries.

COMBINING BATTERIES

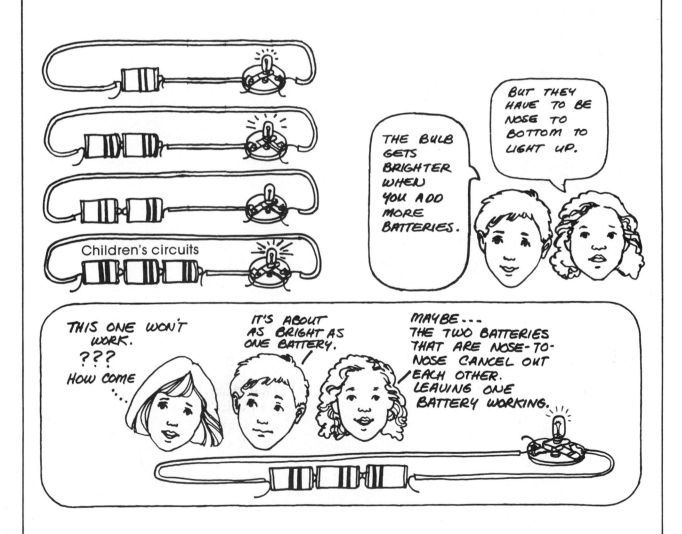

IN WHAT DIFFERENT WAYS CAN YOU PUT ONE BATTERY, TWO BATTERIES AND THREE BATTERIES IN THE CIRCUIT AND STILL LIGHT THE BULB?

HOW DOES THE BULB BRIGHTNESS COMPARE?

Children's circuits

THE BULB GETS BRIGHTER WHEN YOU ADD MORE BATTERIES.

BUT THEY HAVE TO BE NOSE TO BOTTOM TO LIGHT UP.

THIS ONE WON'T WORK. ??? HOW COME ....

IT'S ABOUT AS BRIGHT AS ONE BATTERY.

MAYBE... THE TWO BATTERIES THAT ARE NOSE-TO-NOSE CANCEL OUT EACH OTHER, LEAVING ONE BATTERY WORKING.

EXPLORATION (cont'd)

COMBINING BULBS

WE PUT TWO BULBS IN OUR CIRCUITS. BOTH OF MY BULBS LIT UP!

Jerry

Dale

ONLY ONE OF MINE LIGHTS UP.

THAT'S AN INTERESTING OBSERVATION --- I WONDER IF YOU'RE CIRCUITS ARE REALLY THE SAME.

Other children combine bulbs in a circuit.

YOU'RE USING DIFFERENT BULBS!

IF ONE OF THE BULBS LIGHTS AND THE OTHER DOESN'T, DO YOU HAVE A COMPLETE CIRCUIT? --- HOW DO YOU KNOW?

JERRY, YOU HAVE TWO OF THE SAME BULBS AND DALE HAS ONE OF EACH KIND. WHAT DO YOU THINK WOULD HAPPEN IF YOU PUT TWO OF THE OTHER KIND OF BULB IN THE CIRCUIT?

LATER . . .

HERE'S A BRIGHTNESS METER AND A MAGNIFYING GLASS. SEE IF YOU CAN FIGURE OUT HOW TO USE THEM TO FIND MORE DIFFERENCES BETWEEN THE BULBS.

Increasing layers of waxed paper

AN ACCIDENT

I ACCIDENTALLY DROPPED MY BULB AND IT BROKE ---

I'll GET A BRUSH AND A DUST PAN TO BE SURE THERE ARE NO SLIVERS OF GLASS AROUND.

WHAT DO YOU NEED TO DO TO MAKE IT SAFE FOR OTHERS TO WORK IN THAT AREA?

BLOWING OUT BULBS

Meanwhile other groups are anxious to turn out the lights to highlight their "lanterns." Eventually one group has enough batteries connected to blow out a bulb and cheers when it happens. A second group is anxious to duplicate the results but finds that it needs even more batteries.

TRANSITION TO THE DISCUSSION

The children are given a five-minute signal to finish and return the materials. Since some children would be frustrated at dismantling their circuits they were encouraged to leave them at a side table with their names on them.

Only ten minutes were left in the school day as the class reassembled for discussion. The teacher was aware that the discussion should be limited since different groups were involved in a variety of activities.

Although the discussion was brief, it was productive. It related the work of the different groups and raised other questions for investigation the next day.

*Discussions can occur in all phases of the Learning Cycle with small group interaction the most common. The large group discussion described above is part of the Exploration Phase as its focus was on data gathering and increasing curiosity for further exploration. By contrast, the Invention is an organized intellectual encounter with the specific focus of constructing relationships. Still other group discussions can arise spontaneously which can interrupt the planned cycle.

MATERIALS MANAGEMENT

AFTER SCHOOL

Since the children were beginning to go in different directions and the circuits-in-progress were beginning to spread out beyond the side table, the teacher was very concerned about managing these materials. While surveying the situation, she thought that there were fewer materials than expected. She began to inventory the materials and found that up to eight bulbs and smaller amounts of other materials were missing.

NEXT DAY — BEFORE CHILDREN MADE OUT THEIR INDIVIDUAL SCHEDULES

GROUP MEETING

Most children showed genuine concern for the problem and actively participated in the discussion. Once the problem of missing materials was talked out, the teacher expressed an additional concern.

This touched off additional discussion.

After thirty minutes the following group consensus had been reached.

1. missing materials will be returned to the box in the corner by tommorow morning.
2. materials can be checked out overnight.
3. Its okay to blow out a bulb if its to check a question.
4. Since everyone is working on different circuits they need to have their own basic set and to pick up and store other materials at a central pool.
5. George and Darryl will help set up a system at the pool and to manage it.
6. When there is not enough materials to go around people can schedule time for checking materials out from the pool.

NEXT DAY

Most of the missing materials re-appeared during the morning.

In the afternoon, the children resumed the study of their problems.

This time the teacher did not schedule a discussion. She continued to circulate, observe and leave some materials, or raise questions at crucial points.

The central pool management system was devised by George and Darryl with teacher consultation. It is accessible and visible for quick inventory.

Two empty slots

THE FOLLOWING DAY

Two children didn't want to do the batteries and bulbs activity. One preferred to read. The teacher said it was okay, but encouraged her to rejoin the group when ready. The teacher had noted that the other child had been grouped with someone who had dominated the activity. She suggested that he join a friend who was less dominant in another group. A few minutes later, the teacher noticed that he was actively involved in his new group. Before the end of the period the girl had rejoined her original group.

EXPLORATION (cont'd) — THE IDEA TREE[26]

This time the teacher uses an idea tree as a springboard for generating ideas for changing their circuits.

She asks, "In what different ways might you change the brightness of the bulb?"

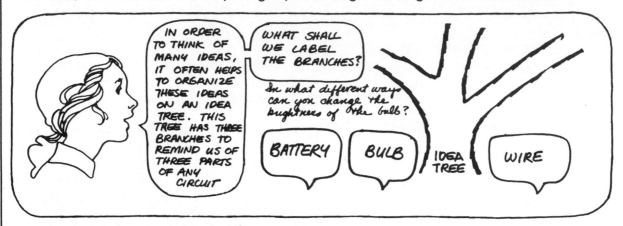

DISCUSSION

The teacher accepts and records the children's ideas as possibilities.

Ideas are also recorded for the two other main variables.

By comparing Explorations 1 and 2 it becomes apparent that the phases of the Learning Cycle can vary in length from 15 minutes to days.

INVENTION OF THE ISOLATING AND CONTROLLING VARIABLES PROCESS

The idea tree was left on the chalkboard until the next day. Children were invited to make additions as new ideas occurred to them.

On the previous day, the teacher accepted all responses uncritically. Today she wants children to focus on the relations between branches. Once the relations are more clearly indicated, the idea can then be more suggestive:

Some entries were relocated at the children's suggestion to emphasize the relationships.

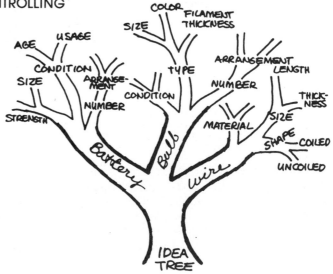

The teacher laid open the possibilities for extending their experience and their under-standing of circuits. Before turning them loose she decided to help them to focus on ways to test their ideas. She was prepared with a chart that illustrated a child's hypothetical test. The children were asked to be critical of the test to find out if the size of the bulb makes a difference in its brightness. (Note that the teacher chose not to invent formal labels in this section.)

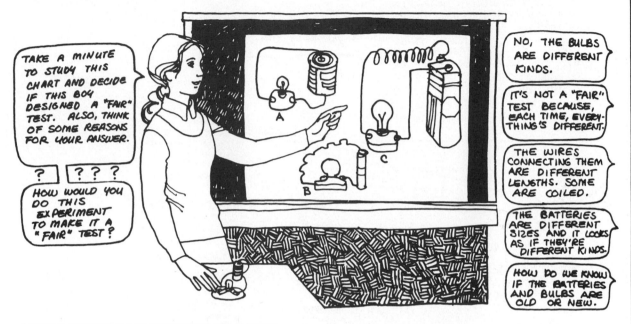

APPLICATIONS AND EXTENSIONS OF THE IDENTIFYING AND CONTROLLING VARIABLES PROCESS

Children were encouraged to team up and test ideas of their choosing. They were also encouraged to keep a record of their procedures and findings.

After that day, children were able to schedule time during any part of the day to continue testing variables. This gave them the freedom to manage their time and to decide on their own problems. During the next couple of weeks, the children were involved with these problems at different times of the day for varied periods.

When the teacher came by, she continued to observe and question. Children who arrived at different conclusions for the same question were encouraged to meet and compare results and procedures. Optional discussions were scheduled on occasion as certain groups wanted to share their findings.

PSYCHOLOGICAL AND PHYSICAL SAFETY

Some of the children discovered that certain factors did not change the brightness of the bulb. The teacher thought that this reflected learning in real life. Since enough time was provided to test a number of possible variables, she felt no pressure to divert them into more "productive" activities. At the same time, she did alert the children to mistakes that could affect their physical safety, such as sticking wires into the wall outlet.

EVALUATION[27]

During these two weeks, in which the children extended their under-standing of the process of identify-ing and controlling variables, the teacher took the opportunity to ob-serve the children working at their problems.

In addition to assessing their level of understanding of isolating and controlling variables, she also noted their inventiveness, critical thinking, and persistence.

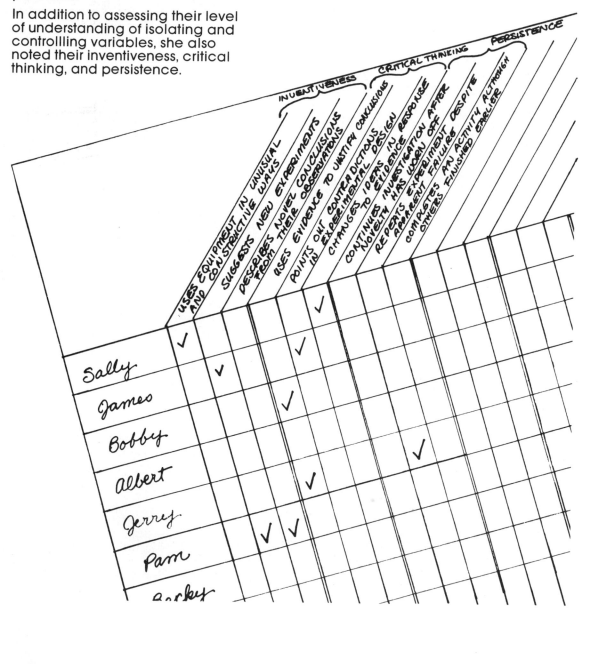

MYSTERY CIRCUITS
Large group lesson

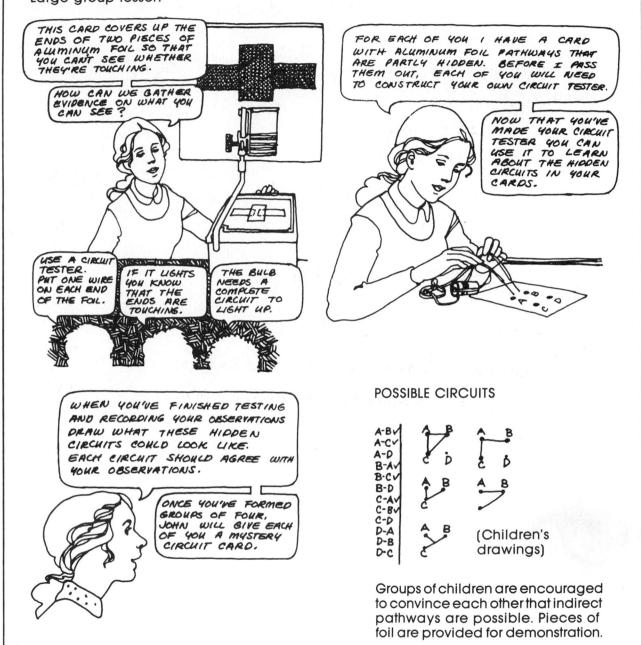

THIS CARD COVERS UP THE ENDS OF TWO PIECES OF ALUMINUM FOIL SO THAT YOU CAN'T SEE WHETHER THEY'RE TOUCHING.

HOW CAN WE GATHER EVIDENCE ON WHAT YOU CAN SEE?

FOR EACH OF YOU I HAVE A CARD WITH ALUMINUM FOIL PATHWAYS THAT ARE PARTLY HIDDEN. BEFORE I PASS THEM OUT, EACH OF YOU WILL NEED TO CONSTRUCT YOUR OWN CIRCUIT TESTER.

NOW THAT YOU'VE MADE YOUR CIRCUIT TESTER YOU CAN USE IT TO LEARN ABOUT THE HIDDEN CIRCUITS IN YOUR CARDS.

USE A CIRCUIT TESTER. PUT ONE WIRE ON EACH END OF THE FOIL.

IF IT LIGHTS YOU KNOW THAT THE ENDS ARE TOUCHING.

THE BULB NEEDS A COMPLETE CIRCUIT TO LIGHT UP.

WHEN YOU'VE FINISHED TESTING AND RECORDING YOUR OBSERVATIONS DRAW WHAT THESE HIDDEN CIRCUITS COULD LOOK LIKE. EACH CIRCUIT SHOULD AGREE WITH YOUR OBSERVATIONS.

ONCE YOU'VE FORMED GROUPS OF FOUR, JOHN WILL GIVE EACH OF YOU A MYSTERY CIRCUIT CARD.

POSSIBLE CIRCUITS

A-B ✓
A-C ✓
A-D
B-A ✓
B-C ✓
B-D
C-A ✓
C-B ✓
C-D
D-A
D-B
D-C

(Children's drawings)

Groups of children are encouraged to convince each other that indirect pathways are possible. Pieces of foil are provided for demonstration.

After the different models are generated, the children hold up their cards to the light. The shadow of the aluminum foil circuit between the card indicates its shape. By exchanging cards they get feedback on their models. Some children also realize that more than one model can account for the same observation.

MYSTERY CIRCUITS (cont'd)

Children are organized into productive grouping's for this problem. Groups are based on children's inquiry attitudes to ensure that each group has sufficient initiative, critical thinking, and persistence to handle a difficult problem.

> NOW WE HAVE CIRCUITS HIDDEN IN A MYSTERY BOX. THEY ARE CONNECTED TO THE BOTTOM OF SOME OF THOSE PAPER FASTENERS THAT ARE SHOWING.

> BEFORE WE START, I NEED TO TELL YOU THAT THERE'S NOTHING INSIDE THAT WE HAVEN'T WORKED WITH BEFORE.

> IT'S IMPORTANT THAT EACH GROUP MAKES AND RECORDS CAREFUL OBSERVATIONS WITH THE CIRCUIT TESTER IN ORDER TO BE ABLE TO NOTICE AN INTERESTING PROBLEM.

> CAN WE OPEN THE BOX TO CHECK?

> THERE'S A BATTERY INSIDE. C-F IS BRIGHTER THAN A-B.

A-B - YES
C-D - NO
C-F - BRIGHTER THAN A-B
E-F - NO

- What are some reasons for opening the box, or not opening the box?

- What would you do as a teacher?

Rather than allowing the children to open the box, she encourages them to gather more evidence to support their ideas about its contens.

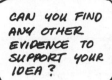

Teacher leaves

Upon returning she checks the children's progress . . .

Left to their own devices, the children review the evidence and discover further support for their idea.

*This method of challenging groups of learners to re-examine their solution in greater depth was first observed in Van Dyk Buchanan's math methods class at California State University, Northridge.

The teacher was aware of the parallel between this activity and scientists' work with theories. They are unable to open their "mystery boxes" to see if they are correct. They can never prove their theories to be right, they can only prove when they are wrong. The work of a scientist may be viewed as one of searching for other ways to test theories. For this reason the teacher never opened the mystery boxes — she only encouraged children to find other evidence for their theories.

During the next week the boxes were available for small group study. Some children began diagraming the position of the hidden battery. Some children constructed physical models of the mystery boxes that behaved in a similar way. Some children lost interest in the activity. Others wondered what other materials could be used to construct mystery circuits.

During the next two weeks, a variety of related activities took place at different times during the day. With the onset of Christmas, children's interests and experience led them to activities involving construction of parallel and series circuit connections, projects involving circuits; a lighting system for: a model house, games of hand steadiness, accuracy of toss, etc., taken from Batteries and Bulbs II[24], Mystery cards and boxes for other children to explore.

The teacher also provided other mystery boxes for those children who were interested. Again, they were reminded that they previously studied all the materials involved.

Another mystery box (provided by the teacher)

After some deliberation . . .

Some time later

The group was in an uproar. It had collected evidence that a bulb was inside. When a large number of batteries were connected in the circuit tester, the outside light suddenly went out. The children concluded that if the bulb on the outside didn't light then the circuit must be broken in the blown-out bulb inside the box.

The last question sent the children back to review their records and to check those of other children who had blown out the two different bulbs as well as those who combined two different bulbs in circuits. After additional investigation of related materials, they were able to arrive at a defensible conclusion.

In the process of conferring with other children the interest was contagious and the size of their group grew.

Varied interest in these activities may reflect varied levels of intellectual development. To explore this possibility further you might examine the intellectual demands of these tasks in relation to the range of intellectual capacities and constraints in a class of eleven- to twelve-year olds.

CONSUMER PRODUCT RESEARCH

AFTER VACATION

The teacher overheard some children complain of the quality of the gifts they had received at Christmas time. She noted a spontaneous interest in Consumer Product Research and organized a meeting to explore the interest further.

At the meeting she asked the children to repeat their concerns and encouraged others to share their experiences.

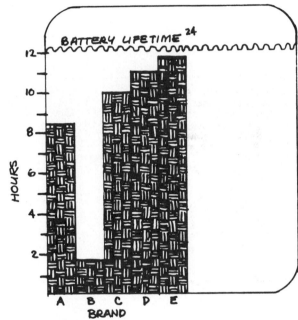

More than one group was organized to study each of the products. Although much of the initial planning was independent, the sharing and comparison of results and procedures at a later stage led to a revision of experiments and further investigation. Each group displayed its results and conclusions, as well as an advertisement for its top product. The latter task led to a study of the persuasion techniques employed in advertising.

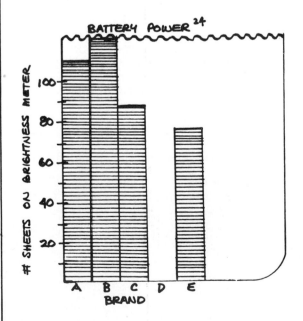

Battery lifetime was measured as the time that a battery will light a flashlight bulb.

Battery power was measured as the number of sheets of paper needed to block out the brightness of the bulb connected to that battery.

Although brand C was given a high overall rating, the group concluded that the best brand might depend on specific use of the battery in the buyer's mind.

The paper towel group tested properties of durability, absorption, and strength (wet and dry).

The pen group tested properties of period of continuous writing, leaking, and horizontal writing ease (writing on a wall).

Such activities with real-life problems provided interesting experiences in which children designed tests, isolated and controlled variables, interpreted data, and evaluated their procedures. These experiments brought some children closer to a formal understanding of controlled experimentation. Although these children may have difficulty in verbalizing a rule or systematically designing all aspects of an experiment by themselves, they were able to participate in the group investigations. Other children's awareness became more sophisticated as they discovered the need to repeat trials and consider the size of the sample tested.

Most children experienced difficulty in trying to respond to the ambiguity of "Which brand of _____ is the best buy?" The number of variables (including cost ratios — cents/hour of light) to be considered simultaneously proved to be mind-boggling for the children.

Putting It Together (Continued)

The Episode can be reread with a different focus each time. Your level of analysis will reflect your understanding of thinking, learning and teaching. The following questions on teaching and their effect on learning illustrated on the first two pages of the Episode may give you an idea of how much food for thought is available:

- Identify ways in which the teacher reduces competition through her introduction to the first activity.

- Contrast the outcomes of the teacher's directions for doing the prediction sheet activity to encouraging children to make all predictions prior to undertaking any test.

- Every class has an "expert" who can arrest the curiosity of his peers with his technical vocabulary. How do the teacher's directions (for constructing a rule) reduce the possibility of this happening and, therefore, facilitate a productive discussion among the children?

- In holding large-group discussions the teacher prefers to move from the materials to another area. Discuss the advantages and disadvantages of this approach.

Forward to Basics[1]
11

First Comes Thinking

Since the introduction of public schooling in America the design and administration of the schools have been based on an industrial model of efficiency reflected in an easily-identified product. The goal of the early schools was teaching the 3R's to a level needed by most industrial workers. Even some of the initiators of public education cautioned against the possibility of overeducation of industrial workers, leading to dissatisfaction with their condition.[2]

Piaget, in his travels and as director of the International Bureau of Education, opined that regardless of the political stance of the government (left- or right-wing), the leaders in education were inevitably conservative in their views on education.[3]

Consider the following questions in the context of the preceding information:

- If children learn according to the ways described by Piaget, they why don't our schools teach accordingly?
- Is our society prepared to nurture logical and critical thought
    in the classroom?
    outside the classroom?
- Who makes the educational decisions?

Educational Goals and the Changing World

Which Goals Are Basic to Survival?

Everyone agrees that children should learn what is basic to their survival, but not everyone agrees on what is basic. Many people are concerned that children, by the time they graduate, have sufficient literacy to read a bus timetable and enough math to make correct change or to balance a checkbook. Some of these people also are concerned with children's retention of basic American values such as honesty and good citizenship. In a climate of change, they are seeking the security of their traditions. Those people who are most concerned with passing on their culture, intact, form the backbone of the *back-to-basics movement*.

Piaget, on the other hand, speaks out for an education that is not only basic to the potential of all humans, but also ensures the quality of their survival:

> **The principal goal of education is to create men who are capable of doing new things, not simply repeating what other generations have done — men who are creative, inventive and discoverers.**[4,p.5]

Piaget's first goal for education is not to perpetuate the existing culture, but to change it. Since the world is already changing rapidly, why be interested in more change? The changes undertaken to date have been largely technological advances. These, however, have been accompanied by an unprecedented number of problems such as pollution, over-population, depletion of nonrenewable energy resources, increases in crime, drug addiction, and "news management." Each of these problems is immersed in a complex web of social, political, and economic forces that cross national boundary lines, and defy solution. In turn, these problems seem to be imbedded in other larger ones.

Piaget's goal for education is to create men and women of vision who can foresee problems and consider the long-term effects of their decisions, who are capable of considering abstractions and multiple variables at the same time that they exercise social responsibility in their decision-making. His goals focus on an alternative set of three *R*'s that are basic to the human potential and essential to the quality of our survival: *reason*, self and mutual *respect*, and self and social *responsibility*.[5]

The news media can replete with opposing views about such serious problems as air pollution and an energy crisis. The surprising thing is that much of the controversy is not over solutions to the problems, but whether they really exist. Expediency seems to color the views of many decision-makers in government and industry. One political leader attempts to make the nation aware of an energy crisis or a related pollution problem, while another states that it is a false issue. The latter politician points out the loss of jobs that would result if changes were undertaken to alleviate the "apparent" problem. While the federal government attempts to reduce air pollution and to alleviate the energy crisis, the vested interests of the American auto manufacturers buy the power of Madison Avenue to sell the public on the virtues of owning large cars. Furthermore, the American auto manufacturers postpone changes that would reduce air pollution, while foreign manufacturers demonstrate the ease of doing so. What standards can the public use to evaluate the statements made by politicians and manufacturers, and the claims of the advertising media?

Piaget's second goal for education speaks directly to the need for critical minds in the survival of a free society:

> **The second goal of education is to form minds that can be critical, can verify, and not accept everything they are offered. The great danger today is of slogans, collective opinions, ready-made trends of thought. We have to be able to resist individually, to criticize, to distinguish between what is proven and what is not. So we need pupils who are active, who learn early to find out by themselves, who learn early to tell what is verifiable and what is simply the first idea to come to them.[4,p.5]**

Attainment of that goal would equip individuals to make intelligent decisions as voters and consumers by providing them with a vision beyond day-to-day survival. Citizens would have personal standards for judging the truth of advertising claims and the claims of political leaders. Consumers and voters, operating from a critical framework, could detect those needs artificially created by big business and the advertising media, and resist such forms of manipulation. Furthermore, Piaget's goal is directed towards learning how to learn and continuing this development beyond the classroom, throughout life.

Which Three R's? — A Values Decision for Teachers and Parents

Both the behaviorist position and Piaget's constructivist-interactionist position can predict and explain certain kinds of learning. Experimental support exists for both positions. The choice of approaches for the classroom must, therefore, be a values decision, based on one's view of people in society and in the universe.[6] The person must decide what is basic — is he interested in skills based on the traditional three *R*'s and the retention

COMPARISON OF PIAGETIAN AND BEHAVIORIST POSITIONS[7]

	Behaviorist Position	Constructivist-interactionist
Goals	Pass on knowledge Emphasis on past/present Training for short-term objectives	Develop knowledge Emphasis on present/future Education for long-term goals
Learning	Knowledge is structured externally. Knowledge is a copy of Reality. Linear/cumulative Passive learner Lack of understanding due only to lack of relevant experiences Small steps—smooth ride on paved road Predictable behavior	Knowledge is structured internally. Knowledge is interpretation of reality. Nonlinear; restructuring necessary Active learner Lack of understanding is due to lack of relevant experiences within developmental constraints Varied steps—roller coaster ride Less predictable behavior
Intelligence	Fixed Collection of skills	Developing Organized, coherent, whole structure
Teaching	Can teach any subject effectively in some intellectually honest form to any child at any age of development by arranging for prerequisite experiences. Teaching by telling is an accepted method. Correct answers are reinforced; wrong answers are not accepted. Locus of evaluation is external—correct answer is only in teacher's head or in the textbook. Promotes extrinsic motivation. Stress memorization.	Basic notions are accessible to children 7–10 years of age, provided that they are divorced from their mathematical expression and studied through materials that a child can handle. Teaching by telling is deemphasized; emphasis is placed on experiences to give meaning to the words prior to their use. All responses are accepted and are related to the materials under study to extend understanding or to develop thinking process. Locus of evaluation is internal—feedback is available from materials and logical consistency. Promotes intrinsic motivation. Stresses development of understanding.
Curriculum	Rigid—structured by adults in a tight sequence that is logical to them. Requires knowledge of subject matter. Usually structured in small steps to encourage immediate success.	Flexible—structured by adults and/or children. When structured by adults it involves the juxtapositioning of children's incomplete thinking patterns. Requires much knowledge of child development, and knowledge of subject matter. Steps are of varied size to encourage involvement in the equilibration process.
Outcomes	Fosters child dependence. Ill-adapted to changing world	Fosters child independence. Well-adapted to changing world.

of traditional American values, or in the development of abilities and attitudes basic to the survival of a free society and the improvement of the quality of life? Each position not only represents a model for different kinds of thinking but also reflects a philosophical position. The following comparison of the two positions may help one decide.

In light of demands for the solution of numerous complex problems to ensure the quality of life and the survival of a free society, the behaviorist position appears ill-adapted for change. The tight, logical sequences with tiny learning steps that characterize the traditional behaviorist curricula find no parallel in the complex web of real-life problems. On the other hand, Piaget's theory supports an education that is well adapted to change. Since children grapple with substantial problems from an early age and actively construct and reconstruct their understandings, they would be capable of creative production and adaptation to change in later life. Similarly, the development of critical minds and ethical standards would support the re-examination of American values in relation to the quality of life. The behaviorist position can support teaching traditional American values as rules handed down from authority to be memorized and obeyed. In this sense, good citizenship is often confused with obedience. The limitations of such an approach to inculcating values are identified by Piaget:

> **Education founded on authority and only unilateral respect, has the same handicaps from the ethical standpoint as from the intellectual standpoint. Instead of leading the individual to work out the rules and the discipline that will obligate him or to work with others to alter them, it imposes a system of ready-made and immediately categorical imperatives on him . . . just as a pupil can recite his lessons without understanding them and can substitute verbalism for rational activity, so a child obeying is sometimes a spirit subjugated to an external conformism, but does not understand the real meaning or facts surrounding the rules he obeys, or the possibility of adapting them or making new ones in different circumstances.**[8,p.118-9]

Using Piaget's theory in the classroom is a forward step towards helping children attain the competence and critical and ethical attitudes of *reasoning, respect,* and *responsibility,* which are basic to human potential and adapted to the needs of achanging world. With this alternative interpretation of what is basic to survival, the way is not back, but *forward to basics!*

The Complexities of Changing the Schools

Where Do We Start?

The complexities of effecting changes in American public schools are comparable to those encountered with the ecological and social problems listed earlier. Change in today's schools is up against a tangled web of political, social, and economic forces that defies innovation. Despite the fact that the development of critical minds is our "single best hope of surviving as a free society,"[9] The task of implementing Piaget's theory in public schools must be approached with caution.

Do Parents Hinder or Help?

Many classrooms exist in which good teaching takes place in behaviorist terms with teachers who enjoy children and are dedicated to their work. Furthermore, all classrooms are not conducted from the extreme and simplified behaviorist position described earlier. In recent years there has been an increasing amount of provision for children's activity. From Piaget's framework, the best in behaviorist education is still limited. Yet, Piaget agrees that parents have the right to influence the kind of education given their children. Currently, many parents support a traditional kind of education with which they can identify readily.

Piaget himself identifies the role of parents as a major obstacle to the implementation of active methods. Their reasons for obstruction are their identification with traditional methods as opposed to experimental ones in which their children serve as "guinea pigs," and their obsession with the fear that their children will turn out "backward." Piaget writes,

> Now the multiple activities of manipulation and construction that are necessary to assure the practical substructure for the whole of later learning seem to parents like a luxury and a waste of time, simply delaying that solemn moment waited for by the entire tribe when the neophyte will know how to read and to count up to twenty! And so it goes with each new stage. . .[3,p.82]

Small groups of vocal parents pressure the schools to accelerate in children certain "prestigious" skills, which they can flaunt before their neighbors, enjoying a moment of superiority. The changes implemented in the schools are often the result of parental ego needs and have little to do with the children's best interests. In this regard, Piaget points out the need for parent education:

> They have the right to be, if not educated, at least informed and even instructed about better education that their children should receive.[3,p.83]

Parent education is basic to changing schools.

Do Any Innovations Survive the Filter of Resistance?

During the past 20 years there has been a flurry of activity in curriculum development. The federal government has contributed millions of dollars towards the development of innovative programs in science, mathematics, and the social sciences. Scientists, mathematicians, and other academic scholars were actively involved in this development and, more recently, were joined in their ventures by psychologists. Several programs developed for elementary school children, for example, Elementary Science Study (E.S.S.) and Science Curriculum Improvement Study (S.C.I.S.), are particularly child-centered and could fit within Piaget's framework. These programs emphasized involvement of children with materials and replaced textbooks with teacher's guides. Despite the quality of these programs, they have made few lasting inroads into the classroom. Typical of most innovations introduced into the public school system, these programs must be filtered through system constraints and often turn out to be unrecognizable to the developers even after teachers receive special training for their implementation. The constraints of the system allow few of the positive features of these programs to surface. Thus, despite the flurry of curriculum development that produced some high-quality programs, no major impact has resulted on the school curriculum and the act of teaching remains almost untouched in many classrooms.

Any serious application of Piaget's methods to all areas of the curriculum is likely to face the same vigorous resistance experienced by other worthwhile innovation. The full range of resistance which may be experienced is outlined by Peter Wolff.

> *A rigorously planned curriculum is well-entrenched by tradition and will not be easily dislodged by a flexible program that depends more on the teacher's imagination and good sense than the curriculum planner's schedule. The academic achievement tests inevitably loom as an annual threat over every teacher who wanders from the beaten path. Thirty-five bored, sedated, unruly, television-sated children are likely to rebel against any effort on the teacher's part to encourage spontaneous discovery. School principals who must account to their local PTA will not be delighted with new programs which cannot be "measured" objectively; and politically appointed school committees may view the education of children to ask good questions as a seditious act that threatens their vested interest.* [9,pp.13-14]

Although worthwhile innovations seldom survive the firmly entrenched system, and the act of teaching has changed little, the veneer of rhetoric has undergone considerable change, as each district claimed the latest innovations.

Are Good Intentions Enough?

The number of classrooms where good teaching takes place in behaviorist terms far exceeds the number of classrooms it takes place within Piaget's framework. Many teachers enter the classroom enthused about active methods, but prepared with only a minimal exposure to Piaget's theory. As a result, misapplications of his theory abound in classrooms, particularly when active methods are attempted within a system entrenched in behaviorism. Wolff offers a graphic description of how good intentions for using active methods can get engulfed by the system:

> *Once the curriculum prescribes what, when, how, and how quickly children should be taught, the opportunity to ask questions and to follow up is lost for the sake of technical efficiency and behavioral control . . . When the year's curriculum becomes so cluttered with behavioral objectives that there is no time to pursue interesting problems, school becomes a social arrangement by and for adults, in which the children have no stakes other than to fulfill behavioral objectives. To make this arrangement work, the teacher must motivate the child to learn by offering tokens of approval and assigning marks or grades since the intrinsic curiosity of children has been dissipated. Earning good grades becomes the end, and "learning" becomes the means. However, a system of grading can only be effective as a "secondary reinforcer" if some children get bad grades, so that others will work for better grades. Having lost the child's interest in knowing, the school must foster competition. This arrangement, no doubt, prepares children for life in a commercial society, but the preparation has little to do with knowing.* [9,p.19]

Despite the teacher's good intentions and the availability of thought-provoking materials, the level of inquiry will be stifled by the time-consuming demands to meet endless short-term objectives and by the pressures for approval within both the classroom and the system. The materials will be available for only one-exposure learning or for those occasions when all other "academic" requirements have been completed. In this way, the academically slower children may not gain access to the materials, even though they need them the most. The full potential of Piaget's methods can only be approached in classrooms without pressures of time and with constant restraints of praise and other forms of evaluation. Under the existing constraints, attempts to implement active methods too often become either superficial applications or total misapplications.

Who Makes the Classroom Decisions?

At the same time that children are restrained from freedom of thought, the teacher is restrained from academic freedom to explore methods of his choice in any depth. The teacher is required to make most of his classroom decisions based on external demands rather than on his academic background and the children's immediate needs. Many decisions are made externally by administrators, parents, legislators, textbook publishers, university professors, and school-board members. Often decisions are based on protection or promotion of vested interests. At the same time, many decision-makers who are truly interested in children are also steeped in behaviorist tradition which limits their view of children. Attempts to solve many of society's problems are transferred to the schools through new programs. Many such programs are supported with federal funds, which are provided only when specific guidelines are followed. Too often these funds are absorbed by an expanding network of administrative paper shuffling. What finally trickles down to the children in the classroom can have little positive effect in terms of the program goals. Involvement in the program, however, has left another of layer of external constraints on the kind of teaching that can take place in the classroom.

As stated aptly by David Elkind, "When the government or the society gets sick, children take the medicine."[10] He views the political exploitation of children as the most serious obstacle to establishing child-centered schools. Unfortunately, when the government or the society gets sick, teachers are required to administer the medicine. Such pressures stifle a teacher's academic freedom and creative intelligence.

How Capable Are Teachers of Making Decisions?

Piaget expresses concern whether teaching has reached the status of a profession. A medical doctor, considered a professional, makes autonomous decisions, consulting a wide range of techniques and procedures approved by a governing body of peers. With their

highly specialized training, doctors receive little input from the public on the appropriateness of their methods. On the other hand, the teacher's position is far from autonomous.
Since almost everyone has spent a number of years in a classroom, they hesitate little in
voicing opinions on teachers' methods. A general impression exists that all an elementary
school teacher needs is some elementary knowledge, which she then can transmit to children. Traditional behaviorist conceptions of the classroom have confined the teacher to a
transmitting role, according to Piaget:

> Those old educational conceptions, having made the
> teachers into mere transmitters of elementary or only slightly more than
> elementary general knowledge, without allowing them any opportunity for
> initiative and even less for research and discovery, have thereby imprisoned
> them in their lowly status.[3,p.124]

Although Piaget questions the status of teaching as a profession, he does not hold teachers
solely responsible for the problem. Since teachers' status is so low, many decisions about
the operation of the classroom are made by others without teachers' input.

Is There Any Parallel Between the Position of a Child-Oriented Teacher and Piaget's Position?

The position of a classroom teacher who attempts to work from Piaget's framework
within the constraints of a system steeped in behavioristic tradition resembles Piaget's
position among psychologists, the great majority of whom were educated in behaviorist
methods. The teacher is pressured to conform as his children are expected to perform
easily measured paper-and-pencil tasks as indicators of basic competence. Their visible
achievement is tied to the limitations of the test. The subtler long-range indicators of
children's learning are hidden by such measures. Piaget also was pressured to conform to
the behaviorist methods. The behaviorist psychologists viewed his clinical method from
their framework, and even tried to replicate his studies from this framework. Piaget was
criticized for his "nonconformist" clinical methods but has persevered for over 50 years.
On the other hand, many qualified teachers have been unable to resist the pressure and
have conformed to the system. Pressures from ambitious parents, a lack of understanding
and support from colleagues and administration, over-sized classes, and a lack of funds for
materials have contributed to this. Yet, a small number of teachers do operate within
Piaget's framework. This requires an unusual sensitivity to children, considerable courage,
and boundless energy. These teachers' commitment is nothing short of heroic since they
maintain their child-centered teaching style despite numerous imposing roadblocks within
the system.

A supporting community of teachers is basic to changing schools[1]

Why Does Piaget Consider Active Teaching So Difficult?

Piaget concludes that although his ideas are becoming more widely accepted, another major obstacle to widespread adoption of active methods in the classroom is their difficulty in comparison to traditional methods. The active methods not only require more intense involvement with individuals and small groups of children, but also on-the-spot curriculum decisions. Such methods cannot be readily packaged in a teacher's guide or kit. Piaget writes,

> In the first place they require a much more varied and much more concentrated kind of work from the teacher, whereas giving lessons is much less tiring and corresponds to a much more natural tendency in the adult, in general, and in the adult pedagogue, in particular.
>
> Secondly, and above all, an active pedagogy presupposes a much more advanced kind of training, and without adequate knowledge of child psychology the teacher cannot properly understand the students' spontaneous procedures, and therefore fails to take advantage of reactions that appear to him quite insignificant and a waste of time. The heartbreaking difficulty in pedagogy, as indeed in medicine and in many other branches of knowledge that partake at the same time of art and science, is in fact, that the best methods are also the most difficult ones . . .[3,p.69]

He urges that teachers be child development specialists and that active methods be employed in their training. Rather than having teachers listen to lectures on child development, he advocates at least one year of clinical experience with children. This would not only involve administering classical Piagetian tasks to individual children, but also original research projects on children's thinking. Whereas the beginnings of the classical tasks have become almost standardized, the original research would focus on developing an ability to phrase questions to contact the thinking of different children.[2] With this background in child development, teachers would be better prepared in areas of assessment, analysis of curricula, and classroom practice. Equally important, teachers, as child development specialists, would have an academic background that is not common knowledge in the public. Their ability to defend their methods against the traditional views of parents and administrators would be a step towards greater autonomy and thus raise their status as professionals.

Autonomous professionalism is basic to changing schools.

Do Universities Have a Responsibility for Ending the Cycle of Mindless Memorization?

The difficulty of teaching within Piaget's framework is that it requires not only a depth of understanding of child development, but also of subject matter and teaching methods. The education of teachers in science and mathematics must also be approached from Piaget's framework in order to be effective. Although many liberal arts and education majors function at a formal operational level in some areas, their thinking in science and mathematics is often concrete operational. It is difficult for scientists and mathematicians who function at a formal operational level in their subject areas to realize that they cannot directly transmit abstract lectures to the minds of their students and expect any true understanding. As a result of the inability of professors to adapt their methods to the thinking level of their students, many graduates participate in a mindless certification process, receiving degrees though intellectually deprived. Many of these graduates then become teachers despite serious emotional blocks and negative attitudes towards learning in the areas of science and mathematics. This problem is revealed when these teachers are exposed to thought-provoking materials and given an opportunity to construct their own knowledge. A surprising number seem paralyzed in their inability to ask questions that interest them and to investigate a possible answer.[11] Perhaps this should not be surprising, since their experiences for at least 16 years have convinced them that questions come from teachers and the answers are found in the teacher's lecture or neatly organized in a textbook.

How can this cycle be stopped? At each level, from kindergarten through university, teachers assume that if the student has come this far he should be able to do certain things. Too many people look to a scope-and-sequence chart (published or assumed), rather than to the student. Teaching below the "expected" level is considered degrading by many university professors and teachers at other levels. Thanks to the pioneering efforts by Robert Karplus[12] and Arnold Arons,[13] two university physics professors, a growing number of university professors are acknowledging the problem and beginning to adapt their methods to student needs.* Unfortunately, once that problem is recognized, there still a problem of time. University courses have a limited time period, yet active methods consume huge amounts of time. Furthermore, the many intelligent students who experience severe emotional blocks to learning require considerably more time than 15 weeks to relearn how to learn in the "real" sense. Provision for this time factor appears critical in

*Recent attempts to overcome math anxiety have involved teams of university math instructors and psychotherapists.

the education of teachers with positive attitudes in the areas of science and mathematics, lest they have a negative influence on the learning of their children in these areas.

Relearning how to learn by teachers is basic to changing schools.

How Many Children Are Too Many?

Another major obstacle to innovation is the unwieldy class size. The abilities of a professional teacher are greatly diluted in dealing with thirty-five children. However, classroom research shows little evidence that either the class achievement increases or that teachers do anything differently when class size is reduced. Change will only come if the

AN EXAMPLE OF INDIVIDUALIZED INSTRUCTION[14]

In Mr. Carson's fifth-grade classroom each child works at his own pace on materials prescribed for him using books, headphones, filmstrips, etc. This frees the teacher from presentation of subject matter and allows him time to interact with students as they work on content. He moves about the room examining the work of various children.

GOOD, BETH.

DONNA, THAT'S NOT WHAT YOU'RE SUPPOSED TO BE DOING. PAY ATTENTION TO THE DIRECTIONS.

A LITTLE LESS DREAMING, LARRY OR YOU'LL NEVER FINISH YOUR WORK.

LOOK HOW MESSY THAT WORK IS BILLY. I'M SURE YOU DON'T WANT YOUR WORK LOOKING LIKE THAT.

WHAT'S THE PROBLEM OVER HERE?

YES, I SEE THAT YOUR ANSWERS ARE WRONG, GLORIA. YOU NEED TO CHECK BACK TO SEE WHERE THE PROBLEM LIES. AS USUAL YOU GO TOO FAST.

Just as more time alloted for teacher help may not mean more helpful teachers, fewer children in a classroom may not be accompanied by improved teaching.[15,p.10]

teacher conceptualizes the learning and teaching acts differently.[15,16] Few universities help teacher to develop a conceptual framework for learning and teaching. Nor do they assist teachers in developing skills in working with individual children at a level that Piaget has demonstrated to be possible, or in developing human relations skills essential to creating a classroom atmosphere that facilitates higher levels of thinking.

A framework for conceptualizing the learning and teaching acts differently is basic to changing schools.

Needless to say, the skills involved in teaching successfully with Piaget's active methods are comparable in complexity to any other existing profession and require considerably more preparation than is presently available. Piaget points out that even an appreciable number of educational authorities and teachers themselves are not aware of the complexity of the teaching act.[3]

Which Comes First, Conclusive Evidence or a Fair Trial?

The true potential of Piaget's active methods has yet to be observed in public school classrooms. As a practical theory, it has face validity and a growing number of committed practitioners. Most of the supporting research has been conducted outside the classroom in interviews with individual children. Supporting classroom research is scattered, but growing in quantity. Although a conclusive body of supportive classroom research is lacking, the structure of the public school system does not allow a fair trial of these methods.

The goals of Piaget's active methods are long-term and involve behavioral changes that, at present, cannot be measured by traditional evaluative instruments. Any attempt to organize an evaluation research study, therefore, must encompass several years and a variety of evaluation techniques. In addressing the problem of evaluating active methods in science, Phillip Morrison writes,

> It may be that a series of in-depth interviews by scientifically trained questioners, with psychiatric consultation, might provide the information we need. I can imagine a random set of children chosen from populations exposed to a sample of this curriculum and to any other, the children followed through the years of school, with judgments given on the knowledge and the attitudes they tend to show in science and elsewhere as the years go by. The tests and interviews would likely require the active use of apparatus, of words, games, drawing, computing, and so on. [17,p.68]

Such long-term studies are critical for evaluating the long-term goals of Piaget's methods. As Morrison states, "We want the child to change not for the examination week but for life."

A broader framework for evaluating innovations is a basic for changing schools.

Need for Change vs. Cost of Change — A Matter of Priorities.

Organizational change involves high costs, since a number of current costs for remediation of educational malpractice are misplaced. The unprecedented number of "academic failures" in today's schools are reflected in serious discipline problems, school vandalism, and violence. Many social problems in society have roots in the classroom. Considering the cost of educational malpractice in terms of ensuing social problems such as drug addiction, jail custody, welfare for unemployable dropouts, and other self-alienated people in the existing system, it behooves the public to seriously consider an alternative system of schools. Despite the dire need for child-centered schools, the complexities of achieving change suggest that nothing short of raising the national consciousness could initiate any widespread application of Piaget's active methods. Since the condition of today's schools reflects the values of society, the concern for quality of life and thinking must extend beyond the classroom before any major changes can be initiated.

A re-examination of societal priorities is a basic for changing schools.

A Recap of Basics

This chapter began by identifying Piaget's basic goals for education: *reasoning, respect, responsibility,* and *learning how to learn* as alternatives to the traditional three R's. Although it has since focused on the complexities of changing schools in terms of Piaget's basic goals of education, it has also identified some criteria that are basic to initiating any major change in public schools:

- Society needs to re-examine its priorities.
- Parents should be schooled in alternative approaches to education.
- Teachers in training need to relearn how to learn, and to develop a framework for conceptualizing the learning and teaching acts differently.
- A supporting community of teachers is needed who are committed to change and to developing professional autonomy in making educational decisions.
- In educational research, a broader framework should be developed from which to evaluate innovation.

An Alternative Proposal

Only a concerted effort on all fronts can support a quality education in Piaget's terms. Since the existing structure of public schools is so resistant to change, new and autonomous organizational patterns must be developed which are conducive to innovation and which offer parents viable alternatives in the education of their children.

Although part of a larger school system, these alternative schools would be autonomous in their operation. They would have autonomy in fiscal matters; in staffing; in establishing class size; in setting their own goals and curricula; from external achievement tests; of location separate from regular schools.

Autonomy in fiscal matters and curriculum selection would facilitate the introduction of a variety of thought-provoking materials into the classrooms. Similarly, it would influence the class size, which could be reduced to 12 to 15 children. Autonomy in staffing would allow for careful screening of administrators and teachers, who would be required to be child development specialists. The teachers would have the freedom to set their goals based on the children's needs and interests, and to select and develop the curriculum with input from children and parents. Textbooks would be used selectively, not to establish the content of a curriculum. Rather than dominate the curriculum, behaviorist methods might be selectively applied in the service of active methods.* Parent education and participation in volunteer work in and out of the classrooms would be critical to parents' understanding of the essence of the active-methods learning process, and of the school's operation. Autonomy from external standardized achievement tests would permit a focus on a variety of evaluative methods as a natural part of the day-to-day teaching-learning process. Lastly, the size of each school would be kept below 250 children to encourage the feeling of an intimate community rather than an impersonal institution.

What to Do Until The Revolution Comes

Changing the public school system is a very complex and gradual process and many teachers have conformed to the system in their frustration. Here are some ideas of what can be done until the revolution comes.

Be selective about the courses and workshops you take.

- Find a child development course based on working with individual children rather than on just listening to lectures.

    Children have a lot to teach us.

- Find math and science (content and method) courses that let you relearn how to learn by exploring materials.

    You'll only be able to allow children freedom to explore materials to the extent that you feel free.

Share your interest.

- Find a colleague who shares your interest in children's thinking. Try some of the ideas in this book with children and compare your experiences to Piaget's theory.

    Piaget's framework can give you a basis for expanding what you already know intuitively.

- Organize a study-and-support group for implementing Piaget's active methods in your classroom, school or district.

    Social interaction is an effective way of expanding your understanding and group support is essential for withstanding external pressures to conform to traditional methods.

---

*See Mary Baratta-Lorton's place value sequence in Chapter 9 for an example of an effective combination of behaviorist and active methods.

- Share this book with a parent, an administrator, or colleague. Take time to talk about it.

    Piaget's framework can give you a basis for communicating ideas that you already have about materials and children.

Volunteer your time.

- Work on textbook evaluation committees and vote against the use of textbooks that lack awareness of children's needs. Investigate the possibilities of using materials in their place.

    Some states have expanded the options for adoption to include kits of materials as well as textbooks.

- Organize parent workshops so they can investigate materials. Alert parents to the level of thinking involved in their "play."

    Parents can be convinced if they find these activities not only to be fun but also challenging their thinking.

In many ways, initiating change is a do-it-yourself job.

Your education as a teacher does not end with a certain sequence of courses. It will continue as long as you interact with children and are challenged by searching beyond their apparent understanding to make contact with their thinking. Still, much is not known but Piaget has provided you with a framework for making further discoveries. On many occasions you will reflect on a child's way of *learning* and your method of *teaching*. You may want to discuss this with your colleagues, or refer back to Piaget's writings before returning to the child with new insights. Much *thinking* is involved in *teaching* and, in turn, it provides you with many opportunities for *learning* in this spiral of mutually supporting processes.

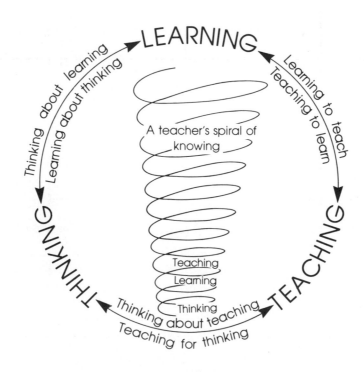

Putting It All Together

Reflect on any of your conceptions of thinking, learning, and teaching which may have changed as a result of interacting with children and with the ideas in this book. Now, consider your teaching in terms of what you want to change, what you want it to be and what you are going to do to make that change. The following table may help you to organize your thoughts and make some important decisions.[14] You may decide that the result is worth the risk. Changing your teaching or changing the schools, like learning, are do-it-yourself jobs.

WHAT I WANT TO CHANGE	WHAT I WANT IT TO BE	HOW TO GET THERE	RISKS/ RESISTANCE/ CATASTROPHIC EXPECTATIONS
EXAMPLE: I teach only with textbooks, workbooks, and AV aids.	I want to provide children with opportunities to interact with thought-provoking materials.	1. Take an E.S.S. workshop where I'll have a chance to explore materials myself. 2. Get moral support from other teachers in workshop.	1. My principal might complain about my noisy classroom. 2. Parents might complain about the children's "play."

References
and
Bibliography

Chapter 1

1. Hermine Sinclair, "Recent Piagetian Research in Learning Studies," in M. Schwebel and J. Raph (eds.), *Piaget in the Classroom* New York: Basic Books, 1973, pp. 57–72.

2. Marilyn Appel et al., *Science Teaching and the Development of Reasoning*, Part I, Berkeley; AESOP, University of California, 1976.

Chapter 2

1. David Elkind, *Child Development and Education: A Piagetian Perspective*. New York: Oxford University Press, 1976.

2. George Hein, "Piaget, Materials and the Open Classroom," *EDC News*, Winter, 1973, pp. 7–10.

3. Evelyn Sharp, *Thinking is Child's Play*, New York: Dutton, 1969.

4. Herbert Ginsburg and Sylvia Opper, *Piaget's Theory of Intellectual Development: An Introduction,* Englewood Cliffs: Prentice-Hall, 1979.

5. Barbel Inhelder, "Memory and Intelligence in the Child," in D. Elkind and J. Flavell (eds.), *Studies in Cognitive Development: Essays in Honor of Jean Piaget,* New York: Oxford University Press, 1979, pp. 337–64.

6. Edward Palmer, "Accelerating the Child's Cognitive Attainments Through the Inducement of Cognitive Conflict: An Interpretation of Piaget's Position," *Journal of Research in Science Teaching,* vol 3, pp. 318–25, 1965.

7. Barry Wadsworth, *Piaget's Theory of Cognitive Development,* New York: McKay, 1971.

8. Edward de Bono, *Lateral Thinking: Creativity Step by Step,* New York: Harper & Row, 1970, pp. 32–35.

9. Richard Gorman, *Discovering Piaget: A Guide for Teachers,* Columbus: Merrill, 1972.

10. Milton Schwebel and Jane Raph, *Piaget in the Classroom,* New York: Basic Books, 1973.

11. John Flavell, *The Developmental Psychology of Jean Piaget,* Princeton: Van Nostrand, 1963.

12. John Phillips, *The Origins of Intellect: Piaget's Theory,* San Francisco: W. H. Freeman, 1975.

13. Jeanette Gallagher and Kim Reid, "The Revised Model of Equilibration and the Concept of Phenocopy," a paper presented to the Jean Piaget Society, Philadelphia, May, 1977.

14. D. Price-Williams et al., "Skill and Conservation: A Study of Pottery-Making Children," *Developmental Psychology,* vol. 1, no. 6, 1969, p. 769.

15. Jean Piaget, "Development and Learning," in R. Ripple and V. Rockcastle (eds.) *Piaget Rediscovered,* Ithaca: Cornell University, 1964, pp. 7–20.

16. H. Shaw, "Mirror Topic," London: Invicta Plastics.

17. Marilyn Appel et al., *Science Teaching and the Development of Reasoning,* Part 2, Berkeley: AESOP, University of California, 1976.

Chapter 3

1. Hermine Sinclair, "Recent Piagetian Research in Learning Studies," in M. Schwebel and J. Raph (eds.) *Piaget in the Classroom,* New York: Basic Books, 1973, pp. 57–72.

2. Barbel Inhelder, Hermine Sinclair, and Magali Bovet, *Learning and the Development of Cognition,* Cambridge: Harvard University Press, 1974.

3. Constance Kamii, "Piaget's Interactionism and the Process of Teaching Young Children," in M. Schwebel and J. Raph (eds.) *Piaget in the Classroom,* New York: Basic Books, 1973, pp. 216–30.

Chapter 4

1. Jean Piaget, *The Origins of Intelligence in Children,* International University Press, 1952.

2. Ina Uzgiris, and J. McVicker Hunt, *Ordinal Scales of Development,* Urbana: University of Illinois Press, 1975.

3. Robert McColl, Dorothy Eichorn, and Pamela Hogarty, "Transitions in Early Mental Development," *Monographs of the Society for Research in Child Development,* vol. 43, no. 3, Serial No. 171, 1977.

4. Jean Piaget and Barbel Inhelder, *The Psychology of the Child,* New York: Basic Books, 1969.

5. Herbert Ginsburg and Sylvia Opper, *Piaget's Theory of Intellectual Development: An Introduction,* Englewood Cliffs: Prentice-Hall, 1969.

6. Jean Piaget, *Play, Dreams and Imitation in Childhood,* New York: Norton, 1962.

7. Mary Ann Spencer Pulaski, *Understanding Piaget: An Introduction to Children's Cognitive Development,* New York: Harper & Row, 1971.

8. Jean Piaget, *The Child and Reality: Problems of Genetic Psychology,* New York: Grossman, 1972.

9. John L. Phillips, *The Origins of Intellect: Piaget's Theory,* San Francisco: W. H. Freeman, 1975.

10. Elementary Science Study, *Kitchen Physics,* New York: McGraw-Hill, Webster Division, 1967. (Developed by Education Development Center, Inc.)

11. Jean Piaget, *The Child's Conception of Number,* New Jersey, Humanities Press, 1964.

12. Barbel Inhelder and Jean Pieget, *The Growth of Logical Thinking: From Childhood to Adolescence,* translated by Anne Parsons and Stanley Milgrave, New York: Basic Books, 1958. (Based on Chapters 3, 4, 7 and 11.)

13. Jean Piaget, *Judgment and Reasoning in the Child,* Totowa, N.J.: Littlefield, Adams and Company, 1960 (reprint of 1928 edition).

14. Lawrence Lowery, *Learning About Learning: Classification Abilities,* Berkeley: University of California, 1974.

15. Jean Piaget, *Six Psychological Studies,* New York: Random House, 1967.

16. Richard Copeland, *How Children Learn Mathematics: Teaching Implications of Piaget's Research,* New York: Macmillan, 1970.

17. Jean Piaget, *The Child's Conception of Physical Causality,* Totowa, N. J.: Littlefield, Adams and Company, 1960 (reprint of 1930 edition).

18. Henry Maier, *Three Theories of Child Development,* New York: Harper & Row, 1965.

19. Jean Piaget and R. Garcia, *Understanding Causality,* New York: Norton, 1974.

20. Jean Piaget and Barbel Inhelder, *The Growth of Logical Thinking: From Childhood to Adolescence,* New York: Basic Books, 1958.

21. Mary Sime, *A Child's Eye View,* New York: Harper & Row, 1973.

22. Richard Gorman, *Discovering Piaget: A Guide for Teachers,* Columbus: Merrill, 1972.

23. Len Ennever and Wynne Harlen, *With Objectives in Mind: Guide to Science 5–13,* London: Macdonald Educational, 1972.

24. Jean Piaget, "Intellectual Evolution from Adolescence to Adulthood," *Human Development,* January, 1972, pp. 1–12.

25. Lawrence Kohlberg and Rochelle Mayer, "Development as the Aim of Education," *Harvard Educational Review*, November, 1972, pp. 449–453.

26. Anton Lawson and Warren Wollman, "Encouraging the Transition from Concrete to Formal Cognitive Functioning—An Experiment", *Journal of Research in Science Teaching,* September 1976, pp. 413–430.

27. For a theoretical discussion of stage models, see John Flavell, "Stage-related Properties of Cognitive Development," *Cognitive Psychology,* 1971, *2*, 421–453.

28. Jean Piaget and Eleanor Duckworth, "Piaget Takes a Teacher's Look," *Learning,* October, 1973, pp. 22–27.

29. Lawrence Lowery, *Learning About Learning: Conservation Abilities,* Berkeley: University of California, 1974.

Chapter 5

1. Jean Piaget and Barbel Inhelder, *The Psychology of the Child,* New York: Basic Books, 1969.

2. Evelyn Sharp, *Thinking is Child's Play,* New York: Dutton, 1969.

3. Glenadine Gibb and Alberta Castenada, "Experiences for Young Children," in Joseph Payne (ed.), *Mathematics Learning in Early Childhood,* Washington: National Council of Teachers of Mathematics, 1975.

4. Hermine Sinclair, "Some Remarks on the Genevan Point of View on Learning With Special Reference to Language," in R. Hinde and J. Stephenson (eds.), *Constraints on Learning: Limitations and Predispositions,* New York: Academic Press, 1973, pp. 397–413.

5. Constance Kamii and Rheta DeVries, *Piaget, Children and Number,* Washington: National Association for Education of Young Children, 1976.

6. Jean Piaget, *The Child's Conception of Number,* New York: Norton, 1965.

7. Richard Copeland, *How Children Learn Mathematics,* New York: Macmillan, 1969.

8. Mary Baratta-Lorton, *Mathematics: Their Way,* Menlo Park: Addison-Wesley, 1976.

9. H. Van Engen and L. P. Steffe, *First Grade Children's Concept of Addition of Natural Numbers,* Madison: University of Wisconsin, Research & Development Center for Learning and Re-Education, 1964.

10. Jean Piaget, "Development and Learning," in R. Ripple and V. Rockcastle (eds.), *Piaget Rediscovered,* Ithaca: Cornell University, 1964, pp. 7–19.

11. Jean Piaget, *To Understand Is to Invent,* New York: Viking, 1973.

12. Jean Piaget, *Genetic Epistemology,* New York: Columbia University Press, 1970.

Chapter 6

1. Hermine Sinclair, "Epistemology and the Study of Language," in B. Inhelder and H. Chipman (eds.), *Piaget and His School: A Reader in Developmental Psychology,* New York: Springer-Verlag, 1976, pp. 205–18.

2. Irving Sigel and Rodney Cocking, *Cognitive Development from Childhood to Adolescence: A Constructivist Perspective,* New York: Holt, Rinehart & Winston, 1977.

3. Jean Piaget and Barbel Inhelder, *The Psychology of the Child,* New York, Basic Books, 1969.

4. Jean Piaget, *Plays, Dreams and Imitation in Childhood,* New York: Norton, 1962.

5. Hanne Sonquist, and Constance Kamii, "Applying Some Piagetian Concepts in the Classroom for the Disadvantaged," in J. Frost (ed.), *Early Childhood Education Rediscovered,* New York: Holt, Rinehart & Winston, 1968, p. 171.

6. David Elkind, "We Can Teach Reading Better," *Today's Education,* November–December 1975, pp. 33–38.

7. Jean Piaget, *The Child and Reality: Problems of Genetic Psychology,* New York: Viking Press, 1974.

8. Hermine Sinclair, "Developmental Psycholinguistics," in B. Inhelder and H. Chipman (eds.), *Piaget and His School: A Reader in Developmental Psychology*, New York: Springer-Verlag, 1976, pp. 189–204.

9. Irving Sigel, "The Piagetian System and the World of Education," in David Elkind and Jim Flavell (eds.), *Studies in Cognitive Development: Essays in Honor of Jean Piaget*, New York: Oxford University Press, 1969, pp. 465–89.

10. Jean Piaget, *Six Psychological Studies*, New York: Random House, 1967.

11. Hans Furth, *Piaget for Teachers*, Englewood Cliffs: Prentice-Hall, 1970.

12. Eleanor Duckworth, "Language and Thought," in M. Schwebel and J. Raph (eds.), *Piaget in the Classroom*, New York: Basic Books, 1973, pp. 132–54.

13. Hermine Sinclair, "Piaget's Theory and Language Acquisition," in M. Rosskopf et al. (eds.), *Piagetian Cognitive-Development Research*, Washington: National Council of Teachers of Mathematics, 1971, pp. 149–59.

14. Jean Piaget, *Science of Education and the Psychology of the Child*, New York: Viking Press, 1972.

15. Eleanor Duckworth, "Piaget Rediscovered," in R. Ripple and V. Rockcastle (eds.), *Piaget Rediscovered*, Ithaca: Cornell University, 1964. pp. 1–5.

Chapter 7

1. Barbel Inhelder, Hermine Sinclair, and Magali Bovet, *Learning and the Development of Cognition*, Cambridge: Harvard University Press, 1974.

2. Barbel Inhelder, "Information Processing Tendencies in Recent Experiments in Cognitive Learning-Empirical Studies," in S. Farnhan-Diggory (ed.), New York: Academic Press: 1973.

3. Barbel Inhelder and Hermine Sinclair, "Learning Cognitive Structures," in P. Mussen, J. Langer, and M. Covington (eds.) *Trends and Issues in Developmental Psychology*, New York: Holt, Rinehart & Winston, 1969, pp. 2–21.

4. Hermine Sinclair and Constance Kamii, "Some Implications of Piaget's Theory for Teaching Young Children," *School Review*, February 1970, pp. 169–83.

5. Hermine Sinclair, "Number and Measurement," in M. Rosskopf, L. Steffe, and S. Taback (eds.), *Piagetian Cognitive-Developmental Research and Mathematical Education*, Washington: National Council of Teachers of Mathematics, 1971, pp. 149–59.

6. Hermine Sinclair, "Recent Research in Piagetian Learning Studies," in M. Schwebel and J. Raph (eds.), *Piaget in the Classroom*, New York: Basic Books, 1973, pp. 57–73.

7. Hermine Sinclair, "Some Remarks on the Genevan Point of View on Learning With Special Reference to Language Learning," in R. Hinde and J. Stephenson-Hinde (eds.), *Constraints on Learning: Limitations and Predispositions*, New York: Academic Press, 1973, pp. 57–73.

8. Leon Ukens, "How Would You Respond?" *Science and Children*, March 1974, pp. 27–28.

9. Jean Piaget, Barbel Inhelder and Alina Szeminska, *The Child's Concept of Geometry*, New York: Harper and Row, 1964.

Chapter 8

1. John Phillips, *The Origins of Intellect: Piaget's Theory,* San Francisco: W. H. Freeman, 1975.

2. Irving Sigel and Rodney Cocking, *Cognitive Development from Childhood to Adolescence: A Constructivist Perspective,* New York: Holt, Rinehart & Winston, 1977.

3. Bob Samples, Cheryl Charles, and Dick Barnhart, *The Wholeschool Book,* Reading: Addison-Wesley, 1977.

4. Herbert Ginsburg and Sylvia Opper, *Piaget's Theory of Intellectual Development: An Introduction,* Englewood Cliffs: Prentice-Hall, 1969.

5. Jean Piaget, *The Child's Conception of Number,* New York: Norton, 1965.

6. Eleanor Duckworth, "Language and Thought," in M. Schwebel and J. Raph (eds.), *Piaget in the Classroom,* New York: Basic Books, 1973, pp. 132–54.

7. Jean Piaget, "Development and Learning," in R. Ripple and V. Rockcastle (eds.), *Piaget Rediscovered,* Ithaca: Cornell University, 1964, pp. 7–20.

8. Jean Piaget and Barbel Inhelder, "The Gaps in Empiricism," in B. Inhelder and H. Chipman (eds.), *Piaget and His School: A Reader in Developmental Psychology,* New York: Springer-Verlag, 1976, pp. 24–35.

9. Constance Kamii and Rheta DeVries, "Piaget for Early Education" in M. C. Day and R. K. Parker (eds.), *The Preschool in Action: Exploring Early Childhood Programs,* Boston: Allyn & Bacon, 1977, pp. 365–420.

10. Robert Gagné, "Contributions of Learning to Human Development," A paper presented at the meeting of the American Association for the Advancement of Science, December 1966, 30 pp.

11. Siegfried Engelmann, "Does the Piagetian Approach Imply Instruction?" in Donald Green, et al. (eds.), *Measurement and Piaget,* New York: McGraw-Hill, 1971.

12. Barbel Inhelder, Hermine Sinclair, and Magali Bovet, *Learning and the Development of Cognition,* Cambridge: Harvard University Press, 1974.

13. Barry Wadsworth, *Piaget's Theory of Cognitive Development,* New York: McKay, 1971.

14. Jean Piaget, *The Science of Education and the Psychology of the Child,* New York: Viking, 1971.

15. Hermine Sinclair, "Recent Developments in Genetic Epistemology," The *Genetic Epistemologist,* July 1977, p. 1.

16. Jean Piaget, "Biology and Cognition," in B. Inhelder and H. Chipman (eds.), *Piaget and His School: A Reader in Developmental Psychology,* New York: Springer-Verlag, 1976, pp. 45–62.

17. A title used by Peter Wolff in an address given to the Piaget Conference on Piagetian Theory for the Helping Professions, Los Angeles, 1974.

18. Elizabeth Hall, "A Conversation with Jean Piaget and Barbel Inhelder," *Psychology Today,* May 1970, pp. 25–28.

19. Marianne Denis-Pinzhorn, Constance Kamii, and Pierre Monoud, "Pedagogical Applications of Piaget's Theory," an unpublished paper.

Chapter 9

1. Elementary Science Study, "How Do They Think?" *E.S.S. Newsletter,* Newton, Mass.: Education Development Center, March 1968.

2. David Elkind, *Child Development and Education.* New York: Oxford University Press, 1976.

3. Jean Piaget and Eleanor Duckworth, "Piaget Takes a Teacher's Look," *Learning,* October 1973, pp. 22–27.

4. Robert Wirtz, *CDA Math, Drill and Practice at the Problem Solving Level: An Alternative,* Washington, D.C.: Curriculum Development Associates, 1974.

5. Jean Piaget, *To Understand Is to Invent: The Future of Education,* New York: Grossman, 1973.

6. Irving Sigel and Rodney Cocking, *Cognitive Development from Childhood to Adolescence: A Constructivist Perspective,* New York: Holt, Rinehart & Winston, 1977.

7. Jean Piaget and Barbel Inhelder, *The Psychology of the Child,* New York: Basic Books, 1969.

8. Mary Sime, *A Child's Eye View,* New York: Harper and Row, 1973.

9. Mary Baratta-Lorton, *Mathematics Their Way,* Menlo Park: Addison-Wesley, 1976.

10. Constance Kamii and Rheta DeVries, "Piaget for Early Education," in M. Parker and R. Parker (eds.), *The Preschool in Action: Exploring Early Childhood Programs,* Boston: Allyn & Bacon, 1977, pp. 365–420.

11. George Hein, "Piaget, Materials and the Open Classroom," *EDC News,* Newton, Mass.: Education Development Center, Winter 1973, pp. 7–10.

12. Elementary Science Study, *Sand,* New York: McGraw-Hill, Webster Division, 1970.

13. George Forman, and David Kuschner, *The Child's Construction of Knowledge: Piaget for Teaching Children,* Monterey: Brooks/Cole, 1977.

14. Science Curriculum Improvement Study, *Interaction and Systems,* Chicago: Rand McNally, 1970.

15. Science Curriculum Improvement Study, *Relativity,* Chicago: Rand McNally, 1968.

16. Roach Van Allen, "A Language Experience Approach to Reading," in M. Douglas (ed.), *Claremont Reading Conference Twenty-fifth Yearbook,* Claremont: Claremont University College, 1961, pp. 59–72.

17. Kenneth Goodman, *Reading: A Conversation with Kenneth Goodman,* Evanston: Scott Foresman, 1976.

18. Jean Piaget, "Comments on Mathematical Education," in H. Gruber and J. Voneche (eds.), *The Essential Piaget: An Interpretive Reference and Guide,* New York: Basic Books, 1977, pp. 726–32.

19. Mary Baratta-Lorton. *Workjobs II, Number Activities for Early Childhood,* Menlo Park: Addison-Wesley, 1978.

20. Jean Piaget, *Six Psychological Studies,* New York: Random House, 1967.

21. Eleanor, Duckworth, "Piaget Rediscovered," in R. Ripple and V. Rockcastle (eds.), *Piaget Rediscovered,* Ithaca: Cornell University, 1964, pp. 1–5.

22. Mary Baratta-Lorton, *Mathematics Their Way Newsletter,* Issue No. 4, Saratoga, California: Center for Innovation in Education, 1977.

23. Jean Piaget, "Development and Learning," in R. Ripple and V. Rockcastle (eds.), *Piaget Rediscovered,* Ithaca: Cornell University, 1964, pp. 7–20.

24. Jean Piaget, *The Science of Education and the Psychology of the Child,* New York: Viking, 1971.

25. Randall Souviney, "A New Commitment to Developmental Learning," *Learning,* March 1975, pp. 36–40.

26. Jean Piaget, *The Child and Reality,* New York: Grossman, 1973, p. 30.

27. Carolyn Aho, Carne Barnett, Wallace Judd, and Sharon Young, *Measure Matters,* Palo Alto: Creative Publications, 1976.

28. Nuffield Mathematics Program, *Green Problems,* New York: Wiley and Sons, 1967.

29. Anton Lawson and Warren Wallman, "Encouraging Transition from Concrete to Formal Operational Functioning—An Experiment," *Journal of Research in Science Teaching,* September 1976, pp. 413–30.

30. Verne Rockcastle, "Curriculum in the Open Classroom: Structure or Stricture?" *Science and Children,* September 1974, pp. 9–13.

31. Lawrence Lowery, *A Sourcebook for Everyday Science,* Boston: Allyn & Bacon, 1978.

32. Elementary Science Study, *Kitchen Physics,* New York: McGraw-Hill, Webster Division, 1967.

33. Ronald Good, *How Children Learn Science: Conceptual Development and Implications for Teaching,* New York: Macmillan, 1977.

34. David Welton and John Mallan, *Children and Their World: Teaching Elementary Social Studies,* Chicago: Rand McNally, 1976.

35. Elementary Science Study, *Teacher's Guide to Mapping,* New York: McGraw-Hill, Webster Division, 1971.

36. Victor Perkes, "The Tyranny of Words—Nonsense, Pseudo-explanations, and the Stifling of Curiosity," *Science and Children,* September 1971, pp. 17–18.

37. Elizabeth Hall, "A Conversation with Jean Piaget and Barbel Inhelder," *Psychology Today,* May 1970, pp. 25–32.

38. Irving Sigel, "The Piagetian System and the World of Education," in D. Elkind and J. Flavell (eds.), *Studies in Cognitive Development: Essays in Honor of Jean Piaget,* New York: Oxford University Press, 1969, pp. 465–89.

39. Evelyn Nuefeld, A presentation made at a Piaget conference held at Stanford University, August, 1977.

40. Illa Podendorf, "Alternatives in Reading," *Science and Children,* April 1973, pp. 14–16.

41. Arnold Arons, "Cultivating the Capacity for Formal Reasoning: Objectives and Procedures in an Introductory Physical Science Course," *American Journal of Physics,* September 1976, pp. 834–38.

42. Elementary Science Study, *Mystery Powders,* New York: McGraw-Hill, Webster Division, 1967.

43. Observed at a presentation by Mary Budd Rowe at the National Science Teachers Association conference held in Chicago, March 1974.

44. Mary Budd Rowe, "Help is Denied to Those in Need," *Science Teacher,* March 1975.

45. Jerome Bruner, *The Process of Education,* New York: Vintage Books, 1960.

Chapter 10

1. Eleanor Duckworth, "Piaget Rediscovered," in R. Ripple and V. Rockcastle (eds.), *Piaget Rediscovered,* Ithaca: Cornell University, 1964, pp. 1–5.

2. Jean Piaget and Eleanor Duckworth, "Piaget Takes a Teacher's Look," *Learning,* October 1973, pp. 22–27.

3. David Wickens, "Piagetian Theory as a Model For Open Systems of Education," in M. Schwebel and R. Raph (eds.), *Piaget in the Classroom,* New York: Basic Books, 1973, pp. 179–98.

4. Elementary Science Study, *Sink or Float*, New York: McGraw-Hill, Webster Division, 1970.

5. Mary Budd Rowe, *Teaching Science as Continuous Inquiry,* New York: McGraw-Hill, 1973.

6. Elementary Science Study, *A Materials Book for the Elementary Science Study,* Newton, Mass.: Education Development Center, 1972.

7. P. Richmond, *An Introduction to Piaget,* New York: Basic Books, 1971.

8. Brenda Lansdown, Paul Blackwood, and Paul Brandwein, *Teaching Elementary Science Through Investigation and Colloquim*, New York: Harcourt Brace Jovanovich, 1971.

9. Lazer Goldberg, *Children and Science,* New York: Scribner's, 1970.

10. Jean Piaget, *To Understand Is to Invent: The Future of Education,* New York: Grossman, 1973.

11. Constance Kamii and Rheta DeVries, "Piaget for Early Education," in M. C. Day and R. K. Parker (eds.), *The Preschool in Action: Exploring Early Childhood Programs,* Boston: Allyn & Bacon, 1977, pp. 365–420.

12. Thomas Gordon, *Teacher Effectiveness Training,* New York: Wyden, 1974.

13. Elizabeth Hall, "A Conversation with Jean Piaget and Barbel Inhelder," *Psychology Today,* May 1970, pp. 25–52.

14. Eleanor Duckworth, "The Having of Wonderful Ideas," in M. Schwebel and R. Raph (eds.), *Piaget in the Classroom,* New York: Basic Books, 1973, pp. 258–77.

15. T. C. Campbell and R. G. Fuller, "A Teacher's Guide to the Learning Cycle, A Piagetian Approach to College Instruction," in *Multidisciplinary Piagetian-based Programs for College Freshmen,* Lincoln: ADAPT Project, University of Nebraska, 1977, pp. 7–26.

16. Lawrence Lowery, *Learning about Instruction: Questioning Strategies,* Berkeley: University of California, 1975.

17. Peter Wolff, "What Piaget Did Not Intend." in G. Lubin (ed.), *Fourth Annual Piagetian Conference Proceedings,* Los Angeles: University of Southern California, 1974, pp. 3–14.

18. Richard Sprinthall and Norman Sprinthall, *Educational Psychology: A Developmental Approach,* Reading: Addison-Wesley, 1974.

19. Charles Matthews and Darrell Phillips, *Child Structured Learning in Science,* Tallahassee: Florida State University, 1969.

20. Constance Kamii, "Pedagogical Principles Derived from Piaget's Theory: Relevance for Educational Practice," in M. Schwebel and J. Raph (eds.), *Piaget in the Classroom,* New York: Basic Books, 1973, pp. 199–215.

21. Ann Bingham-Newman and Ruth Saunders, "Take a New Look at Your Children with Piaget as a Guide," *Young Children,* May 1977, pp. 62–72.

22. William Hull, "Things to Think About While Observing," *E.S.S. Reader,* Newton, Mass.: Education Development Center, 1970.

23. Elementary Science Study, *Teacher's Guide for Batteries and Bulbs,* New York: McGraw-Hill, Webster Division, 1968.

24. Elementary Science Study, *Batteries and Bulbs II: An Electrical Gadget Suggestion Book,* New York: McGraw-Hill, Webster Division, 1971.

25. United Science and Mathematics for Elementary Schools, *Consumer Research-Product Testing: Teacher's Resource Book,* Newton, Mass.: Education Development Center, 1973.

26. Ed Labinowicz, "In How Many Different Ways . . . ? Divergent Questions as Springboards for 'Opening' Your Classroom," *Science and Children.* October 1973, pp. 18–21.

27. Science Curriculum Improvement Study, *Models and Magnetic Interactions: Evaluation Supplement,* Berkeley: University of California, 1972.

Chapter 11

1. Title adapted from papers by Robert Wirtz, LACTMA Conference, Los Angeles, and Thomas O'Brien at Jean Piaget Society Conference in Philadelphia in 1977.

2. Milton Schwebel and Jane Raph, *Piaget in the Classroom,* New York, Basic Books, 1973.

3. Jean Piaget, *Science of Education and the Psychology of the Child,* New York: Viking Press, 1971.

4. Eleanor Duckworth, "Piaget Rediscovered," in R. Ripple and V. Rockcastle (eds.), *Piaget Rediscovered,* Ithaca: Cornell University, 1964, pp. 1–5.

5. These are goals identified by the Sherman Oaks Elementary School, Los Angeles Unified School District.

6. Elizabeth Hitchfield, "The Implications of Piagetian Research for Education," An interview conducted by Thomas O'Brien, Belleville Area Teachers' Center.

7. Adapted and expanded from Robert Reyes and Thomas Post, *The Mathematics Laboratory: Theory to Practice,* Boston: Prindle, Weber and Schmidt, 1973.

8. Jean Piaget, *To Understand Is to Invent: The Future of Education,* New York: Grossman, 1973.

9. Peter Wolff, "What Piaget Did Not Intend," in G. Lubin (ed.), *Fourth Annual Piagetian Conference Proceedings,* Los Angeles: University of Southern California, 1974 pp. 3–14.

10. David Elkind, *Child Development and Education: A Piagetian Perspective,* New York: Oxford University Press, 1976.

11. Frances Hawkins, *The Logic of Action,* New York: Random House, 1969.

12. Marilyn Appel, Robert Bernoff, Ann Howe, Robert Karplus, Anton Lawson, et al., *Science Teaching and the Development of Reasoning,* Berkeley: AESOP, University of California, 1976.

13. Arnold Arons, "Towards Wider Public Understanding of Science," *American Journal of Physics,* June 1973, pp. 769–82.

14. Elizabeth Hunter, *Encounter in the Classroom: New Way of Teaching,* New York: Holt, Rinehart & Winston, 1972.

15. Ed Labinowicz, "Affective-Cognitive Integration in Science Education for Facilitation of Teacher Change," *Science Education,* October 1976, pp. 513–19.

16. Lawrence Lowery, Personal correspondence, 1978.

17. Phillip Morrison, "Tensions of Purpose," *ESI Quarterly Report,* Spring/Summer 1966, pp. 67–70.

Appendix A
Outline for Introductory Course, Beginners' Bibliography, and Student Project

Note: Although THE PIAGET PRIMER is intended for everyone who is interested in Piaget, the following outline is suggested for an introductory course, which might be titled "Classroom Applications of Piaget's Theory of Cognitive Development, in which THE PIAGET PRIMER would be the basal text. The PRIMER is suitable for use in courses in educational methods, educational psychology, child development, and psychology.

Introductory Course Outline For

CLASSROOM APPLICATIONS OF PIAGET'S THEORY OF COGNITIVE DEVELOPMENT

Psychological Theory	Educational Applications

1. Four factors influencing intellectual development
—biological maturation
—physical experiences   (Chapt.
—social interaction   1,2,3,7)
—equilibrium
  —equilibration as the coordinating factor in interaction with the environment.
	—Organizing a classroom environment which provides for all four factors in intellectual development.
	—Analyzing methods of teaching which trigger the equilibration mechanism, e.g.,
	  —discrepant events (Chapt. 10)
	  —novelty
	  —juxtaposing opposing viewpoints in groups

2. Four stages of intellectual development —sensori-motor stage —preoperational stage (Chapt. 4) —concrete operational stage —formal operational stage. Discontinuous/continuous duality of development. —intellectual tasks and age ranges as convenient benchmarks —integration of successive stage structures.	—Evaluating curricula based on an analysis of intellectual demands of school tasks in relation to children's natural capacities and constraints —Designing developmental learning sequences in which "concrete-to-abstract" is a long-range goal rather than a lesson objective. Applying these developmental learning sequences to individualizing classroom learning. (Chapt. 9)
3. Methods of investigation (Chapt. —naturalistic observation 1,2,3,4, —clinical method of assessment 7,8) —recent learning experiments	—Expanding a classroom teacher's repertoire of assessment techniques. —Extrapolating the facilitating behaviors of the clinical interviewer to clinical teaching situations. —Adapting models which provoke children's thinking. (Chapt. 7,9,10)
4. In-depth studies (Chapt. —language development 5,6) —number concept	—Evaluating the implications for language usage in teaching and language emphasis in primary grades, and for grade placement of math concepts and methods of teaching. (Chapt. 9)
5. Contrast to other theories (Chapt. 8) —interactionist and constructivist view in developmental psychology —contrast with behaviorist assumptions, theories, and methods. —limitations of a theory —issues —recent shifts in emphasis in Piaget's theory	—Evaluating the desirability and complexities of changing schools in a behaviorist system. (Analyzing the basis for educational policy.) —Justifying the need for a viable alternative based on Piaget's theory of intellectual development. —Analyzing the limitations of extrapolating a psychological theory to an educational setting. —Designing evaluation studies from an expanded frame of reference. (Chapt. 8,11)

EVALUATION:
to be based on class participation, written tests, and project analyzing children's thinking and interviewer behaviors. These are end products of the following student actions:

Piaget's Observations, Theory, and Methods

(define
(describe
(explain
(contrast
(outline
(demonstrate

apply)
analyze)
evaluate)
justify)
design)
adapt)
organize)

based on understanding of Piaget's theory and methods.

Beginner's Bibliography

Required Text: Labinowicz, Ed. *The Piaget Primer: Thinking, Learning, Teaching.* Menlo Park: Addison Wesley, 1980.

Optional Texts: One text will be selected from each group of primary and secondary sources. Students using different texts will be grouped to encourage sharing and comparing interpretations of different authors and exchanging books.

1. Piaget, Jean and Inhelder, Barbel. *The Psychology of the Child.* New York: Basic, 1969.

   Piaget, Jean. *The Child and Reality*, New York: Viking, 1972.

   To Understand Is to Invent. New York: Grossman, 1972.
   Science of Education and the Psychology of the Child New York: Viking, 1972.

2. Gorman, Richard. *Discovering Piaget: A Guide for Teachers.* Columbus: Charles Merrill, 1972.

   Phillips, John. *The Origins of Intellect.* San Francisco: Freeman, 1969.

   Pulaski, Mary Ann. *Understanding Piaget: An Introduction to Children's Cognitive Development.* New York: Harper and Row, 1971.

   Sund, Robert. *Piaget for Educators.* Columbus: Charles Merrill, 1976.

   Wadsworth, Barry. *Piaget's Theory of Cognitive Development: An Introduction for Students of Psychology and Education.* New York: McKay, 1972.

Major References (books of intermediate difficulty placed on library reserve).

Gruber, Howard and Voneche, Jacques (eds.) *The Essential Piaget: An Interpretive Reference and Guide,* New York: Basic Books, 1977.

Cowan, Phillip. *Piaget with Feeling: Cognitive, Social and Emotional Dimensions,* New York: Holt, 1978.

Ginsburg, Herbert and Opper, Sylvia. *Piaget's Theory of Intellectual Development: An Introduction,* Englewood Cliffs, New Jersey: Prentice-Hall, 1969.

Schwebel, Milton and Raph, Jane (eds.). *Piaget in the Classroom.* New York: Basic Books, 1973.

Student Project

During the course, students will be required to undertake a first-hand study of children's thinking through an application of Piaget's methods. In this project, taped interviews will be analyzed, not only for the processes and levels of children's thinking, but also for the processes of questioning, listening, and responding by the interviewer.

Appendix B
Films, Videotapes,
and Other Media Sources

Films

Davidson Films, *Piaget's Developmental Theory Series:*
   Classification (19 minutes)
   Conservation (29 minutes)
   Formal Thought (33 minutes)
   Growth of Intelligence in the Preschool Years (31 minutes)
These films show a range of children's responses to classical Piagetian tasks administered by
Celia Stendler Lavatelli, Robert Karplus and others. The commentary discusses these
responses in terms of Piaget's theory.

Phoenix Films, *Learning About Thinking and Vice Versa* (32 minutes)

This black-and-white film describes a teacher's workshop for studying children's thinking
and relates the teachers' experiences to their classrooms. Eleanor Duckworth is the
workshop leader.

Videotapes

Far West Laboratory, *The Growing Mind: A Piagetian View of Young Children Series*
   The Development of Classification (30 minutes)
   The Development of Order Relations — Seriation (27 minutes)
   The Development of Quantitative Relations — *Conservation* (32 minutes)
   The Development of Spatial Relations (29 minutes)
These videotapes are of commercial quality and are accompanied by substantive study
guides which assist the viewer with theoretical background, analysis of the videotapes and
suggestions for beginning own investigations of children's thinking. The study guides are
prepared by Keith Alward. Videotapes and study guides are available from the Far West
Laboratory, 1855 Folsom Street, San Francisco, CA 94103.

Filmstrips

Robert Sund. *Piaget for Educators: A Multimedia Program,* Columbus, Ohio: Charles Merrill Publishers, 1976.

> *Piaget's Theory of Cognitive Development*
> *The Preoperational Period*
> *The Concrete Operational Period*
> *The Formal-Operational Period*
> *General Implications for Education*
> *Moral Education*

The text coordinates usage of the audiovisual media, provides useful summaries and numerous examples of Piagetian interview activities. The *Formal Operational Period* filmstrip is an excellent introduction to a difficult area of study.

Print

Lawrence, Lowery, *The Learning About Learning Series*

> *Conservation*
> *Classification*
> *Propositional Abilities*

These self-directed, study modules provide opportunities to increase theoretical understanding in each area, to conduct related investigations of children's thinking and to apply this knowledge and skills for diagnosis, and selection of curriculum materials in the classroom. Other modules related to teaching are also available. These study modules are available from Tolman Hall, University of California, Berkeley, CA 94720.

Index

thinking in the, 77

transitivity in the, 77

variables, isolating and controlling, in the, 83

Conflict resolution, 218~221, 246

Connecting level, in number learning, 178, 180~181

Consensus, encouraging, 218~219

Conservation/Conservation concepts/Conservation
tasks, 73, 89, 93~95, 158

development related to, 94~95

of amount, 25, 73

gradual development of, 89

gaps between, 91~92

intellectual development and, 94~95

of length, 122~125

misinterpretation in research on, 150

of number, 100~101, 108, 123~125, 165

road building, 124~141

at stages, 73

of volume, 25, 73

Conserver/-s

language usage, 116~117

in measurement activities, 192

Conserver level, of task response, 94~95

Constraints, capacities and, 160~167

Construction

of concept, 29~30

games of, 69, 124~141

of puzzle solutions, 31~34

of reality, 28, 34, 156

Constructivist position, 46, 146~152, 267

Consumer product research, 239, 260~261

Continuity, 37

Contradictions

awareness of, 53~55, 137~138

eliminating, 81

Counting

number concepts and, 97~99

as one-to-one correspondence, 100

as ordering, 98

physical, 96, 97~99

verbal, 96, 97~99

Curriculum/-a

behaviorist, 267

innovation and resistance, 270

Piagetian, 267

preschool, 170~175

restructuring, 169~191

de Bono, Edward, 31~33

Decision making, in schools and classrooms,
167~168, 271~273

Definitions

introducing lessons with, 203~204

as ready-made truths, 203

Demonstrating, in the teaching process, 18

Description, learning of, 173~175

DeVries, Rheta, 170, 173, 174

Disequilibrium

awareness of contradiction as, 53~55, 137~138

dealing with, 224~225

definition of, 36

encounters arranged to create, 213

examples of, 40~41, 47~50, 53~55, 128~130

intellectual development and, 35

in learning, 154

in mirror tasks, 47~50

problem recognition as, 53

tension in, 238

See also Equilibration; Equilibrium

Displacement volume, 1~18, 25, 36,
52~55, 73, 94

volume and, 1~18, 36,
52~55

Division, arithmetical, 97, 110

Duckworth, Eleanor, 209

Education

basic issue in, 265~268

basics of, 264~281

DATE DUE

1/02/03			
MY 13 '03			
SE 12 '03			
SE 23 '04			
NO 18 '04			
NO 18 04			
FE 5 '05			1908
SE 04 '06			
AG 27 '07			8
			100
MR 09 '08			
			01

▲▼ Addison-Wesley Publishing Company

ISBN-0-201-040